MARY SHELLEY

Frankenstein or The Modern Prometheus

Cornelsen

MARY SHELLEY **Frankenstein or The Modern Prometheus**

Annotationen und Zusatzmaterialien: Lars Schüler
Verlagsredaktion: Elke Lehmann (Redaktionsleitung), Dr. Jan Dreßler
Umschlagkonzept: Cornelsen Verlag GmbH
Umschlaggestaltung: Klein & Halm Grafikdesign
Umschlagfoto: Shutterstock.com/Richard Bowden
Layout und technische Umsetzung: L101 Mediengestaltung, Fürstenwalde

www.cornelsen.de

1. Auflage, 1. Druck 2020

This edition is the complete and unabridged text of the novel.

Alle Drucke dieser Auflage sind inhaltlich unverändert und können im Unterricht nebeneinander verwendet werden.

Druck: H. Heenemann, Berlin

ISBN 978-3-06-036205-9

PEFC/04-31-1156

PEFC zertifiziert
Dieses Produkt stammt aus nachhaltig bewirtschafteten Wäldern und kontrollierten Quellen.

www.pefc.de

Contents

Note on the Text

Frankenstein was first published in 1818. The text of this edition is based on the third, revised edition published in 1831.

Abbreviations and Annotations

adj	adjective
derog	derogatory
e.g.	exempli gratia; for example
etw.	*etwas*
fig	figurative(ly)
Fr.	French
i.e.	id est, that is
interj	interjection
Ital.	Italian
jdm./jdn.	*jemand(em/n)*
n	noun
pl	plural
prep	preposition
sb.	somebody
sth.	something
usu.	usually
v	verb

The annotations are arranged chronologically; the first time a word is used is where you will find it explained.

Note on the Text

Did I request thee[1], Maker, from my clay[2]
To mould[3] Me man? Did I solicit[4] thee
From darkness to promote[5] me? –
Paradise Lost.[6]

TO
WILLIAM GODWIN[7]
AUTHOR OF POLITICAL JUSTICE, CALEB WILLIAMS, &C.

THESE VOLUMES
ARE RESPECTFULLY INSCRIBED[8]
BY
THE AUTHOR

1 thee (poetic): you **2** clay: *Ton* **3** mould sth.: form sth. into a specific shape **4** solicit sb. to do sth.: (here) ask sb. to do sth. **5** promote sb./sth.: (here) bring sb./sth. into being **6** *Paradise Lost*: epic poem by English poet John Milton (1608–1674) which expands on the biblical story of the creation of Adam and Eve and their subsequent expulsion from Paradise **7** William Godwin: Mary Shelley's father (1756–1836), sociologist and writer who strongly opposed governmental or institutionalized interference into the individual's life in his works of fiction and nonfiction **8** inscribe sth. to sb.: *(hier) jdm. etw. widmen*

Introduction (1831)

The Publishers of the Standard Novels, in selecting *Frankenstein* for one of their series, expressed a wish that I should furnish[1] them with some account of the origin of the story. I am the more willing to comply[2], because I shall thus give a general answer to the question, so very frequently asked me – 'How I, then a young girl, came to think of and to dilate[3] upon so very hideous[4] an idea?' It is true that I am very averse[5] to bringing myself forward in print; but as my account will only appear as an appendage[6] to a former production, and as it will be confined[7] to such topics as have connection with my authorship alone, I can scarcely accuse myself of a personal intrusion[8].

It is not singular that, as the daughter of two persons of distinguished literary celebrity, I should very early in life have thought of writing. As a child I scribbled[9]; and my favourite pastime, during the hours given me for recreation, was to 'write stories.' Still I had a dearer pleasure than this, which was the formation of castles in the air – the indulging[10] in waking dreams – the following up trains of thought[11], which had for their subject the formation of a succession of imaginary incidents. My dreams were at once more fantastic and agreeable than my writings. In the latter I was a close imitator – rather doing as others had done, than putting down the suggestions of my own mind. What I wrote was intended at least for one other eye – my Childhood's companion and friend; but my dreams were

1 furnish sb. with sth.: (here) give sth. to sb. **2** comply: do what you are asked to do **3** dilate upon sth.: talk/write at length about sth. **4** hideous [ˈhɪdiəs]: gruesome, ugly **5** be averse to sth.: dislike sth. **6** appendage: add-on
7 confine sth. to sth.: restrict sth. to sth. **8** intrusion: *Aufdrängen* **9** scribble: write or draw quickly and in a sloppy way **10** indulge in sth.: do sth. enjoyable
11 train of thought: *Gedankengang*

all my own; I accounted[1] for them to nobody; they were my refuge[2] when annoyed – my dearest pleasure when free.

I lived principally in the country as a girl, and passed a considerable time in Scotland. I made occasional visits to the more picturesque parts; but my habitual residence was on the blank and dreary[3] northern shores[4] of the Tay, near Dundee. Blank and dreary on retrospection I call them; they were not so to me then. They were the eyry[5] of freedom, and the pleasant region where unheeded[6] I could commune[7] with the creatures of my fancy[8]. I wrote then – but in a most common-place[9] style. It was beneath the trees of the grounds belonging to our house, or on the bleak sides of the woodless mountains near, that my true compositions, the airy flights of my imagination, were born and fostered[10]. I did not make myself the heroine of my tales. Life appeared to me too common-place an affair as regarded myself. I could not figure to myself that romantic woes[11] or wonderful[12] events would ever be my lot; but I was not confined to my own identity, and I could people[13] the hours with creations far more interesting to me at that age, than my own sensations.

After this my life became busier, and reality stood in place of fiction. My husband[14], however, was from the first, very anxious that I should prove myself worthy of my parentage[15], and enrol[16] myself on the page of fame. He was for ever inciting[17] me to obtain literary reputation, which even on my own part I cared for then, though since I have become infinitely indifferent[18] to it. At this time he desired that I should write, not so much with the idea that I could produce any

1 account for sth.: justify (yourself for) sth. **2** refuge ['refju:dʒ]: place that provides shelter and protection **3** dreary: bleak, depressing **4** shore: *Ufer* **5** eyry: nest of a predatory bird **6** unheeded: with nobody watching **7** commune with sb. (v): (here) communicate with sb. in thought **8** fancy (n): imagination **9** common-place: simple, ordinary **10** foster sth.: (here) promote the development of sth. **11** woe [wəʊ] (n): condition of deep suffering, unhappiness **12** wonderful: (here) strange, wondrous **13** people (v): *bevölkern* **14** my husband: Percy Bysshe [bɪʃ] Shelley (1792–1822): influential English Romantic poet, married Mary Shelley (née Godwin) in 1816 **15** parentage: family background **16** enrol yourself: (here) permanently insert your name **17** incite sb. to do sth.: encourage sb. to do sth. **18** indifferent: not interested, unmoved

thing worthy of notice, but that he might himself judge how far I possessed the promise of better things hereafter. Still I did nothing. Travelling, and the cares of a family, occupied my time; and study, in the way of reading, or improving my ideas in communication with his far more cultivated mind, was all of literary employment[1] that engaged[2] my attention.

In the summer of 1816, we visited Switzerland, and became the neighbours of Lord Byron[3]. At first we spent our pleasant hours on the lake, or wandering on its shores; and Lord Byron, who was writing the third canto of *Childe Harold*[4], was the only one among us who put his thoughts upon paper. These, as he brought them successively to us, clothed in all the light and harmony of poetry, seemed to stamp[5] as divine[6] the glories of heaven and earth, whose influences we partook[7] with him.

But it proved a wet, ungenial[8] summer, and incessant rain often confined us for days to the house. Some volumes of ghost stories, translated from the German into French, fell into our hands. There was the *History of the Inconstant Lover*, who, when he thought to clasp[9] the bride to whom he had pledged his vows, found himself in the arms of the pale ghost of her whom he had deserted. There was the tale of the sinful founder of his race, whose miserable doom[10] it was to bestow[11] the kiss of death on all the younger sons of his fated house, just when they reached the age of promise[12]. His gigantic, shadowy form, clothed like the ghost in *Hamlet*, in complete armour, but with the beaver up, was seen at midnight, by the moon's fitful beams, to advance slowly along the gloomy avenue. The shape

1 employment: (here) activity, occupation **2** engage sth.: (here) captivate sth.
3 George Gordon Byron, known as Lord Byron (1788–1824): English poet of aristocratic descent and leading figure in the English Romantic movement; lived in a mansion close to the shore of Lake Geneva from June to November 1816
4 *Childe Harold's Pilgrimage*: autobiographical narrative poem by Byron
5 stamp sth. (v): (here) characterize sth. **6** divine: relating to God (or a god)
7 partake sth. with sb.: share sth. with sb., participate in sth. with sb.
8 ungenial: unpleasant **9** clasp sb.: (here) hug sb. **10** doom (n): (unhappy) destiny **11** bestow sth. on sb.: give sth. to sb. (as a gift) **12** age of promise: age when young people start into their adult lives

was lost beneath the shadow of the castle walls; but soon a gate swung back, a step was heard, the door of the chamber opened, and he advanced to the couch of the blooming youths, cradled in healthy sleep. Eternal sorrow sat upon his face as he bent down and kissed the forehead of the boys, who from that hour withered[1] like flowers snapt upon the stalk. I have not seen these stories since then; but their incidents are as fresh in my mind as if I had read them yesterday.

'We will each write a ghost story,' said Lord Byron; and his proposition was acceded to. There were four of us. The noble author began a tale, a fragment of which he printed at the end of his poem of *Mazeppa*. Shelley, more apt[2] to embody ideas and sentiments in the radiance of brilliant imagery, and in the music of the most melodious verse that adorns our language, than to invent the machinery of a story, commenced[3] one founded on the experiences of his early life. Poor Polidori[4] had some terrible idea about a skull-headed lady, who was so punished for peeping through a key-hole – what to see I forget – something very shocking and wrong of course; but when she was reduced to a worse condition than the renowned Tom of Coventry[5], he did not know what to do with her, and was obliged to despatch[6] her to the tomb of the Capulets[7], the only place for which she was fitted. The illustrious poets[8] also, annoyed by the platitude of prose, speedily relinquished[9] their uncongenial task.

I busied myself *to think of a story*, – a story to rival those which had excited us to this task. One which would speak to the mysterious fears of our nature, and awaken thrilling horror – one to make the reader dread[10] to look round, to curdle[11] the blood, and quicken

1 wither: weaken, waste away **2** apt: suitable **3** commence: begin **4** John William Polidori (1795–1821): Byron's personal physician (during Byron's travels throughout Europe) and aspiring writer **5** Tom of Coventry ('Peeping Tom'): legendary character who was blinded or killed as a punishment for spying on a naked lady **6** despatch sth./sb.: send away sth./sb. quickly **7** tomb of the Capulets: reference to the underground family grave of the Capulet family in William Shakespeare's *Romeo and Juliet* **8** illustrious poets: (here) Byron and P.B. Shelley **9** relinquish sth.: give sth. up **10** dread [dred] (v): fear greatly **11** curdle sth.: *etw. gerinnen lassen*

the beatings of the heart. If I did not accomplish these things, my ghost story would be unworthy of its name. I thought and pondered[1] – vainly[2]. I felt that blank incapability of invention which is the greatest misery of authorship, when dull Nothing replies to our anxious[3] invocations[4]. 'Have you thought of a story?' I was asked each morning, and each morning I was forced to reply with a mortifying negative.

Every thing must have a beginning, to speak in Sanchean phrase[5]; and that beginning must be linked to something that went before. The Hindoos give the world an elephant to support it, but they make the elephant stand upon a tortoise. Invention, it must be humbly admitted, does not consist in creating out of void, but out of chaos; the materials must, in the first place, be afforded[6]: it can give form to dark, shapeless substances, but cannot bring into being the substance itself. In all matters of discovery and invention, even of those that appertain[7] to the imagination, we are continually reminded of the story of Columbus and his egg[8]. Invention consists in the capacity of seizing on the capabilities[9] of a subject, and in the power of moulding and fashioning ideas suggested to it.

Many and long were the conversations between Lord Byron and Shelley, to which I was a devout but nearly silent listener. During one of these, various philosophical doctrines were discussed, and among others the nature of the principle of life, and whether there was any probability of its ever being discovered and communicated. They talked of the experiments of Dr. Darwin[10],

1 ponder sth.: think about sth. **2** vainly (also: in vain): without success **3** anxious: fearful **4** invocation: *Beschwörung, Anrufung* **5** Sanchean phrase: reference to a specific passage from the famous novel *Don Quijote* by Spanish author Miguel de Cervantes (1547–1616) where the protagonist, Sancho Panza, is made to state what is actually quite obvious **6** afford sth.: (here) give sth. **7** appertain to sth. [ˌæpəˈteɪn]: belong to sth. **8** Columbus and his egg: reference to an anecdote about Christopher Columbus who found a solution to the problem of making an egg stand on its tip by tapping it on the table and thus flattening the shell at the tip **9** capabilities: (here) qualities, options **10** Dr. Erasmus Darwin (1731–1802): famous British physician, natural philosopher and poet; grandfather of Charles Darwin

(I speak not of what the Doctor really did, or said that he did, but, as more to my purpose, of what was then spoken of as having been done by him,) who preserved a piece of vermicelli[1] in a glass case, till by some extraordinary means it began to move with voluntary motion. Not thus, after all, would life be given. Perhaps a corpse would be re-animated; galvanism[2] had given token[3] of such things: perhaps the component parts of a creature might be manufactured, brought together, and endued[4] with vital[5] warmth.

Night waned[6] upon this talk, and even the witching hour had gone by, before we retired[7] to rest. When I placed my head on my pillow, I did not sleep, nor could I be said to think. My imagination, unbidden[8], possessed and guided me, gifting the successive images that arose in my mind with a vividness far beyond the usual bounds of reverie[9]. I saw – with shut eyes, but acute[10] mental vision, – I saw the pale student of unhallowed[11] arts kneeling beside the thing he had put together. I saw the hideous phantasm[12] of a man stretched out, and then, on the working of some powerful engine, show signs of life, and stir with an uneasy, half vital motion. Frightful must it be; for supremely frightful would be the effect of any human endeavour[13] to mock[14] the stupendous[15] mechanism of the Creator of the world. His success would terrify the artist; he would rush away from his odious[16] handywork, horror-stricken. He would hope that, left to itself, the slight spark of life which he had communicated would fade; that this thing, which had received such imperfect animation, would

1 vermicelli: spaghetti-like pasta **2** galvanism: contractions of muscles stimulated by electric current; named after the Italian physician Luigi Galvani (1737–1798) who researched the effect of electricity on dissected animals, e.g. frog's legs. In 1803, Galvani's nephew Giovanni Aldini tried (unsuccessfully) to re-animate corpses by applying electricity to them. **3** give token of sth.: give evidence of sth. **4** endue with sth.: equip with sth. **5** vital: possessing life **6** wane: decrease in size, e.g. the moon; (here) come to an end **7** retire: *sich zurückziehen* **8** unbidden: unasked for **9** reverie: dreams, imagination **10** acute: sharp, very accurate **11** unhallowed: forbidden, morally unacceptable **12** phantasm: *geisterhafte Erscheinung* **13** endeavour [ɪnˈdevə(r)] (n): attempt **14** mock sb./sth.: ridicule sb./sth. **15** stupendous: enormous **16** odious: disgusting, appalling

subside[1] into dead matter; and he might sleep in the belief that the silence of the grave would quench[2] for ever the transient[3] existence of the hideous corpse which he had looked upon as the cradle[4] of life. He sleeps; but he is awakened; he opens his eyes; behold[5] the horrid[6] thing stands at his bedside, opening his curtains, and looking on him with yellow, watery, but speculative eyes.

I opened mine in terror. The idea so possessed my mind, that a thrill of fear ran through me, and I wished to exchange the ghastly image of my fancy for the realities around. I see them still; the very room, the dark *parquet*, the closed shutters[7], with the moonlight struggling through, and the sense I had that the glassy lake and white high Alps were beyond. I could not so easily get rid of my hideous phantom; still it haunted[8] me. I must try to think of something else. I recurred to my ghost story, – my tiresome unlucky ghost story! Oh! if I could only contrive[9] one which would frighten my reader as I myself had been frightened that night!

Swift[10] as light and as cheering was the idea that broke in upon me. 'I have found it! What terrified me will terrify others; and I need only describe the spectre[11] which had haunted my midnight pillow.' On the morrow[12] I announced that I had *thought of a story*. I began that day with the words, 'It was on a dreary night of November,' making only a transcript[13] of the grim terrors of my waking dream.

At first I thought but of a few pages – of a short tale; but Shelley urged me to develope the idea at greater length. I certainly did not owe the suggestion of one incident, nor scarcely of one train of feeling, to my husband, and yet but for[14] his incitement, it would never have taken the form in which it was presented to the world. From

1 subside into sth.: (here) turn into sth. **2** quench sth.: (here) erase sth., kill sth. **3** transient: short(-lived) **4** cradle: *Wiege* **5** behold (interj): *Siehe!* **6** horrid: shocking, horrible **7** shutter: *Fensterladen* **8** haunt sb.: *(hier) jdn. verfolgen, jdn. heimsuchen* **9** contrive sth.: create or think of sth. by clever use of the imagination **10** swift: quick **11** spectre: ghost **12** morrow: morning **13** transcript: (here) notes **14** but for: (here) without

this declaration I must except the preface[1]. As far as I can recollect, it was entirely written by him.

And now, once again, I bid my hideous progeny[2] go forth and prosper[3]. I have an affection for it, for it was the offspring[4] of happy days, when death and grief[5] were but words, which found no true echo in my heart. Its several pages speak of many a walk, many a drive, and many a conversation, when I was not alone; and my companion was one who, in this world, I shall never see more. But this is for myself; my readers have nothing to do with these associations.

I will add but one word as to the alterations[6] I have made. They are principally those of style. I have changed no portion of the story, nor introduced any new ideas or circumstances. I have mended[7] the language where it was so bald[8] as to interfere with the interest of the narrative; and these changes occur almost exclusively in the beginning of the first volume. Throughout they are entirely confined to such parts as are mere adjuncts[9] to the story, leaving the core and substance of it untouched.

M. W. S.[10]
London, October 15. 1831.

1 preface [ˈprefəs]: *Vorwort* **2** progeny: *Nachkomme, Abkömmling* **3** go forth and prosper: *geh hin und vermehre dich* **4** offspring: *Nachwuchs* **5** grief: *Schmerz, Trauer* **6** alteration: change **7** mend sth.: (here) improve sth. **8** bald: (here) simple **9** adjunct: add-on **10** M.W.S.: the 'W' in Mary Shelley's name is for 'Wollstonecraft', her mother's last name

Preface (by P. B. Shelley, 1818)

The event on which this fiction is founded, has been supposed, by Dr. Darwin, and some of the physiological writers[1] of Germany, as not of impossible occurrence. I shall not be supposed as according[2] the remotest degree of serious faith to such an imagination; yet, in assuming it as the basis of a work of fancy, I have not considered myself as merely[3] weaving[4] a series of supernatural terrors. The event on which the interest of the story depends is exempt[5] from the disadvantages of a mere tale of spectres or enchantment[6]. It was recommended by the novelty of the situations which it developes; and, however impossible as a physical fact, affords a point of view to the imagination for the delineating[7] of human passions more comprehensive[8] and commanding[9] than any which the ordinary relations[10] of existing events can yield[11].

I have thus endeavoured[12] to preserve the truth of the elementary principles of human nature, while I have not scrupled[13] to innovate upon their combinations. *The Iliad*[14], the tragic poetry of Greece, – Shakespeare, in *The Tempest*, and *Midsummer Night's Dream*[15], – and most especially Milton, in *Paradise Lost*, conform[16] to this rule; and

1 physiological writers: scientists and physicians who published the results of their research **2** accord faith to sth.: fully believe in sth. **3** merely: only **4** weave sth. (fig): form sth. by interlacing strands, create sth. by connecting *(weben)* **5** exempt from sth. (adj): free from sth. **6** enchantment: power of magic and illusion **7** delineating (n): description **8** comprehensive: *umfassend* **9** commanding (adj): (here) impressive **10** relation: (here) report, narration **11** yield sth. (v): bring sth. forth **12** endeavour to do sth.: try to do sth. **13** scruple to do sth. (v): be uncertain about doing sth. **14** *The Iliad*: ancient Greek epic poem by Homer **15** *A Midsummer Night's Dream*: play by William Shakespeare (1546–1616) that contains supernatural occurences and characters **16** conform to sth.: (here) follow sth.

the most humble[1] novelist, who seeks to confer[2] or receive amusement from his labours[3], may, without presumption[4], apply to prose fiction a licence[5], or rather a rule, from the adoption[6] of which so many exquisite combinations of human feeling have resulted in the highest specimens[7] of poetry.

The circumstance on which my story rests was suggested in casual conversation. It was commenced partly as a source of amusement, and partly as an expedient[8] for exercising any untried resources of mind. Other motives were mingled[9] with these, as the work proceeded[10]. I am by no means indifferent to the manner in which whatever moral tendencies exist in the sentiments or characters it contains shall affect the reader; yet my chief concern in this respect has been limited to the avoiding the enervating[11] effects of the novels of the present day, and to the exhibition of the amiableness[12] of domestic affection[13], and the excellence of universal virtue[14]. The opinions which naturally spring from the character and situation of the hero are by no means to be conceived[15] as existing always in my own conviction[16]; nor is any inference[17] justly to be drawn from the following pages as prejudicing[18] any philosophical doctrine[19] of whatever kind.

It is a subject also of additional interest to the author, that this story was begun in the majestic region where the scene is principally laid, and in society which cannot cease[20] to be regretted. I passed the summer of 1816 in the environs of Geneva. The season was cold and rainy, and in the evenings we crowded around a blazing wood fire, and occasionally amused ourselves with some German stories of ghosts, which happened to fall into our hands. These tales excited

1 humble: *bescheiden* **2** confer sth.: give sth. **3** labour: hard and unpleasant work **4** presumption: arrogance **5** (poetic) licence: artistic freedom **6** adoption of sth.: decision to take up sth. **7** specimen: example **8** expedient (n): way, means **9** mingle sth. with sth.: mix sth. with sth. **10** proceed: go on **11** enervating: causing the loss of energy and vitality **12** amiableness: *Liebenswürdigkeit* **13** domestic affection: *häusliche bzw. eheliche Zuneigung* **14** virtue: *Tugend* **15** conceive sth.: (here) understand sth. **16** conviction: opinion, view **17** inference: *Rückschluss* **18** prejudice sth. (v): attach a prejudice / a negative view to sth. **19** doctrine: (here) position, theory **20** cease (v): stop

in us a playful desire of imitation. Two other friends (a tale from the pen of one of whom would be far more acceptable to the public than any thing I can ever hope to produce) and myself agreed to write each a story, founded on some supernatural occurrence.

The weather, however, suddenly became serene[1]; and my two friends left me on a journey among the Alps, and lost, in the magnificent scenes which they present, all memory of their ghostly visions. The following tale is the only one which has been completed.

Marlow[2], September, 1817

1 serene (adj): clear and calm **2** Marlow: town 50 km west of London

Letter 1

To Mrs. Saville, England.

St. Petersburgh, Dec. 11th, 17–.

You will rejoice[1] to hear that no disaster has accompanied the commencement of an enterprise[2] which you have regarded with such evil forebodings[3]. I arrived here yesterday, and my first task is to assure my dear sister of my welfare and increasing confidence in the success of my undertaking.

I am already far north of London, and as I walk in the streets of Petersburgh, I feel a cold northern breeze play upon my cheeks, which braces[4] my nerves and fills me with delight. Do you understand this feeling? This breeze, which has travelled from the regions towards which I am advancing, gives me a foretaste of those icy climes[5]. Inspirited[6] by this wind of promise, my daydreams become more fervent[7] and vivid. I try in vain[8] to be persuaded that the pole is the seat of frost and desolation; it ever presents itself to my imagination as the region of beauty and delight. There, Margaret, the sun is forever visible, its broad disk just skirting the horizon and diffusing a perpetual[9] splendour. There – for with your leave[10], my sister, I will put some trust in preceding[11] navigators – there snow and frost are banished; and, sailing over a calm sea, we may be wafted[12] to a land surpassing in wonders and in beauty every region hitherto[13] discovered on the habitable globe[14]. Its productions[15] and features

1 rejoice to do sth.: be happy about doing sth. **2** enterprise: large project **3** foreboding: feeling that sth. dangerous or bad is about to happen **4** brace sth.: prepare sth. (for a difficult situation) **5** clime: region with a particular climate **6** inspirit sb./sth. (old use): give strength to sb./sth., motivate sb./sth. **7** fervent: enthusiastic **8** in vain: without success **9** perpetual: unending **10** with your leave: if you allow me to **11** preceding: *vorherig* **12** waft sth.: carry sth. **13** hitherto: until now **14** habitable globe: those parts of the earth where humans can live and survive **15** production: *(hier) Beschaffenheit*

may be without example, as the phenomena of the heavenly bodies undoubtedly are in those undiscovered solitudes. What may not be expected in a country of eternal light? I may there discover the wondrous power which attracts the needle and may regulate a thousand celestial[1] observations that require only this voyage to render their seeming eccentricities[2] consistent[3] forever. I shall satiate[4] my ardent[5] curiosity with the sight of a part of the world never before visited, and may tread a land never before imprinted by the foot of man. These are my enticements[6], and they are sufficient to conquer all fear of danger or death and to induce[7] me to commence this labourious[8] voyage with the joy a child feels when he embarks in a little boat, with his holiday mates, on an expedition of discovery up his native river. But supposing all these conjectures[9] to be false, you cannot contest[10] the inestimable benefit which I shall confer[11] on all mankind, to the last generation, by discovering a passage near the pole to those countries, to reach which at present so many months are requisite[12]; or by ascertaining[13] the secret of the magnet, which, if at all possible, can only be effected by an undertaking such as mine.

These reflections have dispelled[14] the agitation with which I began my letter, and I feel my heart glow with an enthusiasm which elevates[15] me to heaven, for nothing contributes so much to tranquillize[16] the mind as a steady purpose[17] – a point on which the soul may fix its intellectual eye. This expedition has been the favourite dream of my early years. I have read with ardour[18] the accounts of the various voyages which have been made in the prospect[19] of arriving at the North Pacific Ocean through the seas which surround the pole.

1 celestial: relating to heaven or to the sky **2** eccentricities (pl): *(hier) Widersprüchlichkeiten* **3** to render sth. consistent: *etw. in Einklang bringen* **4** satiate sth.: satisfy sth. **5** ardent: passionate **6** enticement: *Verlockung* **7** induce sb. to do sth.: make sb. do sth., bring sb. to do sth. **8** labourious [lə'bɔːriəs]: hard and strenuous **9** conjecture (n): speculation **10** contest sth. (v): (here) deny sth. **11** confer sth. on sb.: give sth. to sb. (as a present) **12** requisite: necessary **13** ascertain sth.: (here) find out about sth. **14** dispel sth.: get rid of sth. **15** elevate sb./sth.: lift up sb./sth. **16** tranquillize sb./sth.: make sb./sth. calmer **17** purpose: aim **18** ardour: great energy/intensity **19** in the prospect of doing sth.: with the idea/goal of doing sth.

You may remember that a history of all the voyages made for purposes of discovery composed the whole of our good Uncle Thomas' library. My education was neglected[1], yet I was passionately fond of reading. These volumes were my study day and night, and my familiarity with them increased that regret which I had felt, as a child, on learning that my father's dying injunction[2] had forbidden my uncle to allow me to embark in a seafaring life.

These visions faded when I perused[3], for the first time, those poets whose effusions[4] entranced my soul and lifted it to heaven. I also became a poet and for one year lived in a paradise of my own creation; I imagined that I also might obtain a niche in the temple[5] where the names of Homer and Shakespeare are consecrated. You are well acquainted[6] with my failure and how heavily I bore[7] the disappointment. But just at that time I inherited the fortune of my cousin, and my thoughts were turned into the channel of their earlier bent[8].

Six years have passed since I resolved[9] on my present undertaking. I can, even now, remember the hour from which I dedicated myself to this great enterprise. I commenced by inuring[10] my body to hardship. I accompanied the whale-fishers on several expeditions to the North Sea; I voluntarily endured[11] cold, famine[12], thirst, and want[13] of sleep; I often worked harder than the common sailors during the day and devoted[14] my nights to the study of mathematics, the theory of medicine, and those branches of physical science from which a naval[15] adventurer might derive[16] the greatest practi-

1 neglect sth./sb. (v): fail to pay enough attention to sth./sb. **2** dying injunction: firm wish made briefly before dying **3** peruse sth. [pəˈruːz] (v): read sth., study sth. **4** effusions (n, pl): (fig) *Ergüsse* **5** obtain a niche in the temple where [...]: (here) have the same (artistic) qualities as **6** be acquainted with sth.: be familiar with sth. **7** bear sth. (bore – borne): *etw. ertragen* **8** channel of their earlier bent: (here) direction of their original inclinations **9** resolve on sth.: decide (on) sth. **10** inure sth. to sth.: make sth. fit to withstand sth. **11** endure sth.: bear sth. **12** famine: hunger **13** want of sth. (n): lack of sth. **14** devote yourself to sth.: *sich etw. widmen* **15** naval (adj): relating to seafaring **16** derive sth. from sth.: get sth. from / out of sth.

cal advantage. Twice I actually hired myself as an under-mate[1] in a Greenland whaler, and acquitted[2] myself to admiration. I must own[3] I felt a little proud when my captain offered me the second dignity[4] in the vessel[5] and entreated[6] me to remain with the greatest earnestness, so valuable did he consider my services.

And now, dear Margaret, do I not deserve to accomplish some great purpose? My life might have been passed in ease and luxury, but I preferred glory to every enticement that wealth placed in my path. Oh, that some encouraging voice would answer in the affirmative[7]! My courage and my resolution is firm; but my hopes fluctuate, and my spirits are often depressed. I am about to proceed on a long and difficult voyage, the emergencies of which will demand all my fortitude[8]: I am required not only to raise the spirits of others, but sometimes to sustain[9] my own, when theirs are failing.

This is the most favourable period for travelling in Russia. They fly quickly over the snow in their sledges[10]; the motion is pleasant, and, in my opinion, far more agreeable than that of an English stagecoach[11]. The cold is not excessive, if you are wrapped in furs – a dress which I have already adopted, for there is a great difference between walking the deck and remaining seated motionless for hours, when no exercise prevents the blood from actually freezing in your veins. I have no ambition to lose my life on the post-road between St. Petersburgh and Archangel[12].

I shall depart for the latter town in a fortnight[13] or three weeks; and my intention is to hire a ship there, which can easily be done by paying the insurance for the owner, and to engage as many sailors as I think necessary among those who are accustomed to the whale-

1 under-mate: low-ranking deck officer on a ship **2** acquit yourself of sth.: take care of sth. (a job) **3** own sth. (v): (here) admit sth. **4** second dignity: higher ranking deck officer **5** vessel: ship **6** entreat sb. to do sth.: appeal to sb. to do sth. **7** answer in the affirmative: give a positive answer **8** fortitude: strength **9** sustain sth.: keep sth. up **10** sledge: *Schlitten* **11** stagecoach: horse-drawn carriage running on a regular schedule **12** Archangel: city in the north of European Russia at the delta of the Dvina River, close to the White Sea **13** fortnight: period of two weeks

fishing. I do not intend to sail until the month of June; and when shall I return? Ah, dear sister, how can I answer this question? If I succeed, many, many months, perhaps years, will pass before you and I may meet. If I fail, you will see me again soon, or never.

Farewell, my dear, excellent Margaret. Heaven shower down blessings on you, and save me, that I may again and again testify[1] my gratitude for all your love and kindness.

Your affectionate brother,
R. WALTON

1 testify sth.: show sth., express sth.

Letter 2

To Mrs. Saville, England.

Archangel, March 28th, 17–.

How slowly the time passes here, encompassed as I am by frost and snow! Yet a second step is taken towards my enterprise. I have hired a vessel and am occupied in collecting my sailors; those whom I have already engaged appear to be men on whom I can depend and are certainly possessed of dauntless[1] courage.

But I have one want which I have never yet been able to satisfy, and the absence of the object of which I now feel as a most severe evil. I have no friend, Margaret: when I am glowing with the enthusiasm of success, there will be none to participate my joy; if I am assailed[2] by disappointment, no one will endeavour to sustain[3] me in dejection[4]. I shall commit my thoughts to paper, it is true; but that is a poor medium for the communication of feeling. I desire the company of a man who could sympathise with me, whose eyes would reply to mine. You may deem[5] me romantic, my dear sister, but I bitterly feel the want of a friend. I have no one near me, gentle yet courageous, possessed of a cultivated as well as of a capacious[6] mind, whose tastes are like my own, to approve or amend my plans. How would such a friend repair the faults of your poor brother! I am too ardent[7] in execution[8] and too impatient of difficulties. But it is a still greater evil to me that I am self-educated: for the first fourteen years of my life I ran wild on a common[9] and read nothing but our Uncle Thomas' books of voyages. At that age I became acquainted with the celebrated poets of our own country; but it was only when

1 dauntless: fearless **2** be assailed by sth.: (here) be overcome by sth.
3 sustain sb.: (here) cheer sb. up **4** dejection: sadness **5** deem sth./sb. sth.: consider sth./sb. to be sth. **6** capacious [kəˈpeɪʃəs]: *(hier) aufnahmefähig*
7 ardent: (here) quick **8** execution: *Ausführung* **9** run wild on a common: have fun in a public, park-like place

it had ceased to be in my power to derive its most important benefits from such a conviction that I perceived[1] the necessity of becoming acquainted with more languages than that of my native country. Now I am twenty-eight and am in reality more illiterate[2] than many schoolboys of fifteen. It is true that I have thought more and that my daydreams are more extended and magnificent, but they want (as the painters call it) *keeping*[3]; and I greatly need a friend who would have sense enough not to despise[4] me as romantic, and affection enough for me to endeavour to regulate my mind.

Well, these are useless complaints; I shall certainly find no friend on the wide ocean, nor even here in Archangel, among merchants and seamen. Yet some feelings, unallied to the dross[5] of human nature, beat even in these rugged bosoms[6]. My lieutenant, for instance, is a man of wonderful courage and enterprise[7]; he is madly desirous of glory, or rather, to word my phrase more characteristically, of advancement in his profession. He is an Englishman, and in the midst of national and professional prejudices, unsoftened by cultivation[8], retains[9] some of the noblest endowments[10] of humanity. I first became acquainted with him on board a whale vessel; finding that he was unemployed in this city, I easily engaged him to assist in my enterprise.

The master[11] is a person of an excellent disposition[12] and is remarkable in the ship for his gentleness and the mildness of his discipline. This circumstance, added to his well-known integrity[13] and dauntless courage, made me very desirous to engage him. A youth passed in solitude, my best years spent under your gentle and feminine fosterage[14], has so refined the groundwork of my character

1 perceive sth.: *etw. erkennen, etw. wahrnehmen* **2** illiterate: (here) having little education **3** keeping: maintaining the proper relation between near and more distant objects; *(hier) Bezug zur Realität* **4** despise sth./sb.: look down on sth./sb. **5** unallied to the dross: *fern der Niederungen* **6** rugged bosoms: *raue Kerle* **7** enterprise: (hier) *Tatendrang* **8** unsoftened by cultivation: *nicht durch Bildung abgemildert* **9** retain sth.: keep sth. **10** endowment: quality, talent **11** master (or sailing master): officer responsible for the navigation of a sailing boat **12** disposition: (here) character **13** integrity: goodness, decency **14** fosterage: *(hier) Obhut, Pflegschaft*

that I cannot overcome an intense distaste to the usual brutality exercised on board ship: I have never believed it to be necessary, and when I heard of a mariner equally noted for his kindliness of heart and the respect and obedience[1] paid to him by his crew, I felt myself peculiarly[2] fortunate in being able to secure his services. I heard of him first in rather a romantic manner, from a lady who owes to him the happiness of her life. This, briefly, is his story. Some years ago he loved a young Russian lady of moderate[3] fortune, and having amassed a considerable sum in prize-money[4], the father of the girl consented[5] to the match. He saw his mistress once before the destined ceremony; but she was bathed in tears, and throwing herself at his feet, entreated him to spare her, confessing at the same time that she loved another, but that he was poor, and that her father would never consent to the union. My generous friend reassured the suppliant[6], and on being informed of the name of her lover, instantly abandoned his pursuit[7]. He had already bought a farm with his money, on which he had designed[8] to pass the remainder[9] of his life; but he bestowed the whole on his rival, together with the remains of his prize-money to purchase stock[10], and then himself solicited[11] the young woman's father to consent to her marriage with her lover. But the old man decidedly refused, thinking himself bound in honour to my friend, who, when he found the father inexorable[12], quitted his country, nor returned until he heard that his former mistress was married according to her inclinations. 'What a noble fellow!' you will exclaim. He is so; but then he is wholly uneducated: he is as silent as a Turk, and a kind of ignorant carelessness attends him, which,

1 obedience: *Gehorsam* **2** peculiar: particular, odd **3** moderate (adj): (here) little **4** prize-money: money paid to the crew of a ship for capturing or destroying an enemy ship **5** consent to sth. (v): approve of sth. **6** suppliant: sb. who asks/begs for sth. **7** abandon your pursuit: give up your undertaking/plan **8** design to do sth.: plan to do sth. **9** remainder: rest **10** stock (n): (here) farm animals **11** solicit sb. to do sth.: ask sb. to do sth. **12** inexorable: unstoppable, relentless

while it renders[1] his conduct[2] the more astonishing, detracts from the interest and sympathy which otherwise he would command[3].

Yet do not suppose, because I complain a little or because I can conceive a consolation for my toils[4] which I may never know, that I am wavering in my resolutions. Those are as fixed as fate, and my voyage is only now delayed until the weather shall permit my embarkation. The winter has been dreadfully severe, but the spring promises well, and it is considered as a remarkably early season, so that perhaps I may sail sooner than I expected. I shall do nothing rashly: you know me sufficiently to confide in my prudence[5] and considerateness whenever the safety of others is committed to my care.

I cannot describe to you my sensations on the near prospect of my undertaking. It is impossible to communicate to you a conception of the trembling sensation, half pleasurable and half fearful, with which I am preparing to depart. I am going to unexplored regions, to 'the land of mist and snow,' but I shall kill no albatross; therefore do not be alarmed for my safety or if I should come back to you as worn and woeful[6] as the 'Ancient Mariner.'[7] You will smile at my allusion[8], but I will disclose[9] a secret. I have often attributed my attachment to, my passionate enthusiasm for, the dangerous mysteries of ocean to that production of the most imaginative of modern poets. There is something at work in my soul which I do not understand. I am practically industrious[10] – painstaking[11]; – a workman to execute with perseverance[12] and labour – but besides this there is a love for the marvellous[13], a belief in the marvellous, intertwined in all my projects, which hurries me out of the common

1 render sb./sth.: (here) make sb./sth. be or become sth. **2** conduct (n): behaviour **3** command sth. (v): (here) deserve sth. **4** toil (n): long, hard, exhausting work **5** prudence [ˈpruːdns]: carefulness, caution **6** woeful: sad **7** 'the land of mist and snow' ... 'Ancient Mariner.': references to the ballad 'The Rime of the Ancient Mariner' by the poet S.T. Coleridge (1772–1834) **8** allusion: hint **9** disclose sth.: reveal sth. **10** industrious: *fleißig* **11** painstaking (adj): working very precisely **12** perseverance [ˌpɜːsəˈvɪərəns]: *Durchhaltewillen* **13** marvellous (n): quality of the miraculous and supernatural

pathways of men, even to the wild sea and unvisited regions I am about to explore.

But to return to dearer considerations. Shall I meet you again, after having traversed immense seas, and returned by the most southern cape of Africa or America? I dare not expect such success, yet I cannot bear to look on the reverse of the picture. Continue for the present to write to me by every opportunity: I may receive your letters on some occasions when I need them most to support my spirits. I love you very tenderly. Remember me with affection, should you never hear from me again.

Your affectionate brother,
ROBERT WALTON.

Letter 3

To Mrs. Saville, England.

July 7th, 17–.

My dear Sister,

I write a few lines in haste to say that I am safe – and well advanced on my voyage. This letter will reach England by a merchantman[1] now on its homeward voyage from Archangel; more fortunate than I, who may not see my native land, perhaps, for many years. I am, however, in good spirits: my men are bold[2] and apparently firm of purpose[3], nor do the floating sheets of ice that continually pass us, indicating the dangers of the region towards which we are advancing, appear to dismay them. We have already reached a very high latitude[4]; but it is the height of summer, and although not so warm as in England, the southern gales[5], which blow us speedily towards those shores[6] which I so ardently desire to attain[7], breathe a degree of renovating[8] warmth which I had not expected.

No incidents have hitherto befallen us that would make a figure[9] in a letter. One or two stiff gales and the springing of a leak[10] are accidents which experienced navigators scarcely remember to record, and I shall be well content if nothing worse happen to us during our voyage.

Adieu, my dear Margaret. Be assured that for my own sake, as well as yours, I will not rashly encounter danger. I will be cool, persevering, and prudent.

But success *shall* crown my endeavours. Wherefore not? Thus far I have gone, tracing a secure way over the pathless seas, the very

1 merchantman: ship used in commerce **2** bold: fearless **3** firm of purpose: confident and determined **4** (degree of) latitude: *Breitengrad* **5** gale: storm **6** shore: coast **7** attain sth.: reach sth. **8** renovating: giving new strength **9** make a figure: (here) be worth mentioning **10** leak (n): crack or hole that allows water to rush in

stars themselves being witnesses and testimonies[1] of my triumph. Why not still proceed over the untamed[2] yet obedient element? What can stop the determined heart and resolved will of man?

My swelling heart involuntarily pours[3] itself out thus. But I must finish. Heaven bless my beloved[4] sister!

R.W.

1 testimony [ˈtestɪməni]: (here) proof **2** untamed: wild **3** pour sth.: transfer sth. (i.e. a liquid) from one container to another one **4** beloved [bɪˈlʌvd]: much loved

Letter 4

To Mrs. Saville, England.

August 5th, 17–.

So strange an accident has happened to us that I cannot forbear[1] recording it, although it is very probable that you will see me before these papers can come into your possession.

Last Monday (July 31st) we were nearly surrounded by ice, which closed in the ship on all sides, scarcely leaving her the sea-room in which she floated. Our situation was somewhat dangerous, especially as we were compassed[2] round by a very thick fog. We accordingly lay to[3], hoping that some change would take place in the atmosphere and weather.

About two o'clock the mist cleared away, and we beheld[4], stretched out in every direction, vast and irregular plains of ice, which seemed to have no end. Some of my comrades groaned[5], and my own mind began to grow watchful with anxious[6] thoughts, when a strange sight suddenly attracted our attention and diverted our solicitude[7] from our own situation. We perceived a low carriage[8], fixed on a sledge and drawn by dogs, pass on towards the north, at the distance of half a mile; a being which had the shape of a man, but apparently of gigantic stature, sat in the sledge and guided the dogs. We watched the rapid progress of the traveller with our telescopes until he was lost among the distant inequalities[9] of the ice.

This appearance excited our unqualified[10] wonder. We were, as we believed, many hundred miles from any land; but this appari-

1 forbear (forbore – forborn): hold yourself back **2** compassed round by sth.: encompassed by sth., surrounded by sth. **3** lay to: stop (a ship) **4** behold (beheld – beheld) sb./sth.: see sb./sth. **5** groan (v): produce a sound of annoyance **6** anxious: fearful **7** solicitude: worries **8** carriage: *(hier) Gefährt* **9** inequalities: *(hier) Unregelmäßigkeiten* **10** unqualified: (here) great

tion[1] seemed to denote[2] that it was not, in reality, so distant as we had supposed. Shut in, however, by ice, it was impossible to follow his track, which we had observed with the greatest attention.

About two hours after this occurrence we heard the ground sea[3], and before night the ice broke and freed our ship. We, however, lay to until the morning, fearing to encounter in the dark those large loose masses which float about after the breaking up of the ice. I profited of this time to rest for a few hours.

In the morning, however, as soon as it was light, I went upon deck and found all the sailors busy on one side of the vessel, apparently talking to someone in the sea. It was, in fact, a sledge, like that we had seen before, which had drifted towards us in the night on a large fragment of ice. Only one dog remained alive; but there was a human being within it whom the sailors were persuading to enter the vessel. He was not, as the other traveller seemed to be, a savage inhabitant of some undiscovered island, but a European. When I appeared on deck the master said, 'Here is our captain, and he will not allow you to perish[4] on the open sea.'

On perceiving me, the stranger addressed me in English, although with a foreign accent. 'Before I come on board your vessel,' said he, 'will you have the kindness to inform me whither[5] you are bound?'

You may conceive my astonishment on hearing such a question addressed to me from a man on the brink of destruction and to whom I should have supposed that my vessel would have been a resource[6] which he would not have exchanged for the most precious wealth the earth can afford. I replied, however, that we were on a voyage of discovery towards the northern pole.

Upon hearing this he appeared satisfied and consented to come on board. Good God! Margaret, if you had seen the man who thus capitulated for his safety[7], your surprise would have been bound-

1 apparition: *Erscheinung* **2** denote: indicate **3** ground sea: (here) swelling of the sea level causing a strong landward wave **4** perish: die **5** whither: where (to) **6** resource: (here) place of rescue **7** who thus capitulated for his safety: *der so seiner Rettung zustimmte*

less. His limbs were nearly frozen, and his body dreadfully emaciated[1] by fatigue[2] and suffering. I never saw a man in so wretched[3] a condition. We attempted to carry him into the cabin, but as soon as he had quitted the fresh air he fainted. We accordingly brought him back to the deck and restored him to animation by rubbing him with brandy and forcing him to swallow a small quantity. As soon as he showed signs of life we wrapped him up in blankets and placed him near the chimney of the kitchen stove. By slow degrees he recovered and ate a little soup, which restored him wonderfully.

Two days passed in this manner before he was able to speak, and I often feared that his sufferings had deprived[4] him of understanding. When he had in some measure recovered, I removed him to my own cabin and attended[5] on him as much as my duty would permit. I never saw a more interesting creature: his eyes have generally an expression of wildness, and even madness, but there are moments when, if anyone performs an act of kindness towards him or does him the most trifling[6] service, his whole countenance[7] is lighted up, as it were, with a beam of benevolence[8] and sweetness that I never saw equalled. But he is generally melancholy and despairing, and sometimes he gnashes his teeth[9], as if impatient of the weight of woes that oppresses him.

When my guest was a little recovered I had great trouble to keep off the men, who wished to ask him a thousand questions; but I would not allow him to be tormented by their idle[10] curiosity, in a state of body and mind whose restoration evidently depended upon entire repose[11]. Once, however, the lieutenant asked why he had come so far upon the ice in so strange a vehicle.

His countenance instantly assumed an aspect[12] of the deepest gloom[13], and he replied, 'To seek one who fled from me.'

1 emaciated: *ausgemergelt* **2** fatigue (n): tiredness **3** wretched (adj): miserable, awful **4** deprive sb. of sth.: take away sth. from sb. **5** attend (on) sb.: care for sb. **6** trifling: insignificant **7** countenance: facial expression **8** benevolence: grace, kindness **9** gnash your teeth: *mit den Zähnen knirschen* **10** idle: (here) pointless **11** repose (n): rest, sleep **12** aspect: (here) appearance, look **13** gloom (n): desolation, unhappiness

'And did the man whom you pursued[1] travel in the same fashion?'

'Yes.'

'Then I fancy we have seen him, for the day before we picked you up we saw some dogs drawing a sledge, with a man in it, across the ice.'

This aroused the stranger's attention, and he asked a multitude of questions concerning the route which the daemon, as he called him, had pursued. Soon after, when he was alone with me, he said, 'I have, doubtless, excited your curiosity, as well as that of these good people; but you are too considerate to make inquiries[2].'

'Certainly; it would indeed be very impertinent[3] and inhuman of me to trouble you with any inquisitiveness[4] of mine.'

'And yet you rescued me from a strange and perilous[5] situation; you have benevolently restored me to life.'

Soon after this he inquired[6] if I thought that the breaking up of the ice had destroyed the other sledge. I replied that I could not answer with any degree of certainty, for the ice had not broken until near midnight, and the traveller might have arrived at a place of safety before that time; but of this I could not judge.

From this time a new spirit of life animated the decaying frame[7] of the stranger. He manifested[8] the greatest eagerness to be upon deck to watch for the sledge which had before appeared; but I have persuaded him to remain in the cabin, for he is far too weak to sustain[9] the rawness of the atmosphere. I have promised that someone should watch for him and give him instant notice if any new object should appear in sight.

Such is my journal of what relates to this strange occurrence up to the present day. The stranger has gradually improved in health but is very silent and appears uneasy when anyone except myself

1 pursue sb./sth.: follow sb./sth. **2** make inquiries: ask questions **3** impertinent: *aufdringlich* **4** inquisitiveness: nosiness, excessive curiosity **5** perilous: dangerous **6** inquire: ask **7** decaying frame: (here) unhealthy condition **8** manifest sth. (v): show sth., display sth. **9** sustain sth.: (here) bear sth., endure sth.

enters his cabin. Yet his manners are so conciliating[1] and gentle that the sailors are all interested in him, although they have had very little communication with him. For my own part, I begin to love him as a brother, and his constant and deep grief fills me with sympathy and compassion. He must have been a noble creature in his better days, being even now in wreck[2] so attractive and amiable.

I said in one of my letters, my dear Margaret, that I should find no friend on the wide ocean; yet I have found a man who, before his spirit had been broken by misery, I should have been happy to have possessed as the brother of my heart.

I shall continue my journal concerning the stranger at intervals, should I have any fresh incidents to record.

August 13th, 17–.

My affection for my guest increases every day. He excites at once my admiration and my pity to an astonishing degree. How can I see so noble a creature destroyed by misery[3] without feeling the most poignant[4] grief? He is so gentle, yet so wise; his mind is so cultivated, and when he speaks, although his words are culled with the choicest art[5], yet they flow with rapidity and unparalleled eloquence[6].

He is now much recovered from his illness and is continually on the deck, apparently watching for the sledge that preceded[7] his own. Yet, although unhappy, he is not so utterly occupied by his own misery but that he interests himself deeply in the projects of others. He has frequently conversed with me on mine, which I have communicated to him without disguise[8]. He entered attentively into all my arguments in favour of my eventual success and into every minute[9] detail of the measures I had taken to secure it. I was easily led by

1 conciliating: *entgegenkommend* **2** in wreck: destroyed, broken **3** misery: *Elend* **4** poignant ['pɔɪnjənt]: strong, heavy **5** his words are culled with the choicest art: he used carefully selected and artful vocabulary **6** eloquence: ability to speak very convincingly **7** precede sth.: come ahead of sth., be earlier than sth. **8** without disguise: (here) without holding anything back **9** minute [maɪ'njuːt]: very small

the sympathy which he evinced[1] to use the language of my heart, to give utterance[2] to the burning ardour of my soul, and to say, with all the fervour[3] that warmed me, how gladly I would sacrifice my fortune, my existence, my every hope, to the furtherance of my enterprise. One man's life or death were but a small price to pay for the acquirement[4] of the knowledge which I sought[5], for the dominion[6] I should acquire and transmit over the elemental foes[7] of our race. As I spoke, a dark gloom spread over my listener's countenance. At first I perceived that he tried to suppress his emotion; he placed his hands before his eyes, and my voice quivered[8] and failed me as I beheld tears trickle fast from between his fingers; a groan burst from his heaving[9] breast. I paused; at length he spoke, in broken accents: 'Unhappy man! Do you share my madness? Have you drunk also of the intoxicating draught[10]? Hear me; let me reveal my tale, and you will dash[11] the cup from your lips!'

Such words, you may imagine, strongly excited my curiosity; but the paroxysm[12] of grief that had seized the stranger overcame his weakened powers, and many hours of repose and tranquil[13] conversation were necessary to restore his composure[14].

Having conquered the violence of his feelings, he appeared to despise himself for being the slave of passion; and quelling[15] the dark tyranny of despair, he led me again to converse concerning myself personally. He asked me the history of my earlier years. The tale was quickly told, but it awakened various trains of reflection. I spoke of my desire of finding a friend, of my thirst for a more intimate sympathy with a fellow mind than had ever fallen to my lot, and expressed my conviction that a man could boast of little happiness who did not enjoy this blessing.

1 evince sth.: demonstrate sth. **2** give utterance to sth.: express sth. in words **3** fervour: enthusiasm **4** acquirement of sth.: act of taking possession of sth. **5** seek sth. (sought – sought): look for sth. **6** dominion: (here) authority **7** foe: enemy **8** quiver (v): shake **9** heave: (here) breathe heavily **10** intoxicating draught: drink containing a drug or poison **11** dash (v): strike **12** paradoxysm: seizure *(Anfall, Krampf)* **13** tranquil: quiet **14** composure: state of being (or appearing to be) in control of yourself **15** quell sth.: suppress sth.

'I agree with you,' replied the stranger; 'we are unfashioned[1] creatures, but half made up, if one wiser, better, dearer than ourselves – such a friend ought to be – do not lend his aid to perfectionate our weak and faulty natures. I once had a friend, the most noble of human creatures, and am entitled[2], therefore, to judge respecting friendship. You have hope, and the world before you, and have no cause for despair. But I – I have lost everything and cannot begin life anew.'

As he said this his countenance became expressive of a calm, settled grief that touched me to the heart. But he was silent and presently retired to his cabin.

Even broken in spirit as he is, no one can feel more deeply than he does the beauties of nature. The starry sky, the sea, and every sight afforded[3] by these wonderful regions seem still to have the power of elevating his soul from earth. Such a man has a double existence: he may suffer misery and be overwhelmed by disappointments, yet when he has retired into himself, he will be like a celestial spirit that has a halo[4] around him, within whose circle no grief or folly[5] ventures[6].

Will you smile at the enthusiasm I express concerning this divine wanderer? You would not if you saw him. You have been tutored and refined by books and retirement[7] from the world, and you are therefore somewhat fastidious[8]; but this only renders you the more fit to appreciate[9] the extraordinary merits[10] of this wonderful man. Sometimes I have endeavoured to discover what quality it is which he possesses that elevates him so immeasurably above any other person I ever knew. I believe it to be an intuitive discernment[11], a quick but never-failing power of judgment, a penetration[12] into the causes of things, unequalled for clearness and precision; add to this

1 unfashioned: imperfect **2** be entitled to do sth.: have a right to do sth.
3 afford sth.: (here) offer sth. **4** halo: *Heiligenschein* **5** folly: craziness
6 venture (somewhere) (v): dare to go (somewhere) **7** retirement: *(hier) Zurückgezogenheit* **8** fastidious: *anspruchsvoll* **9** appreciate sth./sb.: value and admire sth./sb. **10** merit (n): positive quality (of sb.) **11** discernment: *Scharfsinn*
12 penetration: act of getting inside sth.

a facility of expression and a voice whose varied intonations are soul-subduing[1] music.

August 19, 17–.

Yesterday the stranger said to me, 'You may easily perceive, Captain Walton, that I have suffered great and unparalleled misfortunes. I had determined at one time that the memory of these evils should die with me, but you have won me to alter[2] my determination. You seek for knowledge and wisdom, as I once did; and I ardently hope that the gratification[3] of your wishes may not be a serpent[4] to sting you, as mine has been. I do not know that the relation[5] of my disasters will be useful to you; yet, when I reflect that you are pursuing the same course, exposing yourself to the same dangers which have rendered me what I am, I imagine that you may deduce an apt[6] moral from my tale, one that may direct you if you succeed in your undertaking and console[7] you in case of failure. Prepare to hear of occurrences which are usually deemed marvellous. Were we among the tamer[8] scenes of nature I might fear to encounter your unbelief, perhaps your ridicule; but many things will appear possible in these wild and mysterious regions which would provoke the laughter of those unacquainted with the ever-varied powers of nature; nor can I doubt but that my tale conveys[9] in its series internal evidence of the truth of the events of which it is composed.'

You may easily imagine that I was much gratified[10] by the offered communication, yet I could not endure that he should renew his grief by a recital[11] of his misfortunes. I felt the greatest eagerness to hear the promised narrative, partly from curiosity and partly from a strong desire to ameliorate[12] his fate if it were in my power. I expressed these feelings in my answer.

1 soul-subduing: (here) overwhelming **2** alter sth.: change sth. **3** gratification: reward, fulfillment **4** serpent: snake **5** relation: (here) report **6** apt: suitable **7** console sb.: cheer sb. up, give relief to sb.'s trouble **8** tame: *gezähmt*
9 convey sth.: deliver sth. **10** be gratified by sth.: be happy/thankful about sth.
11 recital: telling (of a story) **12** ameliorate sth. [əˈmiːliəreɪt]: improve sth., make sth. better

'I thank you,' he replied, 'for your sympathy, but it is useless; my fate is nearly fulfilled. I wait but for one event, and then I shall repose in peace. I understand your feeling,' continued he, perceiving that I wished to interrupt him; 'but you are mistaken, my friend, if thus you will allow me to name you; nothing can alter my destiny; listen to my history, and you will perceive how irrevocably[1] it is determined.'

He then told me that he would commence his narrative the next day when I should be at leisure[2]. This promise drew from me the warmest thanks. I have resolved every night, when I am not imperatively occupied by my duties, to record[3], as nearly as possible in his own words, what he has related during the day. If I should be engaged, I will at least make notes. This manuscript will doubtless afford you the greatest pleasure; but to me, who know him and who hear it from his own lips – with what interest and sympathy shall I read it in some future day! Even now, as I commence my task, his full-toned voice swells in my ears; his lustrous[4] eyes dwell on me with all their melancholy sweetness; I see his thin hand raised in animation, while the lineaments of his face are irradiated[5] by the soul within. Strange and harrowing[6] must be his story, frightful the storm which embraced[7] the gallant vessel on its course and wrecked it – thus!

1 irrevocable: impossible to take back **2** be at leisure: have time **3** record sth. (v): (here) write down sth. **4** lustrous: reflecting light **5** irradiated: filled with light **6** harrowing: horrible **7** embrace sb./sth.: (here) take hold of sb./sth.

Chapter 1

I am by birth a Genevese, and my family is one of the most distinguished of that republic. My ancestors had been for many years counsellors and syndics[1], and my father had filled several public situations[2] with honour and reputation. He was respected by all who knew him for his integrity and indefatigable[3] attention to public business. He passed his younger days perpetually occupied by the affairs of his country; a variety of circumstances had prevented his marrying early, nor was it until the decline of life that he became a husband and the father of a family.

As the circumstances of his marriage illustrate his character, I cannot refrain from relating them. One of his most intimate friends was a merchant who, from a flourishing state, fell, through numerous mischances, into poverty. This man, whose name was Beaufort, was of a proud and unbending disposition and could not bear to live in poverty and oblivion[4] in the same country where he had formerly been distinguished for his rank and magnificence. Having paid his debts, therefore, in the most honourable manner, he retreated[5] with his daughter to the town of Lucerne, where he lived unknown and in wretchedness[6]. My father loved Beaufort with the truest friendship and was deeply grieved[7] by his retreat in these unfortunate circumstances. He bitterly deplored[8] the false pride which led his friend to a conduct so little worthy of the affection that united them. He lost no time in endeavouring to seek him out, with the hope of persuading him to begin the world again through his credit and assistance.

1 syndics: group of officials in charge of supervising the law in Geneva
2 situation: *(hier) Amt* **3** indefatigable: not becoming tired **4** oblivion: state of being forgotten or unknown **5** retreat: *sich zurückziehen* **6** wretchedness: poverty, misery **7** grieved (adj): sad **8** deplore sth.: *etw. beklagen*

Beaufort had taken effectual measures to conceal[1] himself, and it was ten months before my father discovered his abode[2]. Overjoyed at this discovery, he hastened to the house, which was situated in a mean street near the Reuss[3]. But when he entered, misery and despair alone welcomed him. Beaufort had saved but a very small sum of money from the wreck of his fortunes, but it was sufficient to provide him with sustenance[4] for some months, and in the mean time he hoped to procure[5] some respectable employment in a merchant's house. The interval was, consequently, spent in inaction; his grief only became more deep and rankling[6] when he had leisure for reflection, and at length it took so fast hold of his mind that at the end of three months he lay on a bed of sickness, incapable of any exertion[7].

His daughter attended him with the greatest tenderness, but she saw with despair that their little fund[8] was rapidly decreasing and that there was no other prospect of support. But Caroline Beaufort possessed a mind of an uncommon mould[9], and her courage rose to support her in her adversity[10]. She procured plain work; she plaited[11] straw and by various means contrived to earn a pittance[12] scarcely sufficient to support life.

Several months passed in this manner. Her father grew worse; her time was more entirely occupied in attending him; her means of subsistence[13] decreased; and in the tenth month her father died in her arms, leaving her an orphan[14] and a beggar. This last blow overcame her, and she knelt by Beaufort's coffin weeping bitterly, when my father entered the chamber. He came like a protecting spirit to the poor girl, who committed herself to his care; and after the

1 conceal sb./sth.: hide sb./sth. **2** abode: home **3** Reuss: river running through Lucerne **4** sustenance: money to provide for the basic necessities of life **5** procure sth.: receive sth., take up sth. **6** rankling: frustrating **7** exertion: physical activity **8** fund (n): sum of money **9** mould (n): form, (here) sort **10** adversity: misfortune **11** plait (sth.): *(etw.) flechten* **12** pittance: very small amount of money **13** means of subsistence: *Geldmittel* **14** orphan: child whose parents have died

interment[1] of his friend he conducted her to Geneva and placed her under the protection of a relation[2]. Two years after this event Caroline became his wife.

There was a considerable difference between the ages of my parents, but this circumstance seemed to unite them only closer in bonds of devoted[3] affection. There was a sense of justice in my father's upright mind which rendered it necessary that he should approve highly to love strongly[4]. Perhaps during former years he had suffered from the late-discovered unworthiness of one beloved and so was disposed[5] to set a greater value on tried[6] worth. There was a show of gratitude and worship[7] in his attachment to my mother, differing wholly from the doating[8] fondness[9] of age, for it was inspired by reverence[10] for her virtues and a desire to be the means of, in some degree, recompensing[11] her for the sorrows she had endured, but which gave inexpressible grace to his behaviour to her. Everything was made to yield[12] to her wishes and her convenience. He strove[13] to shelter her, as a fair exotic is sheltered by the gardener, from every rougher wind and to surround her with all that could tend to excite pleasurable emotion in her soft and benevolent[14] mind. Her health, and even the tranquillity of her hitherto constant spirit, had been shaken by what she had gone through. During the two years that had elapsed previous to their marriage my father had gradually relinquished all his public functions; and immediately after their union they sought[15] the pleasant climate of Italy, and the change of scene and interest attendant[16] on a tour through that land of wonders, as a restorative for her weakened frame.

1 interment: funeral **2** relation: (here) relative **3** devoted: faithful, loving
4 that he should approve highly to love strongly: *dass die Achtung vor einem Menschen die Voraussetzung für eine starke Liebe war* **5** be disposed to sth.: have a tendency to sth. **6** tried: *erprobt, bewährt* **7** worship (n): (here) admiration
8 doating: excessive, foolish **9** fondness: love, affection **10** reverence: *Ehrfurcht, Verehrung* **11** recompense sb. for sth.: *(hier) etw. bei jdm. wiedergutmachen*
12 yield to sth.: (here) satisfy sth. **13** strive to do sth. (strove – striven; also strived – strived): make an effort to do sth. **14** benevolent: kindhearted
15 seek (a place) (sought – sought): (here) travel to (a place) **16** attendant on sth. (adj): connected with sth.

From Italy they visited Germany and France. I, their eldest child, was born at Naples, and as an infant accompanied them in their rambles[1]. I remained for several years their only child. Much as they were attached to each other, they seemed to draw inexhaustible stores of affection from a very mine of love to bestow them upon me. My mother's tender caresses[2] and my father's smile of benevolent pleasure while regarding me are my first recollections. I was their plaything and their idol, and something better – their child, the innocent and helpless creature bestowed on them by heaven, whom to bring up to good, and whose future lot[3] it was in their hands to direct to happiness or misery, according as they fulfilled their duties towards me. With this deep consciousness of what they owed towards the being to which they had given life, added to the active spirit of tenderness that animated both, it may be imagined that while during every hour of my infant life I received a lesson of patience, of charity[4], and of self-control, I was so guided by a silken cord that all seemed but one train of enjoyment to me.

For a long time I was their only care. My mother had much desired to have a daughter, but I continued[5] their single offspring. When I was about five years old, while making an excursion beyond the frontiers of Italy, they passed a week on the shores of the Lake of Como. Their benevolent disposition often made them enter the cottages of the poor. This, to my mother, was more than a duty; it was a necessity, a passion – remembering what she had suffered, and how she had been relieved – for her to act in her turn the guardian angel[6] to the afflicted[7]. During one of their walks a poor cot[8] in the foldings of a vale[9] attracted their notice as being singularly disconsolate[10], while the number of half-clothed children gathered about it spoke of penury[11] in its worst shape. One day, when my father had gone by himself to Milan, my mother, accompanied by me, visited

1 ramble (n): aimless, yet pleasurable trip **2** caress (n): act of touching sb. in a tender and loving way **3** future lot: destiny **4** charity: *(hier) Güte*
5 continue: (here) remain **6** guardian angel: *Schutzengel* **7** afflicted (n, pl): people who are poor and/or suffer from a disease **8** cot: hut, small house
9 vale: valley **10** disconsolate: shabby **11** penury: poverty

this abode. She found a peasant and his wife, hard working, bent down by care and labour, distributing a scanty meal to five hungry babes. Among these there was one which attracted my mother far above all the rest. She appeared of a different stock. The four others were dark-eyed, hardy[1] little vagrants[2]; this child was thin and very fair. Her hair was the brightest living gold, and despite the poverty of her clothing, seemed to set a crown of distinction on her head. Her brow was clear and ample, her blue eyes cloudless, and her lips and the moulding of her face so expressive of sensibility and sweetness that none could behold her without looking on her as of a distinct species, a being heaven-sent, and bearing[3] a celestial stamp in all her features.

The peasant woman, perceiving that my mother fixed eyes of wonder and admiration on this lovely girl, eagerly communicated her history. She was not her child, but the daughter of a Milanese nobleman. Her mother was a German and had died on giving her birth. The infant had been placed with these good people to nurse: they were better off then. They had not been long married, and their eldest child was but just born. The father of their charge[4] was one of those Italians nursed[5] in the memory of the antique glory of Italy – one among the *schiavi ognor frementi*[6], who exerted himself to obtain the liberty of his country. He became the victim of its weakness. Whether he had died or still lingered in the dungeons[7] of Austria was not known. His property was confiscated; his child became an orphan and a beggar. She continued with her foster parents and bloomed in their rude abode, fairer than a garden rose among dark-leaved brambles[8].

1 hardy: robust, tough **2** vagrant (n): homeless wanderer **3** bear sth.: (here) have sth. **4** charge: *(hier) Schützling* **5** nurse sb. (v): bring sb. up **6** schiavi ognor frementi (Ital.): 'slaves in permanent uproar'; this phrase refers to the resistance put up by the Northern Italians against Austria which ruled over much of their territory after the Vienna Congress in 1814/15 **7** dungeon: *Kerker* **8** bramble: *Brombeerstrauch*

When my father returned from Milan, he found playing with me in the hall of our villa a child fairer than pictured cherub[1] – a creature who seemed to shed radiance from her looks and whose form and motions were lighter than the chamois[2] of the hills. The apparition was soon explained. With his permission my mother prevailed[3] on her rustic[4] guardians to yield their charge to her. They were fond of the sweet orphan. Her presence had seemed a blessing to them, but it would be unfair to her to keep her in poverty and want when Providence[5] afforded her such powerful protection. They consulted their village priest, and the result was that Elizabeth Lavenza became the inmate[6] of my parents' house – my more than sister – the beautiful and adored companion of all my occupations and my pleasures.

Everyone loved Elizabeth. The passionate and almost reverential[7] attachment with which all regarded her became, while I shared it, my pride and my delight. On the evening previous to her being brought to my home, my mother had said playfully, 'I have a pretty present for my Victor – tomorrow he shall have it.' And when, on the morrow, she presented Elizabeth to me as her promised gift, I, with childish seriousness, interpreted her words literally and looked upon Elizabeth as mine – mine to protect, love, and cherish. All praises bestowed on her I received as made to a possession of my own. We called each other familiarly by the name of cousin. No word, no expression could body forth[8] the kind of relation in which she stood to me – my more than sister, since till death she was to be mine only.

1 cherub: angel **2** chamois ['ʃæmwɑː]: goatlike animal of mountainous regions *(Gemse)* **3** prevail on sb. to do sth.: convince sb. to do sth. **4** rustic (adj): *(hier) bäuerlich* **5** Providence: *(göttliche) Vorsehung* **6** inmate: (here) occupant **7** reverential: deeply admiring **8** body forth sth.: describe sth.

Chapter 2

We were brought up together; there was not quite a year difference in our ages. I need not say that we were strangers to any species of disunion or dispute. Harmony was the soul of our companionship, and the diversity and contrast that subsisted in our characters drew us nearer together. Elizabeth was of a calmer and more concentrated disposition; but, with all my ardour, I was capable of a more intense application[1] and was more deeply smitten[2] with the thirst for knowledge. She busied herself with following the aerial creations of the poets; and in the majestic and wondrous scenes which surrounded our Swiss home – the sublime[3] shapes of the mountains, the changes of the seasons, tempest and calm, the silence of winter, and the life and turbulence of our Alpine summers – she found ample scope[4] for admiration and delight. While my companion contemplated[5] with a serious and satisfied spirit the magnificent appearances of things, I delighted in investigating their causes. The world was to me a secret which I desired to divine[6]. Curiosity, earnest research to learn the hidden laws of nature, gladness akin[7] to rapture[8], as they were unfolded to me, are among the earliest sensations I can remember.

On the birth of a second son, my junior[9] by seven years, my parents gave up entirely their wandering life and fixed themselves in their native country. We possessed a house in Geneva, and a *campagne*[10] on Belrive, the eastern shore of the lake, at the distance of rather more than a league[11] from the city. We resided principally in

1 application: energetic effort **2** be smitten with sth.: have a passion for sth. **3** sublime (adj): awesome, stunning **4** scope (n): opportunity **5** contemplate sth.: think about sth. thoroughly **6** divine sth.: discover sth. by insight **7** akin to sth.: similar to sth. **8** rapture (n): *Verzückung* **9** my junior by seven years: seven years younger than me **10** campagne (Fr.): cottage **11** 1 league = 3 miles (ca. 5 kilometers)

the latter, and the lives of my parents were passed in considerable seclusion[1]. It was my temper to avoid a crowd and to attach myself fervently to a few. I was indifferent, therefore, to my school-fellows in general; but I united myself in the bonds of the closest friendship to one among them. Henry Clerval was the son of a merchant of Geneva. He was a boy of singular talent and fancy. He loved enterprise, hardship, and even danger for its own sake. He was deeply read in books of chivalry[2] and romance. He composed heroic songs and began to write many a tale of enchantment and knightly adventure. He tried to make us act plays and to enter into masquerades, in which the characters were drawn from the heroes of Roncesvalles[3], of the Round Table of King Arthur, and the chivalrous train[4] who shed their blood to redeem[5] the holy sepulchre[6] from the hands of the infidels[7].

No human being could have passed a happier childhood than myself. My parents were possessed by the very spirit of kindness and indulgence[8]. We felt that they were not the tyrants to rule our lot according to their caprice[9], but the agents and creators of all the many delights which we enjoyed. When I mingled with other families I distinctly discerned how peculiarly fortunate my lot was, and gratitude assisted the development of filial love[10].

My temper was sometimes violent[11], and my passions vehement; but by some law in my temperature[12] they were turned not towards childish pursuits[13] but to an eager desire to learn, and not to learn all things indiscriminately[14]. I confess that neither the structure of languages, nor the code of governments, nor the politics of various states possessed attractions for me. It was the secrets of heaven and earth that I desired to learn; and whether it was the outward

1 seclusion: aloneness **2** chivalry: tradition of knights **3** Roncesvalles: town in the (French) Pyrenees and site of a famous battle in 778 **4** train (n): *(hier) Gefolge* **5** redeem sth.: win sth. back **6** sepulchre: grave **7** infidel (n, derog): person who does not believe in God **8** indulgence: kindness **9** caprice [kəˈpriːs]: *Laune, Willkür* **10** filial love: love felt for your parents **11** violent: (here) passionate, wild **12** temperature (old use): (here) temperament **13** pursuits (pl): (here) interests **14** indiscriminate: random

substance of things or the inner spirit of nature and the mysterious soul of man that occupied me, still my inquiries were directed to the metaphysical[1], or in its highest sense, the physical secrets of the world.

Meanwhile Clerval occupied himself, so to speak, with the moral relations of things. The busy stage of life, the virtues of heroes, and the actions of men were his theme; and his hope and his dream was to become one among those whose names are recorded in story as the gallant and adventurous benefactors[2] of our species. The saintly soul of Elizabeth shone like a shrine-dedicated lamp[3] in our peaceful home. Her sympathy was ours; her smile, her soft voice, the sweet glance of her celestial eyes, were ever there to bless and animate us. She was the living spirit of love to soften and attract; I might have become sullen[4] in my study, through the ardour of my nature, but that she was there to subdue[5] me to a semblance of her own gentleness. And Clerval – could aught[6] ill entrench[7] on the noble spirit of Clerval? Yet he might not have been so perfectly humane, so thoughtful in his generosity, so full of kindness and tenderness amidst his passion for adventurous exploit[8], had she not unfolded to him the real loveliness of beneficence[9] and made the doing good the end and aim of his soaring[10] ambition.

I feel exquisite pleasure in dwelling on the recollections of childhood, before misfortune had tainted my mind and changed its bright visions of extensive usefulness into gloomy and narrow reflections upon self. Besides, in drawing the picture of my early days, I also record those events which led, by insensible steps, to my after tale of misery, for when I would account[11] to myself for the birth of that passion which afterward ruled my destiny I find it arise, like a mountain

1 metaphysical (n): part of a reality beyond the observable physical universe **2** benefactor: person who does a good deed for a larger community **3** shrine-dedicated lamp: *ewiges Licht* **4** sullen: cheerless, gloomy **5** subdue sth./sb.: get sb./sth. under control **6** aught: something **7** ill entrench on sth./sb.: have a negative effect on sth./sb. **8** exploit (n): heroic act **9** beneficience: good-heartedness **10** soaring: (here) growing **11** account to sb.: *jdm. Rechenschaft ablegen*

river, from ignoble[1] and almost forgotten sources; but, swelling as it proceeded, it became the torrent[2] which, in its course, has swept away all my hopes and joys.

Natural philosophy[3] is the genius[4] that has regulated my fate; I desire, therefore, in this narration, to state those facts which led to my predilection[5] for that science. When I was thirteen years of age we all went on a party[6] of pleasure to the baths near Thonon[7]; the inclemency[8] of the weather obliged us to remain a day confined to the inn. In this house I chanced[9] to find a volume of the works of Cornelius Agrippa[10]. I opened it with apathy[11]; the theory which he attempts to demonstrate and the wonderful facts which he relates soon changed this feeling into enthusiasm. A new light seemed to dawn upon my mind, and bounding with joy, I communicated my discovery to my father. My father looked carelessly at the title page of my book and said, 'Ah! Cornelius Agrippa! My dear Victor, do not waste your time upon this; it is sad trash.'

If, instead of this remark, my father had taken the pains to explain to me that the principles of Agrippa had been entirely exploded[12] and that a modern system of science had been introduced which possessed much greater powers than the ancient, because the powers of the latter were chimerical[13], while those of the former were real and practical, under such circumstances I should certainly have thrown Agrippa aside and have contented my imagination, warmed as it was, by returning with greater ardour to my former studies. It is even possible that the train of my ideas would never have received the fatal impulse that led to my ruin. But the cursory[14] glance my father had taken of my volume by no means assured me that he

1 ignoble: bad, shameful **2** torrent: violent stream **3** natural philosophy: old term for natural science **4** genius: attendant spirit in ancient Roman religion **5** predilection: preference **6** party: (here) trip with a group of people **7** Thonon: town on the shore of Lake Geneva **8** inclemency: harshness **9** chance to do sth.: happen to do sth., do sth. by coincidence **10** Cornelius Agrippa (1486–1535): German physician and universal scholar who is best known for his works on magic **11** apathy: lack of interest **12** explode sth.: refute sth., show that sth. is wrong **13** chimerical: made-up, imagined **14** cursory: quick, without paying much attention

was acquainted with its contents, and I continued to read with the greatest avidity[1].

When I returned home my first care was to procure the whole works of this author, and afterwards of Paracelsus[2] and Albertus Magnus[3]. I read and studied the wild fancies of these writers with delight; they appeared to me treasures known to few besides myself. I have described myself as always having been imbued[4] with a fervent longing to penetrate the secrets of nature. In spite of the intense labour and wonderful discoveries of modern philosophers, I always came from my studies discontented and unsatisfied. Sir Isaac Newton[5] is said to have avowed[6] that he felt like a child picking up shells beside the great and unexplored ocean of truth. Those of his successors in each branch of natural philosophy with whom I was acquainted appeared even to my boy's apprehensions[7] as tyros[8] engaged in the same pursuit.

The untaught peasant beheld the elements around him and was acquainted with their practical uses. The most learned philosopher knew little more. He had partially unveiled[9] the face of Nature, but her immortal lineaments were still a wonder and a mystery. He might dissect[10], anatomise, and give names; but, not to speak of a final cause, causes in their secondary and tertiary grades were utterly unknown to him. I had gazed upon the fortifications[11] and impediments[12] that seemed to keep human beings from entering the citadel of nature, and rashly and ignorantly I had repined[13].

But here were books, and here were men who had penetrated deeper and knew more. I took their word for all that they averred[14],

1 avidity: (here) enthusiasm **2** Paracelsus (1493–1541): influential Swiss physician and universal scholar **3** Albertus Magnus (1200–1280): German universal scholar and pioneer of modern natural science **4** imbue sb. with sth.: *jdn. mit etw. erfüllen* **5** Isaac Newton (1643–1727): English scientist whose findings laid the foundation for many principles in physics and mathematics **6** avow sth.: admit sth., declare sth. **7** apprehension: understanding **8** tyro: beginner **9** unveil sth.: uncover sth. **10** dissect sth.: cut up sth. into pieces (e.g. an animal's body) **11** fortifications (pl): *Befestigungsanlage* **12** impediment: obstacle **13** repine: feel dissatisfied **14** aver sth.: claim sth.

and I became their disciple[1]. It may appear strange that such should arise in the eighteenth century; but while I followed the routine of education in the schools of Geneva, I was, to a great degree, self-taught with regard to my favourite studies. My father was not scientific, and I was left to struggle with a child's blindness, added to a student's thirst for knowledge. Under the guidance of my new preceptors[2] I entered with the greatest diligence[3] into the search of the philosopher's stone[4] and the elixir of life; but the latter soon obtained my undivided attention. Wealth was an inferior object, but what glory would attend the discovery if I could banish[5] disease from the human frame and render man invulnerable[6] to any but a violent death!

Nor were these my only visions. The raising of ghosts or devils was a promise liberally accorded by my favourite authors, the fulfillment of which I most eagerly sought; and if my incantations[7] were always unsuccessful, I attributed the failure rather to my own inexperience and mistake than to a want of skill or fidelity[8] in my instructors. And thus for a time I was occupied by exploded systems, mingling, like an unadept[9], a thousand contradictory theories and floundering[10] desperately in a very slough[11] of multifarious[12] knowledge, guided by an ardent imagination and childish reasoning, till an accident again changed the current of my ideas.

When I was about fifteen years old we had retired to our house near Belrive, when we witnessed a most violent and terrible thunderstorm. It advanced from behind the mountains of Jura[13], and the thunder burst at once with frightful loudness from various quarters of the heavens. I remained, while the storm lasted, watching

1 disciple [dɪˈsaɪpl]: follower, pupil **2** preceptor: teacher, instructor
3 diligence: *Fleiß* **4** philosopher's stone: unknown substance searched for by scientists for its supposed ability to turn metals like iron into precious ones, especially gold and silver. It was also believed that an elixir of life could be produced with the substance's help. **5** banish sth./sb.: remove sth./sb.
6 invulnerable: incapable of being wounded **7** incantation: *Beschwörung*
8 fidelity: (here) trustworthiness **9** unadept (n): *(hier) Laie* **10** flounder: move with much effort **11** slough: swamp **12** multifarious: having many different forms **13** Jura: mountain range at the French-Swiss border

its progress with curiosity and delight. As I stood at the door, on a sudden I beheld a stream of fire issue[1] from an old and beautiful oak[2] which stood about twenty yards from our house; and so soon as the dazzling light vanished[3], the oak had disappeared, and nothing remained but a blasted stump. When we visited it the next morning, we found the tree shattered in a singular manner. It was not splintered by the shock, but entirely reduced to thin ribbons[4] of wood. I never beheld anything so utterly destroyed.

Before this I was not unacquainted with the more obvious laws of electricity. On this occasion a man of great research in natural philosophy was with us, and excited by this catastrophe[5], he entered on the explanation of a theory which he had formed on the subject of electricity and galvanism, which was at once new and astonishing to me. All that he said threw greatly into the shade[6] Cornelius Agrippa, Albertus Magnus, and Paracelsus, the lords of my imagination; but by some fatality[7] the overthrow[8] of these men disinclined[9] me to pursue my accustomed studies. It seemed to me as if nothing would or could ever be known. All that had so long engaged my attention suddenly grew despicable[10]. By one of those caprices of the mind which we are perhaps most subject to in early youth, I at once gave up my former occupations, set down natural history and all its progeny as a deformed and abortive[11] creation, and entertained the greatest disdain[12] for a would-be science which could never even step within the threshold[13] of real knowledge. In this mood of mind I betook[14] myself to the mathematics and the branches of study appertaining to that science as being built upon secure foundations, and so worthy of my consideration.

1 issue from sth. (v): (here) come out of sth. **2** oak: *Eiche* **3** vanish: disappear **4** ribbon (n): *(hier) Fetzen* **5** catastrophe: (here) signifcant event **6** throw sb./sth. into the shade: prove to be better than sb./sth. **7** by some fatality: by coincidence, as a result of fate **8** overthrow (n): downfall **9** disincline sb. to do sth.: make sb. unwilling to do sth. **10** despicable [dɪˈspɪkəbl]: *verabscheuungswürdig* **11** abortive: failed **12** disdain (n): hatred **13** threshold: *Schwelle* **14** betake yourself to sth. (betook – betaken): commit yourself to sth.

Thus strangely are our souls constructed, and by such slight ligaments[1] are we bound to prosperity or ruin. When I look back, it seems to me as if this almost miraculous change of inclination and will was the immediate suggestion of the guardian angel of my life – the last effort made by the spirit of preservation to avert the storm that was even then hanging in the stars and ready to envelope me. Her victory was announced by an unusual tranquillity and gladness of soul which followed the relinquishing of my ancient and latterly tormenting studies. It was thus that I was to be taught to associate evil with their prosecution[2], happiness with their disregard[3].

It was a strong effort of the spirit of good, but it was ineffectual. Destiny was too potent[4], and her immutable[5] laws had decreed[6] my utter[7] and terrible destruction.

1 ligament: *Band* **2** prosecution: *(hier) Durchführung, Fortführung* **3** disregard (n): lack of interest **4** potent: strong **5** immutable: unchangeable **6** decree sth.: determine sth. **7** utter (adj): absolute

Chapter 3

When I had attained the age of seventeen my parents resolved that I should become a student at the university of Ingolstadt[1]. I had hitherto attended the schools of Geneva, but my father thought it necessary for the completion of my education that I should be made acquainted with other customs than those of my native country. My departure was therefore fixed at an early date, but before the day resolved upon could arrive, the first misfortune of my life occurred – an omen, as it were, of my future misery.

Elizabeth had caught the scarlet fever[2]; her illness was severe, and she was in the greatest danger. During her illness many arguments had been urged to persuade my mother to refrain from attending upon her. She had at first yielded[3] to our entreaties, but when she heard that the life of her favourite was menaced[4], she could no longer control her anxiety. She attended her sickbed; her watchful attentions triumphed over the malignity[5] of the distemper[6] – Elizabeth was saved, but the consequences of this imprudence[7] were fatal to her preserver[8]. On the third day my mother sickened; her fever was accompanied by the most alarming symptoms, and the looks of her medical attendants prognosticated[9] the worst event. On her deathbed the fortitude and benignity[10] of this best of women did not desert her. She joined the hands of Elizabeth and myself. 'My children,' she said, 'my firmest hopes of future happiness were placed on the prospect of your union. This expectation will now be the consolation of your father. Elizabeth, my love, you must supply

1 Ingolstadt: town in central Bavaria, Germany **2** scarlet fever: *Scharlach*
3 yield to sb./sth.: give in to sb./sth. **4** menace sb./sth. (v): threaten sb./sth., put sb./sth. in danger **5** malignity: evilness, hostility; (here) seriousness
6 distemper: (here) disease **7** imprudence: carelessness **8** preserver: saviour
9 prognosticate: foretell **10** benignity [biˈnignətē]: kindness

my place to my younger children. Alas![1] I regret that I am taken from you; and, happy and beloved as I have been, is it not hard to quit you all? But these are not thoughts befitting me; I will endeavour to resign[2] myself cheerfully to death and will indulge[3] a hope of meeting you in another world.'

She died calmly, and her countenance expressed affection even in death. I need not describe the feelings of those whose dearest ties are rent[4] by that most irreparable evil, the void that presents itself to the soul, and the despair that is exhibited on the countenance. It is so long before the mind can persuade itself that she whom we saw every day and whose very existence appeared a part of our own can have departed forever – that the brightness of a beloved eye can have been extinguished and the sound of a voice so familiar and dear to the ear can be hushed, never more to be heard. These are the reflections of the first days; but when the lapse of time proves the reality of the evil, then the actual bitterness of grief commences. Yet from whom has not that rude hand rent away some dear connection? And why should I describe a sorrow which all have felt, and must feel? The time at length arrives when grief is rather an indulgence[5] than a necessity; and the smile that plays upon the lips, although it may be deemed a sacrilege[6], is not banished. My mother was dead, but we had still duties which we ought to perform; we must continue our course with the rest and learn to think ourselves fortunate whilst one remains whom the spoiler[7] has not seized.

My departure for Ingolstadt, which had been deferred[8] by these events, was now again determined upon. I obtained from my father a respite[9] of some weeks. It appeared to me sacrilege so soon to leave the repose[10], akin to death, of the house of mourning[11] and to rush into the thick of life. I was new to sorrow, but it did not the less

1 alas (interj): utterance to express unhappiness or concern *(ach!)* **2** resign yourself to sth.: accept sth. that is unpleasant but inevitable **3** indulge sth.: allow yourself to have sth. **4** rend sth. (rent – rent): tear sth. into pieces
5 indulgence: (here) chosen option, luxury **6** sacrilege: act of disrespect to God
7 spoiler: (here) metaphor for death **8** defer sth.: delay sth. **9** respite: break
10 repose: (here) quietness **11** mourning: time of grief after a person's death

alarm me. I was unwilling to quit the sight of those that remained to me, and above all, I desired to see my sweet Elizabeth in some degree consoled.

She indeed veiled[1] her grief and strove to act the comforter to us all. She looked steadily on life and assumed its duties with courage and zeal[2]. She devoted herself to those whom she had been taught to call her uncle and cousins. Never was she so enchanting as at this time, when she recalled the sunshine of her smiles and spent them upon us. She forgot even her own regret in her endeavours to make us forget.

The day of my departure at length arrived. Clerval spent the last evening with us. He had endeavoured to persuade his father to permit him to accompany me and to become my fellow student, but in vain. His father was a narrow-minded trader and saw idleness[3] and ruin in the aspirations[4] and ambition of his son. Henry deeply felt the misfortune of being debarred[5] from a liberal education. He said little, but when he spoke I read in his kindling eye and in his animated glance a restrained[6] but firm resolve[7] not to be chained to the miserable details of commerce.

We sat late. We could not tear ourselves away from each other nor persuade ourselves to say the word 'Farewell!' It was said, and we retired under the pretence of seeking repose, each fancying that the other was deceived; but when at morning's dawn I descended to the carriage which was to convey me away, they were all there – my father again to bless me, Clerval to press my hand once more, my Elizabeth to renew her entreaties that I would write often and to bestow the last feminine attentions on her playmate and friend.

I threw myself into the chaise[8] that was to convey me away and indulged in the most melancholy reflections. I, who had ever been surrounded by amiable companions, continually engaged in

1 veil sth.: hide sth. **2** zeal: enthusiasm **3** idleness: inactivity, laziness **4** aspiration: strong wish **5** debar sb. from sth.: exclude sb. from sth., deny sth. to sb. **6** restrained (adj): controlled **7** resolve (n): determination **8** chaise (Fr.): two-wheeled, horse-drawn carriage

became more obsessed with science in order to cope?

endeavouring to bestow mutual[1] pleasure – I was now alone. In the university whither I was going I must form my own friends and be my own protector. My life had hitherto been remarkably secluded[2] and domestic[3], and this had given me invincible[4] repugnance[5] to new countenances. I loved my brothers, Elizabeth, and Clerval; these were 'old familiar faces,' but I believed myself totally unfitted for the company of strangers. Such were my reflections as I commenced my journey; but as I proceeded, my spirits and hopes rose. I ardently desired the acquisition of knowledge. I had often, when at home, thought it hard to remain during my youth cooped[6] up in one place and had longed to enter the world and take my station among other human beings. Now my desires were complied with, and it would, indeed, have been folly to repent[7].

I had sufficient leisure for these and many other reflections during my journey to Ingolstadt, which was long and fatiguing. At length the high white steeple[8] of the town met my eyes. I alighted[9] and was conducted to my solitary[10] apartment to spend the evening as I pleased.

The next morning I delivered my letters of introduction and paid a visit to some of the principal professors. Chance – or rather the evil influence, the Angel of Destruction, which asserted omnipotent[11] sway[12] over me from the moment I turned my reluctant steps from my father's door – led me first to M. Krempe, professor of natural philosophy. He was an uncouth[13] man, but deeply imbued in the secrets of his science. He asked me several questions concerning my progress in the different branches of science appertaining to natural philosophy. I replied carelessly, and partly in contempt[14], mentioned

1 mutual: *gegenseitig* **2** secluded: isolated **3** domestic (adj): limited to your home **4** invincible: unbeatable, (here) strong **5** repugnance: dislike **6** coop sb. up: lock sb. up **7** repent: regret **8** steeple: tip of a church tower **9** alight (v): get off **10** solitary: just for one person **11** omnipotent [ɒm'nɪpətənt]: all-powerful **12** assert sway over sb.: take control over sb. **13** uncouth [ʌn'ku:θ]: rude and primitive **14** contempt: dislike for sb./sth. you believe to be unworthy of your respect

the names of my alchemists[1] as the principal authors I had studied. The professor stared. 'Have you,' he said, 'really spent your time in studying such nonsense?'

I replied in the affirmative. 'Every minute,' continued M. Krempe with warmth, 'every instant that you have wasted on those books is utterly and entirely lost. You have burdened your memory with exploded systems and useless names. Good God! In what desert land have you lived, where no one was kind enough to inform you that these fancies which you have so greedily imbibed[2] are a thousand years old and as musty[3] as they are ancient? I little expected, in this enlightened and scientific age, to find a disciple of Albertus Magnus and Paracelsus. My dear sir, you must begin your studies entirely anew.'

So saying, he stepped aside and wrote down a list of several books treating of natural philosophy which he desired me to procure, and dismissed me after mentioning that in the beginning of the following week he intended to commence a course of lectures upon natural philosophy in its general relations, and that M. Waldman, a fellow professor, would lecture upon chemistry the alternate days that he omitted.

I returned home not disappointed, for I have said that I had long considered those authors useless whom the professor reprobated[4]; but I returned not at all the more inclined to recur to these studies in any shape. M. Krempe was a little squat[5] man with a gruff voice and a repulsive countenance; the teacher, therefore, did not prepossess[6] me in favour of his pursuits. In rather a too philosophical and connected a strain[7], perhaps, I have given an account of the conclusions I had come to concerning them in my early years. As a child I had not been content with the results promised by the modern professors of natural science. With a confusion of ideas only to be

1 alchemist: medieval scholar who studied natural substances (mainly with the goal of finding out how to turn them into gold) **2** imbibe sth.: drink sth., soak sth. up **3** musty: *muffig* **4** reprobate sb./sth.: condemn sb./sth. **5** squat (adj): *untersetzt* **6** prepossess sb. in favour of sth.: *jdn. für etw. einnehmen* **7** strain (n): (here) way

accounted for by my extreme youth and my want of a guide on such matters, I had retrod[1] the steps of knowledge along the paths of time and exchanged the discoveries of recent inquirers for the dreams of forgotten alchemists. Besides, I had a contempt for the uses of modern natural philosophy. It was very different when the masters of the science sought immortality and power; such views, although futile[2], were grand; but now the scene was changed. The ambition of the inquirer[3] seemed to limit itself to the annihilation[4] of those visions on which my interest in science was chiefly founded. I was required to exchange chimeras[5] of boundless grandeur for realities of little worth.

Such were my reflections during the first two or three days of my residence at Ingolstadt, which were chiefly spent in becoming acquainted with the localities and the principal residents in my new abode. But as the ensuing[6] week commenced, I thought of the information which M. Krempe had given me concerning the lectures. And although I could not consent to go and hear that little conceited[7] fellow deliver sentences out of a pulpit[8], I recollected what he had said of M. Waldman, whom I had never seen, as he had hitherto been out of town.

Partly from curiosity and partly from idleness, I went into the lecturing room, which M. Waldman entered shortly after. This professor was very unlike his colleague. He appeared about fifty years of age, but with an aspect expressive of the greatest benevolence; a few grey hairs covered his temples, but those at the back of his head were nearly black. His person was short but remarkably erect[9] and his voice the sweetest I had ever heard. He began his lecture by a recapitulation[10] of the history of chemistry and the various improvements made by different men of learning, pronouncing with fervour the names of the most distinguished discoverers. He then took a

1 retread sth. (retrod – retrodden): walk sth. again **2** futile: ineffective
3 inquirer: person asking questions, (here) scientist **4** annihilation: destruction
5 chimera: illusion **6** ensuing: following **7** conceited: having an excessively positive view of yourself **8** pulpit: *Kanzel*; (here) desk from which a professor gives his lecture (*Katheder*) **9** erect (adj): straight **10** recapitulation: summary

cursory view of the present state of the science and explained many of its elementary terms. After having made a few preparatory experiments, he concluded with a panegyric[1] upon modern chemistry, the terms of which I shall never forget: –

'The Ancient teachers of this science,' said he, 'promised impossibilities and performed nothing. The modern masters promise very little; they know that metals cannot be transmuted[2] and that the elixir of life is a chimera but these philosophers, whose hands seem only made to dabble[3] in dirt, and their eyes to pore over the microscope or crucible[4], have indeed performed miracles. They penetrate into the recesses[5] of nature and show how she works in her hiding-places. They ascend into the heavens; they have discovered how the blood circulates, and the nature of the air we breathe. They have acquired new and almost unlimited powers; they can command the thunders of heaven, mimic[6] the earthquake, and even mock the invisible world with its own shadows.'

Such were the professor's words – rather let me say such the words of the fate – enounced[7] to destroy me. As he went on I felt as if my soul were grappling[8] with a palpable[9] enemy; one by one the various keys were touched which formed the mechanism of my being; chord[10] after chord was sounded, and soon my mind was filled with one thought, one conception, one purpose. So much has been done, exclaimed the soul of Frankenstein – more, far more, will I achieve; treading in the steps already marked, I will pioneer a new way, explore unknown powers, and unfold to the world the deepest mysteries of creation.

→ personal intentions can cause harm

1 panegyric [ˌpænəˈdʒɪrɪk]: speech of praise **2** transmute sth.: change sth. (e.g. by magic) **3** dabble in sth.: splash in sth., (here) move around in sth.
4 crucible: container used for melting substances at very high temperatures
5 recess: *(hier) hinterster Winkel* **6** mimic sth.: imitate sth. **7** enounce sth.: state sth. **8** grapple with sb./sth.: wrestle with sb./sth. **9** palpable: *greifbar*
10 sound a chord: *eine Saite anschlagen*

I closed not my eyes that night. My internal being was in a state of insurrection[1] and turmoil[2]; I felt that order would thence[3] arise, but I had no power to produce it. By degrees, after the morning's dawn, sleep came. I awoke, and my yesternight's thoughts were as a dream. There only remained a resolution to return to my ancient studies and to devote myself to a science for which I believed myself to possess a natural talent. On the same day I paid M. Waldman a visit. His manners in private were even more mild and attractive than in public, for there was a certain dignity in his mien[4] during his lecture which in his own house was replaced by the greatest affability[5] and kindness. I gave him pretty nearly the same account of my former pursuits as I had given to his fellow professor. He heard with attention the little narration concerning my studies and smiled at the names of Cornelius Agrippa and Paracelsus, but without the contempt that M. Krempe had exhibited. He said that 'These were men to whose indefatigable zeal modern philosophers were indebted for most of the foundations of their knowledge. They had left to us, as an easier task, to give new names and arrange in connected classifications the facts which they in a great degree had been the instruments of bringing to light. The labours of men of genius, however erroneously[6] directed, scarcely ever fail in ultimately turning to the solid advantage of mankind.' I listened to his statement, which was delivered without any presumption or affectation[7], and then added that his lecture had removed my prejudices against modern chemists; I expressed myself in measured terms, with the modesty and deference[8] due[9] from a youth to his instructor, without letting escape (inexperience in life would have made me ashamed) any of the enthusiasm which stimulated my intended labours. I requested his advice concerning the books I ought to procure.

1 insurrection: rebellion **2** turmoil: *Aufruhr* **3** thence: from there; (here) thereby, by (doing) this **4** mien [mi:n]: facial expression **5** affability: friendliness **6** erroneous [ɪˈrəʊniəs]: mistaken **7** affectation: *Affektiertheit* **8** deference [ˈdefərəns]: great respect **9** due: owed

'I am happy,' said M. Waldman, 'to have gained a disciple; and if your application equals your ability, I have no doubt of your success. Chemistry is that branch of natural philosophy in which the greatest improvements have been and may be made; it is on that account that I have made it my peculiar study; but at the same time, I have not neglected the other branches of science. A man would make but a very sorry[1] chemist if he attended[2] to that department of human knowledge alone. If your wish is to become really a man of science and not merely a petty[3] experimentalist, I should advise you to apply[4] to every branch of natural philosophy, including mathematics.'

He then took me into his laboratory and explained to me the uses of his various machines, instructing me as to what I ought to procure and promising me the use of his own when I should have advanced far enough in the science not to derange[5] their mechanism. He also gave me the list of books which I had requested, and I took my leave.

Thus ended a day memorable to me; it decided my future destiny.

1 sorry (adj): *jämmerlich, armselig* **2** attend to sth.: care for sth., focus on sth.
3 petty: insignificant **4** apply (yourself) to sth.: direct attention to sth.
5 derange sth.: disturb the order or functioning of sth.

Chapter 4

From this day natural philosophy, and particularly chemistry, in the most comprehensive sense of the term, became nearly my sole occupation. I read with ardour those works, so full of genius and discrimination[1], which modern inquirers have written on these subjects. I attended the lectures and cultivated the acquaintance of the men of science of the university, and I found even in M. Krempe a great deal of sound[2] sense and real information, combined, it is true, with a repulsive[3] physiognomy and manners, but not on that account[4] the less valuable. In M. Waldman I found a true friend. His gentleness was never tinged[5] by dogmatism[6], and his instructions were given with an air of frankness[7] and good nature that banished every idea of pedantry[8]. In a thousand ways he smoothed[9] for me the path of knowledge and made the most abstruse[10] inquiries clear and facile[11] to my apprehension. My application was at first fluctuating and uncertain; it gained strength as I proceeded and soon became so ardent and eager that the stars often disappeared in the light of morning whilst I was yet engaged in my laboratory.

As I applied so closely, it may be easily conceived that my progress was rapid. My ardour was indeed the astonishment of the students, and my proficiency[12] that of the masters. Professor Krempe often asked me, with a sly[13] smile, how Cornelius Agrippa went on, whilst M. Waldman expressed the most heartfelt exultation[14] in my

1 discrimination: (here) precision **2** sound (adj): free from error **3** repulsive: unpleasant, off-putting **4** on that account: for this reason **5** tinge sth.: (here) influence sth. **6** dogmatism: set of opinions that have an insufficient basis in facts but are inflexibly held onto and promoted **7** frankness: openness, sincerity **8** pedantery: *Pedanterie, Kleinlichkeit* **9** smooth sth. (v): remove obstacles from sth., make sth. easy **10** abstruse: (here) difficult to understand **11** facile: simple, easy **12** proficiency: competence, knowlegde **13** sly: *verstohlen* **14** exultation: expression of joy and triumph

progress. Two years passed in this manner, during which I paid no visit to Geneva, but was engaged, heart and soul, in the pursuit of some discoveries which I hoped to make. None but those who have experienced them can conceive of the enticements of science. In other studies you go as far as others have gone before you, and there is nothing more to know; but in a scientific pursuit there is continual food for discovery and wonder. A mind of moderate capacity which closely pursues one study must infallibly[1] arrive at great proficiency in that study; and I, who continually sought the attainment of one object of pursuit and was solely wrapped up in this, improved so rapidly that at the end of two years I made some discoveries in the improvement of some chemical instruments, which procured me great esteem[2] and admiration at the university. When I had arrived at this point and had become as well acquainted with the theory and practice of natural philosophy as depended on the lessons of any of the professors at Ingolstadt, my residence there being no longer conducive[3] to my improvements, I thought of returning to my friends and my native town, when an incident happened that protracted[4] my stay.

One of the phenomena which had peculiarly attracted my attention was the structure of the human frame, and, indeed, any animal endued with life. Whence[5], I often asked myself, did the principle of life proceed? It was a bold question, and one which has ever been considered as a mystery; yet with how many things are we upon the brink of becoming acquainted, if cowardice[6] or carelessness did not restrain our inquiries. I revolved these circumstances in my mind and determined thenceforth to apply myself more particularly to those branches of natural philosophy which relate to physiology. Unless I had been animated by an almost supernatural enthusiasm, my application to this study would have been irksome[7]

1 infallible (adj): certain **2** esteem (n): appreciation, respect **3** conducive to sth.: advantageous for sth., helpful for sth. **4** protract sth.: prolong sth.
5 whence (old use): from where **6** cowardice: lack of courage **7** irksome: annoying

and almost intolerable. To examine the causes of life, we must first have recourse[1] to death. I became acquainted with the science of anatomy, but this was not sufficient; I must also observe the natural decay[2] and corruption[3] of the human body. In my education my father had taken the greatest precautions that my mind should be impressed with no supernatural horrors. I do not ever remember to have trembled at a tale of superstition or to have feared the apparition of a spirit[4]. Darkness had no effect upon my fancy, and a churchyard was to me merely the receptacle[5] of bodies deprived of life, which, from being the seat of beauty and strength, had become food for the worm. Now I was led to examine the cause and progress of this decay and forced to spend days and nights in vaults[6] and charnel-houses[7]. My attention was fixed upon every object the most insupportable[8] to the delicacy of the human feelings. I saw how the fine form of man was degraded and wasted; I beheld the corruption of death succeed to the blooming cheek of life; I saw how the worm inherited the wonders of the eye and brain. I paused, examining and analysing all the minutiae[9] of causation, as exemplified in the change from life to death, and death to life, until from the midst of this darkness a sudden light broke in upon me – a light so brilliant and wondrous, yet so simple, that while I became dizzy with the immensity of the prospect which it illustrated, I was surprised that among so many men of genius who had directed their inquiries towards the same science, that I alone should be reserved to discover so astonishing a secret.

Remember, I am not recording the vision of a madman. The sun does not more certainly shine in the heavens than that which I now affirm[10] is true. Some miracle might have produced it, yet the stages of the discovery were distinct and probable. After days and nights of incredible labour and fatigue, I succeeded in discovering the

1 have recourse to sth.: focus attention on sth. **2** decay (n): degeneration, dying **3** corruption: (here) decomposition **4** spirit: (here) ghost **5** receptacle: container **6** vault: underground grave chamber **7** charnel-house: building in which bodies and bones are deposited **8** insupportable: unbearable **9** minutiae: details **10** affirm sth.: state sth., confirm sth.

cause of generation[1] and life; nay, more[2], I became myself capable of bestowing animation upon lifeless matter.

The astonishment which I had at first experienced on this discovery soon gave place to delight and rapture. After so much time spent in painful labour, to arrive at once at the summit[3] of my desires was the most gratifying consummation[4] of my toils. But this discovery was so great and overwhelming that all the steps by which I had been progressively led to it were obliterated[5], and I beheld only the result. What had been the study and desire of the wisest men since the creation of the world was now within my grasp[6]. Not that, like a magic scene, it all opened upon me at once: the information I had obtained was of a nature rather to direct my endeavours so soon as I should point them towards the object of my search than to exhibit that object already accomplished. I was like the Arabian[7] who had been buried with the dead and found a passage to life, aided only by one glimmering and seemingly ineffectual light.

I see by your eagerness and the wonder and hope which your eyes express, my friend, that you expect to be informed of the secret with which I am acquainted; that cannot be; listen patiently until the end of my story, and you will easily perceive why I am reserved upon that subject. I will not lead you on, unguarded and ardent as I then was, to your destruction and infallible misery. Learn from me, if not by my precepts[8], at least by my example, how dangerous is the acquirement of knowledge and how much happier that man is who believes his native town to be the world, than he who aspires to become greater than his nature will allow.

When I found so astonishing a power placed within my hands, I hesitated a long time concerning the manner in which I should

1 generation: (here) creation **2** nay, more: (yes,) even more **3** summit: peak, highest part of a mountain **4** consummation: fulfillment **5** obliterate sth.: completely destroy sth., (here) remove sth. from memory **6** within my grasp: close to be understood **7** Arabian ...: reference to a story from the *Tales of 1001 Nights* in which Sindbad the Sailor is buried alive in a cave with his deceased wife and can only escape by following some weak rays of light shining in from another entrance to the cave **8** precept: rule how people should behave

employ it. Although I possessed the capacity of bestowing animation, yet to prepare a frame for the reception of it, with all its intricacies[1] of fibres[2], muscles, and veins, still remained a work of inconceivable difficulty and labour. I doubted at first whether I should attempt the creation of a being like myself, or one of simpler organisation; but my imagination was too much exalted by my first success to permit me to doubt of my ability to give life to an animal as complete and wonderful as man. The materials at present within my command hardly appeared adequate to so arduous an undertaking, but I doubted not that I should ultimately succeed. I prepared myself for a multitude of reverses[3]; my operations might be incessantly baffled[4], and at last my work be imperfect, yet when I considered the improvement which every day takes place in science and mechanics, I was encouraged to hope my present attempts would at least lay the foundations of future success. Nor could I consider the magnitude and complexity of my plan as any argument of its impracticability[5]. It was with these feelings that I began the creation of a human being. As the minuteness of the parts formed a great hindrance to my speed, I resolved, contrary to my first intention, to make the being of a gigantic stature, that is to say, about eight feet in height, and proportionably large. After having formed this determination and having spent some months in successfully collecting and arranging my materials, I began.

No one can conceive the variety of feelings which bore me onwards, like a hurricane, in the first enthusiasm of success. Life and death appeared to me ideal bounds, which I should first break through, and pour a torrent of light into our dark world. A new species would bless me as its creator and source; many happy and excellent natures would owe their being to me. No father could claim the gratitude of his child so completely as I should deserve theirs. Pursuing these reflections, I thought that if I could bestow

1 intricacies (pl): complexity **2** fibre: *Faser* **3** reverse (n): event that causes a situation to become worse than it was before **4** baffle sth./sb.: prevent sth./sb. from being successful **5** impracticability: impossibility to put into action

animation upon lifeless matter, I might in process of time (although I now found it impossible) renew life where death had apparently devoted the body to corruption.

These thoughts supported my spirits, while I pursued my undertaking with unremitting[1] ardour. My cheek had grown pale with study, and my person had become emaciated with confinement[2]. Sometimes, on the very brink of certainty, I failed; yet still I clung[3] to the hope which the next day or the next hour might realise. One secret which I alone possessed was the hope to which I had dedicated myself; and the moon gazed on my midnight labours, while, with unrelaxed and breathless eagerness, I pursued nature to her hiding-places. Who shall conceive the horrors of my secret toil as I dabbled among the unhallowed damps[4] of the grave or tortured the living animal to animate the lifeless clay? My limbs now tremble, and my eyes swim with the remembrance; but then a resistless and almost frantic[5] impulse urged me forward; I seemed to have lost all soul or sensation but for this one pursuit. It was indeed but a passing trance, that only made me feel with renewed acuteness[6] so soon as, the unnatural stimulus ceasing to operate, I had returned to my old habits. I collected bones from charnel-houses and disturbed, with profane[7] fingers, the tremendous secrets of the human frame. In a solitary chamber, or rather cell, at the top of the house, and separated from all the other apartments by a gallery and staircase, I kept my workshop of filthy creation; my eyeballs were starting[8] from their sockets in attending to the details of my employment. The dissecting room[9] and the slaughter-house furnished many of my materials; and often did my human nature turn with loathing[10] from my occupation, whilst, still urged on by an eagerness which perpetually increased, I brought my work near to a conclusion.

1 unremitting: untiring **2** confinement: (here) solitude **3** cling to sth. (clung – clung): hold on to sth. **4** damps (pl): (here) moist fogginess *(Dünste)* **5** frantic: nervous and desperate **6** acuteness: sharpness **7** profane (adj): (here) unholy **8** start from sth.: (here) jump out of sth. **9** dissecting room: place where medical operations take place **10** loathing (n): deep-rooted dislike

The summer months passed while I was thus engaged, heart and soul, in one pursuit. It was a most beautiful season; never did the fields bestow a more plentiful harvest or the vines yield a more luxuriant vintage[1], but my eyes were insensible to the charms of nature. And the same feelings which made me neglect the scenes around me caused me also to forget those friends who were so many miles absent, and whom I had not seen for so long a time. I knew my silence disquieted them, and I well remembered the words of my father: 'I know that while you are pleased with yourself you will think of us with affection, and we shall hear regularly from you. You must pardon me if I regard any interruption in your correspondence as a proof that your other duties are equally neglected.'

I knew well therefore what would be my father's feelings, but I could not tear my thoughts from my employment, loathsome in itself, but which had taken an irresistible hold of my imagination. I wished, as it were, to procrastinate[2] all that related to my feelings of affection until the great object, which swallowed up every habit of my nature, should be completed.

I then thought that my father would be unjust if he ascribed[3] my neglect to vice[4] or faultiness on my part, but I am now convinced that he was justified in conceiving that I should not be altogether free from blame. A human being in perfection ought always to preserve a calm and peaceful mind and never to allow passion or a transitory desire to disturb his tranquillity. I do not think that the pursuit of knowledge is an exception to this rule. If the study to which you apply yourself has a tendency to weaken your affections and to destroy your taste for those simple pleasures in which no alloy[5] can possibly mix, then that study is certainly unlawful, that is to say, not befitting the human mind. If this rule were always observed; if no man allowed any pursuit whatsoever to interfere with the tranquillity of his domestic affections, Greece had not been enslaved,

1 vintage (n): (here) harvest of grapes **2** procrastinate sth.: delay sth.
3 ascribe sth. to sth.: claim that sth. is responsible for sth. **4** vice: *Untugend, Laster* **5** alloy (n): (here) substance of low quality

Caesar would have spared his country, America would have been discovered more gradually, and the empires of Mexico and Peru had not been destroyed.

But I forget that I am moralising in the most interesting part of my tale, and your looks remind me to proceed.

My father made no reproach[1] in his letters and only took notice of my science by inquiring into my occupations more particularly than before. Winter, spring, and summer passed away during my labours; but I did not watch the blossom or the expanding leaves – sights which before always yielded me supreme delight – so deeply was I engrossed in my occupation. The leaves of that year had withered before my work drew near to a close, and now every day showed me more plainly how well I had succeeded. But my enthusiasm was checked by my anxiety, and I appeared rather like one doomed by slavery to toil in the mines, or any other unwholesome[2] trade than an artist occupied by his favourite employment. Every night I was oppressed by a slow fever, and I became nervous to a most painful degree; the fall of a leaf startled[3] me, and I shunned[4] my fellow creatures as if I had been guilty of a crime. Sometimes I grew alarmed at the wreck I perceived that I had become; the energy of my purpose alone sustained me: my labours would soon end, and I believed that exercise and amusement would then drive away incipient[5] disease; and I promised myself both of these when my creation should be complete.

1 reproach (n): expression of disapproval **2** unwholesome: unhealthy **3** startle sb.: shock sb. **4** shun sb.: avoid meeting sb. **5** incipient: beginning

Chapter 5

It was on a dreary night of November that I beheld the accomplishment of my toils. With an anxiety that almost amounted to agony[1], I collected the instruments of life around me, that I might infuse a spark of being into the lifeless thing that lay at my feet. It was already one in the morning; the rain pattered dismally[2] against the panes[3], and my candle was nearly burnt out, when, by the glimmer of the half-extinguished light, I saw the dull yellow eye of the creature open; it breathed hard, and a convulsive[4] motion agitated its limbs.

How can I describe my emotions at this catastrophe, or how delineate the wretch[5] whom with such infinite pains and care I had endeavoured to form? His limbs were in proportion, and I had selected his features as beautiful. Beautiful! Great God! His yellow skin scarcely covered the work of muscles and arteries beneath; his hair was of a lustrous black, and flowing; his teeth of a pearly whiteness; but these luxuriances only formed a more horrid contrast with his watery eyes, that seemed almost of the same colour as the dun-white[6] sockets in which they were set, his shrivelled[7] complexion[8] and straight black lips.

The different accidents of life are not so changeable as the feelings of human nature. I had worked hard for nearly two years, for the sole purpose of infusing life into an inanimate body. For this I had deprived myself of rest and health. I had desired it with an ardour that far exceeded[9] moderation[10]; but now that I had finished, the beauty of the dream vanished, and breathless horror and disgust filled my heart. Unable to endure the aspect of the being I had

1 agony: intense physical or mental pain **2** dismal: depressing **3** pane: glass part of a window **4** convulsive: *krampfartig* **5** wretch: poor creature **6** dun-white (adj): *mattweiß* **7** shrivelled (adj): heavily wrinkled **8** complexion: skin colour **9** exceed sth.: be greater than sth. **10** moderation: *(hier) Mäßigung*

created, I rushed out of the room and continued a long time traversing my bedchamber, unable to compose[1] my mind to sleep. At length lassitude[2] succeeded to the tumult I had before endured, and I threw myself on the bed in my clothes, endeavouring to seek a few moments of forgetfulness. But it was in vain; I slept, indeed, but I was disturbed by the wildest dreams. I thought I saw Elizabeth, in the bloom of health, walking in the streets of Ingolstadt. Delighted and surprised, I embraced[3] her, but as I imprinted the first kiss on her lips, they became livid[4] with the hue[5] of death; her features appeared to change, and I thought that I held the corpse of my dead mother in my arms; a shroud[6] enveloped her form, and I saw the grave-worms crawling in the folds of the flannel. I started[7] from my sleep with horror; a cold dew[8] covered my forehead, my teeth chattered, and every limb became convulsed; when, by the dim and yellow light of the moon, as it forced its way through the window shutters, I beheld the wretch – the miserable monster whom I had created. He held up the curtain of the bed; and his eyes, if eyes they may be called, were fixed on me. His jaws opened, and he muttered some inarticulate[9] sounds, while a grin wrinkled his cheeks. He might have spoken, but I did not hear; one hand was stretched out, seemingly to detain[10] me, but I escaped and rushed downstairs. I took refuge in the courtyard belonging to the house which I inhabited, where I remained during the rest of the night, walking up and down in the greatest agitation, listening attentively, catching and fearing each sound as if it were to announce the approach of the demoniacal corpse to which I had so miserably given life.

Oh! no mortal could support the horror of that countenance. A mummy again endued with animation could not be so hideous as that wretch. I had gazed on him while unfinished; he was ugly then, but when those muscles and joints[11] were rendered capable

1 compose your mind: calm down **2** lassitude: exhaustion, tiredness **3** embrace sb.: hug sb. **4** livid: pale **5** hue: colour **6** shroud: (here) cloth used to cover or wrap dead bodies **7** start (v): *(hier) hochschrecken* **8** dew: (here) sweat **9** inarticulate: incomprehensible **10** detain sb./sth.: hold sb./sth. **11** joint (n): *Gelenk*

of motion, it became a thing such as even Dante[1] could not have conceived.

I passed the night wretchedly. Sometimes my pulse beat so quickly and hardly that I felt the palpitation[2] of every artery; at others, I nearly sank to the ground through languor[3] and extreme weakness. Mingled with this horror, I felt the bitterness of disappointment; dreams that had been my food and pleasant rest for so long a space were now become a hell to me; and the change was so rapid, the overthrow so complete!

Morning, dismal and wet, at length dawned and discovered[4] to my sleepless and aching eyes the church of Ingolstadt, its white steeple and clock, which indicated the sixth hour. The porter opened the gates of the court, which had that night been my asylum, and I issued into the streets, pacing them with quick steps, as if I sought to avoid the wretch whom I feared every turning of the street would present to my view. I did not dare return to the apartment which I inhabited, but felt impelled[5] to hurry on, although drenched by the rain which poured from a black and comfortless[6] sky.

I continued walking in this manner for some time, endeavouring by bodily exercise to ease the load that weighed upon my mind. I traversed the streets without any clear conception of where I was or what I was doing. My heart palpitated in the sickness of fear, and I hurried on with irregular steps, not daring to look about me:

Like one who, on a lonely road,
Doth[7] walk in fear and dread,
And, having once turned round, walks on,
And turns no more his head;

1 Dante Alighieri (1265–1321): Italian poet and philosopher. The reference is meant to hint at the 'Inferno', i.e. the first part of Dante's famous epic narration *Divina Commedia (The Divine Comedy)* in which the reader is led through different parts of hell where sinners are exposed to severe punishment and torture. **2** palpitation: beating **3** languor: lethargy **4** discover sth. to sb.: show sth. to sb., expose sth. to sb. **5** impelled: forced **6** comfortless: depressing **7** doth (old use): does

Because he knows a frightful fiend[1]
Doth close behind him tread.[*]

Continuing thus, I came at length opposite to the inn at which the various diligences[2] and carriages usually stopped. Here I paused, I knew not why; but I remained some minutes with my eyes fixed on a coach that was coming towards me from the other end of the street. As it drew nearer I observed that it was the Swiss diligence; it stopped just where I was standing, and on the door being opened, I perceived Henry Clerval, who, on seeing me, instantly sprung out. 'My dear Frankenstein,' exclaimed he, 'how glad I am to see you! How fortunate that you should be here at the very moment of my alighting!'

Nothing could equal my delight on seeing Clerval; his presence brought back to my thoughts my father, Elizabeth, and all those scenes of home so dear to my recollection. I grasped his hand, and in a moment forgot my horror and misfortune; I felt suddenly, and for the first time during many months, calm and serene joy. I welcomed my friend, therefore, in the most cordial[3] manner, and we walked towards my college. Clerval continued talking for some time about our mutual friends and his own good fortune in being permitted to come to Ingolstadt. 'You may easily believe,' said he, 'how great was the difficulty to persuade my father that all necessary knowledge was not comprised in the noble art of bookkeeping; and, indeed, I believe I left him incredulous[4] to the last, for his constant answer to my unwearied[5] entreaties was the same as that of the Dutch schoolmaster in *The Vicar of Wakefield*[6]: "I have ten thousand florins[7] a year without Greek, I eat heartily without Greek." But his affection for me at length overcame his dislike of learning, and he has permitted me to undertake a voyage of discovery to the land of knowledge.'

1 fiend: devil or evil person ***** Coleridge's *Ancient Mariner* [author's footnote]
2 diligence: *(hier) Postkutsche* **3** cordial: warm-hearted **4** incredulous: sceptical **5** unwearied: tireless **6** *The Vicar of Wakefield*: popular novel by Irish author Oliver Goldsmith (1730–1774) **7** florin: *Gulden* (former currency in the Netherlands)

'It gives me the greatest delight to see you; but tell me how you left my father, brothers, and Elizabeth.'

'Very well, and very happy, only a little uneasy that they hear from you so seldom. By the by, I mean to lecture you a little upon their account myself. But, my dear Frankenstein,' continued he, stopping short and gazing full in my face, 'I did not before remark how very ill you appear; so thin and pale; you look as if you had been watching for several nights.'

'You have guessed right; I have lately been so deeply engaged in one occupation that I have not allowed myself sufficient rest, as you see; but I hope, I sincerely hope, that all these employments are now at an end and that I am at length free.'

I trembled excessively; I could not endure to think of, and far less to allude[1] to, the occurrences of the preceding night. I walked with a quick pace, and we soon arrived at my college. I then reflected, and the thought made me shiver, that the creature whom I had left in my apartment might still be there, alive and walking about. I dreaded to behold this monster, but I feared still more that Henry should see him. Entreating him, therefore, to remain a few minutes at the bottom of the stairs, I darted[2] up towards my own room. My hand was already on the lock of the door before I recollected[3] myself. I then paused, and a cold shivering came over me. I threw the door forcibly open, as children are accustomed to do when they expect a spectre to stand in waiting for them on the other side; but nothing appeared. I stepped fearfully in: the apartment was empty, and my bedroom was also freed from its hideous guest. I could hardly believe that so great a good fortune could have befallen me, but when I became assured that my enemy had indeed fled, I clapped my hands for joy and ran down to Clerval.

We ascended[4] into my room, and the servant presently brought breakfast; but I was unable to contain myself. It was not joy only that

1 allude to sth. (v): hint at sth. **2** dart up: run up quickly **3** recollect yourself: regain control of yourself **4** ascend: go up

possessed me; I felt my flesh tingle[1] with excess[2] of sensitiveness, and my pulse beat rapidly. I was unable to remain for a single instant in the same place; I jumped over the chairs, clapped my hands, and laughed aloud. Clerval at first attributed my unusual spirits to joy on his arrival, but when he observed me more attentively, he saw a wildness in my eyes for which he could not account, and my loud, unrestrained, heartless laughter frightened and astonished him.

'My dear Victor,' cried he, 'what, for God's sake, is the matter? Do not laugh in that manner. How ill you are! What is the cause of all this?'

'Do not ask me,' cried I, putting my hands before my eyes, for I thought I saw the dreaded spectre glide into the room; '*he* can tell. Oh, save me! Save me!' I imagined that the monster seized me; I struggled furiously and fell down in a fit.

Poor Clerval! What must have been his feelings? A meeting, which he anticipated with such joy, so strangely turned to bitterness. But I was not the witness of his grief, for I was lifeless and did not recover my senses for a long, long time.

This was the commencement of a nervous fever which confined me for several months. During all that time Henry was my only nurse. I afterwards learned that, knowing my father's advanced age and unfitness for so long a journey, and how wretched my sickness would make Elizabeth, he spared them this grief by concealing the extent of my disorder. He knew that I could not have a more kind and attentive nurse than himself; and, firm in the hope he felt of my recovery, he did not doubt that, instead of doing harm, he performed the kindest action that he could towards them.

But I was in reality very ill, and surely nothing but the unbounded[3] and unremitting attentions of my friend could have restored me to life. The form of the monster on whom I had bestowed existence was forever before my eyes, and I raved[4] incessantly concerning him. Doubtless my words surprised Henry; he at first believed them to be

1 tingle (v): *kribbeln* **2** excess: *Übermaß* **3** unbounded: unlimited **4** rave (v): (here) talk as if in a state of mental illness

the wanderings[1] of my disturbed imagination, but the pertinacity[2] with which I continually recurred to the same subject persuaded him that my disorder indeed owed its origin to some uncommon and terrible event.

By very slow degrees, and with frequent relapses[3] that alarmed and grieved my friend, I recovered. I remember the first time I became capable of observing outward objects with any kind of pleasure, I perceived that the fallen leaves had disappeared and that the young buds[4] were shooting forth from the trees that shaded my window. It was a divine spring, and the season contributed greatly to my convalescence[5]. I felt also sentiments of joy and affection revive in my bosom; my gloom disappeared, and in a short time I became as cheerful as before I was attacked by the fatal passion.

'Dearest Clerval,' exclaimed I, 'how kind, how very good you are to me. This whole winter, instead of being spent in study, as you promised yourself, has been consumed in my sick room. How shall I ever repay you? I feel the greatest remorse[6] for the disappointment of which I have been the occasion, but you will forgive me.'

'You will repay me entirely if you do not discompose[7] yourself, but get well as fast as you can; and since you appear in such good spirits, I may speak to you on one subject, may I not?'

I trembled. One subject! What could it be? Could he allude to an object on whom I dared not even think?

'Compose yourself,' said Clerval, who observed my change of colour, 'I will not mention it if it agitates you; but your father and cousin would be very happy if they received a letter from you in your own handwriting. They hardly know how ill you have been and are uneasy at your long silence.'

1 wanderings: *Abschweifungen, Irrungen* **2** pertinacity [ˌpɜːtɪˈnæsəti]: *Hartnäckigkeit* **3** relapse (n): return of a state of bad health after a phase of recovery
4 bud (n): *Knospe* **5** convalescence [ˌkɒnvəˈlesns]: recovery after an illness
6 remorse: feeling of shame and regret **7** discompose yourself: get upset

'Is that all, my dear Henry? How could you suppose that my first thought would not fly towards those dear, dear friends whom I love and who are so deserving of my love?'

'If this is your present temper, my friend, you will perhaps be glad to see a letter that has been lying here some days for you; it is from your cousin, I believe.'

Chapter 6

Clerval then put the following letter into my hands. It was from my own Elizabeth:–

My dearest Cousin,

You have been ill, very ill, and even the constant letters of dear kind Henry are not sufficient to reassure me on your account. You are forbidden to write – to hold a pen; yet one word from you, dear Victor, is necessary to calm our apprehensions[1]. For a long time I have thought that each post would bring this line, and my persuasions have restrained my uncle from undertaking a journey to Ingolstadt. I have prevented his encountering the inconveniences[2] and perhaps dangers of so long a journey, yet how often have I regretted not being able to perform it myself! I figure to myself that the task of attending on your sickbed has devolved[3] on some mercenary[4] old nurse, who could never guess your wishes nor minister to them with the care and affection of your poor cousin. Yet that is over now: Clerval writes that indeed you are getting better. I eagerly hope that you will confirm this intelligence[5] soon in your own handwriting.

Get well – and return to us. You will find a happy, cheerful home and friends who love you dearly. Your father's health is vigorous[6], and he asks but to see you, but to be assured that you are well; and not a care will ever cloud his benevolent countenance. How pleased you would be to remark the improvement of our Ernest! He is now sixteen and full of activity and spirit. He is desirous to be a true Swiss and to enter into foreign service[7], but we cannot part with him, at least until his elder brother return to us. My uncle is not

1 apprehension: worry **2** inconvenience: *Unannehmlichkeit* **3** devolve on sb.: be transferred to sb. **4** mercenary [ˈmɜːsənəri] (adj): greedy **5** intelligence: (here) infomation **6** vigorous: strong **7** service: (here) military service

pleased with the idea of a military career in a distant country, but Ernest never had your powers of application. He looks upon study as an odious fetter[1]; his time is spent in the open air, climbing the hills or rowing on the lake. I fear that he will become an idler[2] unless we yield the point[3] and permit him to enter on the profession which he has selected.

Little alteration, except the growth of our dear children, has taken place since you left us. The blue lake and snowclad mountains – they never change; and I think our placid[4] home and our contented hearts are regulated by the same immutable laws. My trifling occupations take up my time and amuse me, and I am rewarded for any exertions by seeing none but happy, kind faces around me. Since you left us, but one change has taken place in our little household. Do you remember on what occasion Justine Moritz entered our family? Probably you do not; I will relate her history, therefore, in a few words. Madame Moritz, her mother, was a widow with four children, of whom Justine was the third. This girl had always been the favourite of her father, but through a strange perversity, her mother could not endure her, and after the death of M. Moritz, treated her very ill. My aunt observed this, and when Justine was twelve years of age, prevailed on her mother to allow her to live at our house. The republican institutions of our country have produced simpler and happier manners than those which prevail[5] in the great monarchies that surround it. Hence there is less distinction between the several classes of its inhabitants; and the lower orders, being neither so poor nor so despised[6], their manners are more refined and moral. A servant in Geneva does not mean the same thing as a servant in France and England. Justine, thus received in our family, learned the duties of a servant, a condition which, in our fortunate country, does not include the idea of ignorance and a sacrifice of the dignity of a human being.

1 fetter: *(Fuß-)Fessel* **2** idler: lazy person **3** yield the point: give in **4** placid: peaceful **5** prevail: (here) be common **6** despised (adj): looked down on with contempt

Justine, you may remember, was a great favourite of yours; and I recollect you once remarked that if you were in an ill humour[1], one glance from Justine could dissipate[2] it, for the same reason that Ariosto[3] gives concerning the beauty of Angelica – she looked so frank-hearted and happy. My aunt conceived a great attachment for her, by which she was induced to give her an education superior to that which she had at first intended. This benefit was fully repaid; Justine was the most grateful little creature in the world: I do not mean that she made any professions[4]; I never heard one pass her lips, but you could see by her eyes that she almost adored her protectress. Although her disposition was gay[5] and in many respects inconsiderate, yet she paid the greatest attention to every gesture of my aunt. She thought her the model of all excellence and endeavoured to imitate her phraseology[6] and manners, so that even now she often reminds me of her.

When my dearest aunt died every one was too much occupied in their own grief to notice poor Justine, who had attended her during her illness with the most anxious affection. Poor Justine was very ill; but other trials[7] were reserved for her.

One by one, her brothers and sister died; and her mother, with the exception of her neglected daughter, was left childless. The conscience of the woman was troubled; she began to think that the deaths of her favourites was a judgment from heaven to chastise[8] her partiality[9]. She was a Roman Catholic; and I believe her confessor[10] confirmed the idea which she had conceived. Accordingly, a few months after your departure for Ingolstadt, Justine was called home by her repentant[11] mother. Poor girl! She wept when she quitted our

1 ill humour: bad mood **2** dissipate sth.: make sth. disappear, drive sth. off **3** Ludovico Ariosto (1474–1533): Italian author of romance poems such as 'Orlando Furioso' ('The Raging Roland') whose highly desired protagonist, Angelica, is referred to here **4** make a profession: declare sth. openly **5** gay: cheerful **6** phraseology: verbal expression **7** trial: (here) challenge **8** chastise sb.: punish sb. **9** partiality: unjust attititude of showing more support to one person or group than to others **10** confessor: priest taking confession (*Beichtvater*) **11** repentant: regretful

house; she was much altered since the death of my aunt; grief had given softness and a winning mildness to her manners which had before been remarkable for vivacity. Nor was her residence at her mother's house of a nature to restore her gaiety. The poor woman was very vacillating[1] in her repentance. She sometimes begged Justine to forgive her unkindness but much oftener accused her of having caused the deaths of her brothers and sister. Perpetual fretting[2] at length threw Madame Moritz into a decline, which at first increased her irritability, but she is now at peace for ever. She died on the first approach of cold weather, at the beginning of this last winter. Justine has returned to us, and I assure you I love her tenderly. She is very clever and gentle and extremely pretty; as I mentioned before, her mien and her expressions continually remind me of my dear aunt.

I must say also a few words to you, my dear cousin, of little darling William. I wish you could see him; he is very tall of his age, with sweet laughing blue eyes, dark eyelashes, and curling hair. When he smiles, two little dimples[3] appear on each cheek, which are rosy with health. He has already had one or two little *wives*, but Louisa Biron is his favourite, a pretty little girl of five years of age.

Now, dear Victor, I dare say you wish to be indulged in a little gossip concerning the good people of Geneva. The pretty Miss Mansfield has already received the congratulatory visits on her approaching marriage with a young Englishman, John Melbourne, Esq[4]. Her ugly sister, Manon, married M. Duvillard, the rich banker, last autumn. Your favourite schoolfellow, Louis Manoir, has suffered several misfortunes since the departure of Clerval from Geneva. But he has already recovered his spirits, and is reported to be on the point of marrying a very lively, pretty Frenchwoman, Madame Tavernier. She is a widow, and much older than Manoir, but she is very much admired and a favourite with everybody.

1 vacillating (adj): inconsistent, constantly changing your opinion **2** fretting (n): worrying **3** dimple: *Grübchen* **4** Esq ('esquire') [ɪˈskwaɪə^{r}]: abbreviation used after a name of a man of aristocatic descent

I have written myself into better spirits, dear cousin; but my anxiety returns upon me as I conclude. Write, dearest Victor – one line – one word will be a blessing to us. Ten thousand thanks to Henry for his kindness, his affection, and his many letters; we are sincerely grateful. Adieu! My cousin, take care of yourself, and, I entreat you, write!

ELIZABETH LAVENZA
Geneva, March 18th, 17–.

'Dear, dear Elizabeth!' I exclaimed when I had read her letter. 'I will write instantly and relieve them from the anxiety they must feel.' I wrote, and this exertion greatly fatigued me; but my convalescence had commenced, and proceeded regularly. In another fortnight I was able to leave my chamber.

One of my first duties on my recovery was to introduce Clerval to the several professors of the university. In doing this, I underwent[1] a kind of rough usage, ill befitting[2] the wounds that my mind had sustained. Ever since the fatal night, the end of my labours, and the beginning of my misfortunes, I had conceived a violent antipathy even to the name of natural philosophy. When I was otherwise quite restored to health, the sight of a chemical instrument would renew all the agony of my nervous symptoms. Henry saw this, and had removed all my apparatus from my view. He had also changed my apartment, for he perceived that I had acquired a dislike for the room which had previously been my laboratory. But these cares of Clerval were made of no avail[3] when I visited the professors. M. Waldman inflicted[4] torture when he praised, with kindness and warmth, the astonishing progress I had made in the sciences. He soon perceived that I disliked the subject, but not guessing the real cause, he attributed my feelings to modesty and changed the subject from my improvement to the science itself, with a desire, as I

1 undergo rough usage: be badly treated **2** ill befitting: not suiting **3** of no avail: useless **4** inflict sth. (on sb./sth.): cause sth. unpleasant to happen to sb./sth.

evidently saw, of drawing me out[1]. What could I do? He meant to please, and he tormented me. I felt as if he had placed carefully, one by one, in my view those instruments which were to be afterwards used in putting me to a slow and cruel death. I writhed[2] under his words yet dared not exhibit the pain I felt. Clerval, whose eyes and feelings were always quick in discerning the sensations of others, declined[3] the subject, alleging[4], in excuse, his total ignorance; and the conversation took a more general turn. I thanked my friend from my heart, but I did not speak. I saw plainly[5] that he was surprised, but he never attempted to draw my secret from me; and although I loved him with a mixture of affection and reverence that knew no bounds, yet I could never persuade myself to confide to him that event which was so often present to my recollection but which I feared the detail to another would only impress[6] more deeply.

M. Krempe was not equally docile[7]; and in my condition at that time, of almost insupportable sensitiveness, his harsh, blunt[8] encomiums[9] gave me even more pain than the benevolent approbation[10] of M. Waldman. 'D – n the fellow!' cried he. 'Why, M. Clerval, I assure you he has outstripped[11] us all. Ay[12], stare if you please; but it is nevertheless true. A youngster who, but a few years ago, believed in Cornelius Agrippa as firmly as in the Gospel[13], has now set himself at the head of the university; and if he is not soon pulled down, we shall all be out of countenance[14]. Ay, ay,' continued he, observing my face expressive of suffering, 'M. Frankenstein is modest, an excellent quality in a young man. Young men should be diffident[15] of themselves, you know, M. Clerval; I was myself when young; but that wears out[16] in a very short time.'

1 draw sb. out: *jdn. aushorchen* **2** writhe: *sich winden* **3** decline sth.: express politely that you don't want sth. **4** allege sth.: (here) claim sth. **5** plainly: clearly **6** impress (sb.): (here) shock (sb.) **7** docile: easy to control **8** blunt: direct and potentially offensive **9** encomium: enthusiastic praise **10** approbation: praise **11** outstrip sb.: get ahead of sb. **12** ay: yes, absolutely **13** Gospel: New Testament **14** be out of countenance: *(hier) das Gesicht verlieren* **15** diffident: reserved **16** wear out: become weaker and weaker

M. Krempe had now commenced a eulogy[1] on himself, which happily turned the conversation from a subject that was so annoying to me.

Clerval had never sympathised in my tastes for natural science, and his literary pursuits differed wholly from those which had occupied me. He came to the university with the design of making himself complete master of the Oriental languages, as thus he should open a field for the plan of life he had marked out for himself. Resolved to pursue no inglorious[2] career, he turned his eyes towards the East as affording scope[3] for his spirit of enterprise[4]. The Persian, Arabic, and Sanskrit languages engaged his attention, and I was easily induced to enter on the same studies. Idleness had ever been irksome to me, and now that I wished to fly from reflection and hated my former studies, I felt great relief in being the fellow pupil with my friend, and found not only instruction but consolation in the works of the Orientalists. I did not, like him, attempt a critical knowledge of their dialects, for I did not contemplate[5] making any other use of them than temporary amusement. I read merely to understand their meaning, and they well repaid my labours. Their melancholy is soothing[6], and their joy elevating[7], to a degree I never experienced in studying the authors of any other country. When you read their writings, life appears to consist in a warm sun and a garden of roses, in the smiles and frowns of a fair enemy, and the fire that consumes your own heart. How different from the manly and heroical poetry of Greece and Rome!

Summer passed away in these occupations, and my return to Geneva was fixed for the latter end of autumn; but being delayed by several accidents, winter and snow arrived, the roads were deemed impassable, and my journey was retarded[8] until the ensuing[9] spring. I felt this delay very bitterly, for I longed to see my native town and

1 eulogy: speech to express praise **2** inglorious: lacking glory **3** scope: *Betätigungsfeld* **4** spirit of enterprise: *Unternehmungslust* **5** contemplate sth.: (here) consider sth. **6** soothing (adj): calming **7** elevating (adj): uplifting **8** retard sth.: delay sth. **9** ensuing: following

my beloved friends. My return had only been delayed so long from an unwillingness to leave Clerval in a strange place before he had become acquainted with any of its inhabitants. The winter, however, was spent cheerfully, and although the spring was uncommonly late, when it came its beauty compensated for its dilatoriness[1].

The month of May had already commenced, and I expected the letter daily which was to fix the date of my departure, when Henry proposed a pedestrian tour in the environs of Ingolstadt, that I might bid[2] a personal farewell to the country I had so long inhabited. I acceded[3] with pleasure to this proposition: I was fond of exercise, and Clerval had always been my favourite companion in the rambles of this nature that I had taken among the scenes of my native country.

We passed a fortnight in these perambulations[4]; my health and spirits had long been restored, and they gained additional strength from the salubrious[5] air I breathed, the natural incidents of our progress, and the conversation of my friend. Study had before secluded me from the intercourse[6] of my fellow creatures and rendered me unsocial, but Clerval called forth the better feelings of my heart; he again taught me to love the aspect of nature and the cheerful faces of children. Excellent friend! How sincerely did you love me and endeavour to elevate my mind until it was on a level with your own! A selfish pursuit had cramped and narrowed me until your gentleness and affection warmed and opened my senses; I became the same happy creature who, a few years ago, loved and beloved by all, had no sorrow or care. When happy, inanimate[7] nature had the power of bestowing on me the most delightful sensations. A serene sky and verdant[8] fields filled me with ecstasy. The present season was indeed divine; the flowers of spring bloomed in the hedges, while those of summer were already in bud. I was undisturbed by

1 dilatoriness: slowness **2** bid (bid/bade – bid/bidden) a personal farewell: say goodbye **3** accede to sth.: agree to sth. **4** perambulation: walk **5** salubrious: healthy **6** intercourse: interaction, communication **7** inanimate: *(hier) unbeseelt* **8** verdant: green

thoughts which during the preceding year had pressed upon me, notwithstanding[1] my endeavours to throw them off, with an invincible burden.

Henry rejoiced in my gaiety and sincerely sympathised in my feelings; he exerted himself to amuse me, while he expressed the sensations that filled his soul. The resources of his mind on this occasion were truly astonishing; his conversation was full of imagination, and very often, in imitation of the Persian and Arabic writers, he invented tales of wonderful fancy and passion. At other times he repeated my favourite poems or drew me out into arguments, which he supported with great ingenuity[2].

We returned to our college on a Sunday afternoon; the peasants were dancing, and everyone we met appeared gay and happy. My own spirits were high, and I bounded along with feelings of unbridled[3] joy and hilarity[4].

1 notwithstanding: despite **2** ingenuity [ˌɪndʒəˈnjuːəti]: inventiveness
3 unbridled: uncontrolled **4** hilarity: cheerfulness

Chapter 7

On my return, I found the following letter from my father:–

My dear Victor,

You have probably waited impatiently for a letter to fix the date of your return to us; and I was at first tempted[1] to write only a few lines, merely mentioning the day on which I should expect you. But that would be a cruel kindness, and I dare not do it. What would be your surprise, my son, when you expected a happy and glad welcome, to behold, on the contrary, tears and wretchedness? And how, Victor, can I relate our misfortune? Absence cannot have rendered you callous[2] to our joys and griefs; and how shall I inflict pain on my long absent son? I wish to prepare you for the woeful news, but I know it is impossible; even now your eye skims over the page to seek the words which are to convey to you the horrible tidings[3].

William is dead! – that sweet child, whose smiles delighted and warmed my heart, who was so gentle, yet so gay! Victor, he is murdered!

I will not attempt to console you; but will simply relate the circumstances of the transaction[4].

Last Thursday (May 7th), I, my niece[5], and your two brothers, went to walk in Plainpalais[6]. The evening was warm and serene, and we prolonged our walk farther than usual. It was already dusk before we thought of returning; and then we discovered that William and Ernest, who had gone on before, were not to be found. We accordingly rested on a seat until they should return. Presently Ernest came, and enquired if we had seen his brother; he said, that

1 be tempted to do sth.: *versucht sein, etw. zu tun* **2** callous: indifferent
3 tidings (pl): news **4** transaction: (here) incident, event **5** niece: *Nichte*
6 Plainpalais [plɛ̃palɛ]: neighbourhood in Geneva

he had been playing with him, that William had run away to hide himself, and that he vainly sought for him, and afterwards waited for a long time, but that he did not return.

This account rather alarmed us, and we continued to search for him until night fell, when Elizabeth conjectured that he might have returned to the house. He was not there. We returned again, with torches[1]; for I could not rest, when I thought that my sweet boy had lost himself, and was exposed to all the damps and dews[2] of night; Elizabeth also suffered extreme anguish[3]. About five in the morning I discovered my lovely boy, whom the night before I had seen blooming and active in health, stretched on the grass livid and motionless; the print of the murderer's finger was on his neck.

He was conveyed home, and the anguish that was visible in my countenance betrayed[4] the secret to Elizabeth. She was very earnest to see the corpse. At first I attempted to prevent her; but she persisted, and entering the room where it lay, hastily examined the neck of the victim, and clasping her hands exclaimed, 'O God! I have murdered my darling child!'

She fainted, and was restored with extreme difficulty. When she again lived[5], it was only to weep and sigh. She told me, that that same evening William had teased her to let him wear a very valuable miniature that she possessed of your mother. This picture is gone, and was doubtless the temptation which urged the murdered to the deed. We have no trace of him at present, although our exertions to discover him are unremitted[6]; but they will not restore my beloved William!

Come, dearest Victor; you alone can console Elizabeth. She weeps continually, and accuses herself unjustly as the cause of his death; her words pierce my heart. We are all unhappy; but will not that be an additional motive for you, my son, to return and be our comforter? Your dear mother! Alas, Victor! I now say, Thank God

1 torch: *Fackel* **2** damps and dews: moistness **3** anguish: pain **4** betray sth.: (here) give sth. away unintentionally **5** live: (here) be conscious **6** unremitted: constant

she did not live to witness the cruel, miserable death of her youngest darling!

Come, Victor; not brooding[1] thoughts of vengeance[2] against the assassin[3], but with feelings of peace and gentleness, that will heal, instead of festering[4], the wounds of our minds. Enter the house of mourning, my friend, but with kindness and affection for those who love you, and not with hatred for your enemies.

Your affectionate and afflicted father,
ALPHONSE FRANKENSTEIN
Geneva, May 12th, 17–.

Clerval, who had watched my countenance as I read this letter, was surprised to observe the despair that succeeded the joy I at first expressed on receiving news from my friends. I threw the letter on the table, and covered my face with my hands.

'My dear Frankenstein,' exclaimed Henry, when he perceived me weep with bitterness, 'are you always to be unhappy? My dear friend, what has happened?'

I motioned him to take up the letter, while I walked up and down the room in the extremest agitation. Tears also gushed from the eyes of Clerval, as he read the account of my misfortune.

'I can offer you no consolation, my friend,' said he; 'your disaster is irreparable. What do you intend to do?'

'To go instantly to Geneva: come with me, Henry, to order the horses.'

During our walk, Clerval endeavoured to say a few words of consolation; he could only express his heartfelt sympathy. 'Poor William!' said he, dear lovely child, he now sleeps with his angel mother! Who that had seen him bright and joyous in his young beauty, but must weep over his untimely[5] loss! To die so miserably; to feel the murderer's grasp! How much more a murderer that could destroy

1 brood: (here) think gloomily about sth. **2** vengeance: revenge **3** assassin: murderer **4** fester: *eitern* **5** untimely: before the natural time

radiant[1] innocence! Poor little fellow! one only consolation have we; his friends mourn and weep, but he is at rest. The pang[2] is over, his sufferings are at an end for ever. A sod[3] covers his gentle form, and he knows no pain. He can no longer be a subject for pity; we must reserve that for his miserable survivors.'

Clerval spoke thus as we hurried through the streets; the words impressed themselves on my mind and I remembered them afterwards in solitude. But now, as soon as the horses arrived, I hurried into a cabriolet[4], and bade farewell to my friend.

My journey was very melancholy. At first I wished to hurry on, for I longed to console and sympathise with my loved and sorrowing friends; but when I drew near my native town, I slackened[5] my progress. I could hardly sustain the multitude of feelings that crowded into my mind. I passed through scenes familiar to my youth, but which I had not seen for nearly six years. How altered every thing might be during that time! One sudden and desolating[6] change had taken place; but a thousand little circumstances might have by degrees worked other alterations, which, although they were done more tranquilly, might not be the less decisive[7]. Fear overcame me; I dared no advance, dreading a thousand nameless evils that made me tremble, although I was unable to define them.

I remained two days at Lausanne[8], in this painful state of mind. I contemplated the lake: the waters were placid; all around was calm; and the snowy mountains, 'the palaces of nature,'[9] were not changed. By degrees the calm and heavenly scene restored me, and I continued my journey towards Geneva.

The road ran by the side of the lake, which became narrower as I approached my native town. I discovered more distinctly the black sides of Jura, and the bright summit of Mont Blanc[10]. I wept like a

1 radiant (adj): shining **2** pang: moment of extreme pain **3** sod: grass-covered surface **4** cabriolet: (here) two-wheeled carriage **5** slacken: slow down **6** desolating: depressing **7** decisive: *entscheidend* **8** Lausanne: Swiss town on the northern shore of Lake Geneva **9** 'the palaces of nature': quotation from Byron's *Childe Harold's Pilgrimage* **10** Mont Blanc: Europe's highest mountain (4810 m)

child. 'Dear mountains! my own beautiful lake! how do you welcome your wanderer? Your summits are clear; the sky and lake are blue and placid. Is this to prognosticate peace, or to mock[1] at my unhappiness?'

I fear, my friend, that I shall render myself tedious[2] by dwelling on these preliminary[3] circumstances; but they were days of comparative happiness, and I think of them with pleasure. My country, my beloved country! who but a native can tell the delight I took in again beholding thy[4] streams, thy mountains, and, more than all, thy lovely lake!

Yet, as I drew nearer home, grief and fear again overcame me. Night also closed around; and when I could hardly see the dark mountains, I felt still more gloomily. The picture appeared a vast and dim scene of evil, and I foresaw obscurely that I was destined to become the most wretched of human beings. Alas! I prophesied truly, and failed[5] only in one single circumstance, that in all the misery I imagined and dreaded, I did not conceive the hundredth part of the anguish I was destined to endure.

It was completely dark when I arrived in the environs of Geneva; the gates of the town were already shut; and I was obliged to pass the night at Secheron, a village at the distance of half a league from the city. The sky was serene; and, as I was unable to rest, I resolved to visit the spot where my poor William had been murdered. As I could not pass through the town, I was obliged to cross the lake in a boat to arrive at Plainpalais. During this short voyage I saw the lightning playing on the summit of Mont Blanc in the most beautiful figures. The storm appeared to approach rapidly, and, on landing, I ascended a low hill, that I might observe its progress. It advanced; the heavens were clouded, and I soon felt the rain coming slowly in large drops, but its violence quickly increased.

I quitted my seat, and walked on, although the darkness and storm increased every minute, and the thunder burst with a ter-

1 mock at sb./sth.: make fun of sb./sth. **2** tedious: boring **3** preliminary: introductory **4** thy (poetic): your **5** fail: (here) be mistaken

rific crash over my head. It was echoed from Salêve[1], the Juras, and the Alps of Savoy; vivid flashes of lightning dazzled my eyes, illuminating the lake, making it appear like a vast sheet of fire; then for an instant every thing seemed of a pitchy[2] darkness, until the eye recovered itself from the preceding flash. The storm, as is often the case in Switzerland, appeared at once in various parts of the heavens. The most violent storm hung exactly north of the town, over the part of the lake which lies between the promontory[3] of Belrive and the village of Copêt. Another storm enlightened Jura with faint[4] flashes; and another darkened and sometimes disclosed the Môle, a peaked mountain to the east of the lake.

While I watched the tempest, so beautiful yet terrific, I wandered on with a hasty step. This noble war in the sky elevated my spirits; I clasped my hands, and exclaimed aloud, 'William, dear angel! this is thy funeral, this thy dirge[5]!' As I said these words, I perceived in the gloom a figure which stole from behind a clump of trees near me; I stood fixed, gazing intently: I could not be mistaken. A flash of lightning illuminated the object, and discovered its shape plainly to me; its gigantic stature, and the deformity of its aspect, more hideous than belongs to humanity, instantly informed me that it was the wretch, the filthy daemon, to whom I had given life. What did he there? Could he be (I shuddered at the conception) the murderer of my brother? No sooner did that idea cross my imagination, than I became convinced of its truth; my teeth chattered, and I was forced to lean against a tree for support. The figure passed me quickly, and I lost it in the gloom. Nothing in human shape could have destroyed the fair child. *He* was the murderer! I could not doubt it. The mere presence of the idea was an irresistible proof of the fact. I thought of pursuing the devil; but it would have been in vain, for another flash discovered him to me hanging among the rocks of the nearly per-

1 Salêve: mountain range close to Geneva **2** pitchy: *pechartig* **3** promontory: mountainous stretch of land that extends into a lake or the sea **4** faint (adj): weak **5** dirge: mournful piece of music

pendicular[1] ascent of Mont Salêve, a hill that bounds[2] Plainpalais on the south. He soon reached the summit, and disappeared.

I remained motionless. The thunder ceased; but the rain still continued, and the scene was enveloped in an impenetrable darkness. I resolved in my minds the events which I had until now sought to forget: the whole train of my progress toward the creation; the appearance of the works of my own hands at my bedside; its departure. Two years had now nearly elapsed since the night on which he first received life; and was this his first crime? Alas! I had turned loose into the world a depraved[3] wretch, whose delight was in carnage[4] and misery; had he not murdered my brother?

No one can conceive the anguish I suffered during the remainder[5] of the night, which I spent, cold and wet, in the open air. But I did not feel the inconvenience of the weather; my imagination was busy in scenes of evil and despair. I considered the being whom I had cast among mankind, and endowed[6] with the will and power to effect purposes of horror, such as the deed which he had now done, nearly in the light of my own vampire, my own spirit let loose from the grave, and forced to destroy all that was dear to me.

Day dawned; and I directed my steps towards the town. The gates were open, and I hastened to my father's house. My first thought was to discover what I knew of the murderer, and cause instant pursuit[7] to be made. But I paused when I reflected on the story that I had to tell. A being whom I myself had formed, and endued with life, had met me at midnight among the precipices[8] of an inaccessible[9] mountain. I remembered also the nervous fever with which I had been seized just at the time that I dated my creation, and which would give an air of delirium to a tale otherwise so utterly improbable. I well knew that if any other had communicated such a relation to me, I should have looked upon it as the ravings[10] of insanity.

1 perpendicular: upright **2** bound sth.: *etw. abgrenzen* **3** depraved (adj): evil and immoral **4** carnage: *Gemetzel* **5** remainder: rest **6** endow sb. with sth.: provide sb. with. sth., give sth. to sb. **7** pursuit: (here) chase in order to catch sb. **8** precipice: steep place **9** inaccessible: impossible to reach **10** raving(n):crazy and unreasonable story

Besides, the strange nature of the animal would elude[1] all pursuit, even if I were so far credited[2] as to persuade my relatives to commence it. And then of what use would be pursuit? Who could arrest a creature capable of scaling[3] the overhanging sides of Mont Salêve? These reflections determined me, and I resolved to remain silent.

It was about five in the morning when I entered my father's house. I told the servants not to disturb the family, and went into the library to attend their usual hour of rising.

Six years had elapsed, passed in a dream but for one indelible[4] trace, and I stood in the same place where I had last embraced my father before my departure for Ingolstadt. Beloved and venerable[5] parent! He still remained to me. I gazed on the picture of my mother, which stood over the mantel-piece. It was an historical subject, painted at my father's desire, and represented Caroline Beaufort in an agony of despair, kneeling by the coffin of her dead father. Her garb[6] was rustic, and her cheek pale; but there was an air of dignity and beauty, that hardly permitted the sentiment of pity. Below this picture was a miniature of William; and my tears flowed when I looked upon it. While I was thus engaged, Ernest entered: he had heard me arrive, and hastened to welcome me: 'Welcome, my dearest Victor,' said he. 'Ah! I wish you had come three months ago, and then you would have found us all joyous and delighted. You come to us now to share a misery which nothing can alleviate[7]; yet your presence will, I hope, revive our father, who seems sinking under his misfortune; and your persuasions will induce poor Elizabeth to cease her vain[8] and tormenting self-accusations. – Poor William! he was our darling and our pride!'

Tears, unrestrained, fell from my brother's eyes; a sense of mortal agony[9] crept over my frame. Before, I had only imagined the wretchedness of my desolated home; the reality came on me as a new, and

1 elude: escape **2** credit sb./sth. (v): trust sb./sth., believe sb./sth. **3** scale (v): climb **4** indelible: impossible to remove, permanent **5** venerable: respected **6** garb: clothes **7** alleviate sth.: ease sth. **8** vain: (here) useless **9** mortal agony: *Todesangst*

a not less terrible, disaster. I tried to calm Ernest; I enquired more minutely concerning my father, and her I named my cousin.

'She most of all,' said Ernest, 'requires consolation; she accused herself of having caused the death of my brother, and that made her very wretched. But since the murderer has been discovered –'

'The murderer discovered! Good God! how can that be? who could attempt to pursue him? It is impossible; one might as well try to overtake the winds, or confine a mountain-stream with a straw. I saw him too; he was free last night!'

'I do not know what you mean,' replied my brother, in accents[1] of wonder, 'but to us the discovery we have made completes our misery. No one would believe it at first; and even now Elizabeth will not be convinced, notwithstanding all the evidence. Indeed, who would credit that Justine Moritz, who was so amiable, and fond of all the family, could suddenly become so capable of so frightful, so appalling[2] a crime?'

'Justine Moritz! Poor, poor girl, is she the accused? But it is wrongfully; every one knows that; no one believes it, surely, Ernest?'

'No one did at first; but several circumstances came out, that have almost forced conviction upon us; and her own behaviour has been so confused, as to add to the evidence of facts a weight that, I fear, leaves no hope for doubt. But she will be tried[3] to-day, and you will then hear all.'

He then related that, the morning on which the murder of poor William had been discovered, Justine had been taken ill, and confined to her bed for several days. During this interval[4], one of the servants, happening to examine the apparel[5] she had worn on the night of the murder, had discovered in her pocket the picture of my mother, which had been judged to be the temptation[6] of the murderer. The servant instantly showed it to one of the others, who,

1 accents (n, pl): (here) tone **2** appalling: shocking **3** try sb.: judge sb. in a court of law **4** interval: space of time **5** apparel: clothing including jewellery **6** temptation: (here) object that tempted sb. to do sth.

without saying a word to any of the family, went to a magistrate[1]; and, upon their deposition[2], Justine was apprehended[3]. On being charged with the fact, the poor girl confirmed the suspicion in a great measure by her extreme confusion of manner.

This was a strange tale, but it did not shake my faith; and I replied earnestly, 'You are all mistaken; I know the murderer. Justine, poor, good Justine, is innocent.'

At that instant my father entered. I saw unhappiness deeply impressed on his countenance, but he endeavoured to welcome me cheerfully; and, after we had exchanged our mournful greeting, would have introduced some other topic than that of our disaster, had not Ernest exclaimed, 'Good God, papa! Victor says that he knows who was the murderer of poor William.'

'We do also, unfortunately,' replied my father, 'for indeed I had rather have been for ever ignorant than have discovered so much depravity and ungratitude in one I valued so highly.'

'My dear father, you are mistaken; Justine is innocent.'

'If she is, God forbid that she should suffer as guilty. She is to be tried to-day, and I hope, I sincerely hope, that she will be acquitted[4].'

This speech calmed me. I was firmly convinced in my own mind that Justine, and indeed every human being, was guiltless of this murder. I had no fear, therefore, that any circumstantial evidence[5] could be brought forward strong enough to convict her. My tale was not one to announce publicly; its astounding horror would be looked upon as madness by the vulgar[6]. Did any one indeed exist, except I, the creator, who would believe, unless his senses convinced him, in the existence of the living monument of presumption and rash[7] ignorance which I had let loose upon the world?

We were soon joined by Elizabeth. Time had altered her since I last beheld her; it had endowed her with loveliness surpassing the

1 magistrate: judge **2** deposition: formal statement in which sb. gives evidence about a crime **3** apprehend sb.: arrest sb. **4** acquit sb.: state officially that sb. is not guilty of the crime he/she was accused of **5** circumstantial evidence: *Indizien* **6** the vulgar (derog): *gemeines Volk* **7** rash: hasty and incautious

beauty of her childish years. There was the same candour[1], the same vivacity, but it was allied to an expression more full of sensibility and intellect. She welcomed me with the greatest affection. 'Your arrival, my dear cousin,' said she, 'fills me with hope. You perhaps will find some means to justify[2] my poor guiltless Justine. Alas! who is safe, if she be convicted of crime? I rely on her innocence as certainly as I do upon my own. Our misfortune is doubly hard to us; we have not only lost that lovely darling boy, but this poor girl, whom I sincerely love, is to be torn away by even a worse fate. If she is condemned[3], I never shall know joy more. But she will not, I am sure she will not; and then I shall be happy again, even after the sad death of my little William.'

'She is innocent, my Elizabeth,' said I, 'and that shall be proved; fear nothing, but let your spirits be cheered by the assurance of her acquittal.'

'How kind and generous you are! every one else believes in her guilt, and that made me wretched, for I knew that it was impossible: and to see every one else prejudiced[4] in so deadly a manner rendered me hopeless and despairing.' She wept.

'Dearest niece,' said my father, 'dry your tears. If she is, as you believe, innocent, rely on the justice of our laws, and the activity with which I shall prevent the slightest shadow of partiality.'

1 cadour: honesty **2** justify sb. (old use): do justice to sb., (here) clear sb. of a charge **3** condemn sb.: (here) find sb. guilty in court **4** prejudiced ['predʒədɪst]: *voreingenommen*

Chapter 8

We passed a few sad hours until eleven o'clock, when the trial[1] was to commence. My father and the rest of the family being obliged to attend as witnesses, I accompanied them to the court. During the whole of this wretched mockery of justice I suffered living torture. It was to be decided whether the result of my curiosity and lawless devices[2] would cause the death of two of my fellow beings: one a smiling babe full of innocence and joy, the other far more dreadfully murdered, with every aggravation[3] of infamy[4] that could make the murder memorable in horror. Justine also was a girl of merit and possessed qualities which promised to render her life happy; now all was to be obliterated in an ignominious[5] grave, and I the cause! A thousand times rather would I have confessed myself guilty of the crime ascribed to Justine, but I was absent when it was committed, and such a declaration would have been considered as the ravings of a madman and would not have exculpated[6] her who suffered through me.

The appearance of Justine was calm. She was dressed in mourning, and her countenance, always engaging[7], was rendered, by the solemnity[8] of her feelings, exquisitely beautiful. Yet she appeared confident in innocence and did not tremble, although gazed on and execrated[9] by thousands, for all the kindness which her beauty might otherwise have excited was obliterated in the minds of the spectators by the imagination of the enormity she was supposed to have committed. She was tranquil, yet her tranquillity was evidently constrained[10]; and as her confusion had before been adduced[11] as a

1 trial: case in a court of law **2** device: (here) plot, scheme, dishonest plan
3 aggravation: process of making sth. worse **4** infamy: *Niederträchtigkeit*
5 ignominious [ˌɪgnəˈmɪniəs]: shameful **6** exculpate sb.: clear sb. of a charge
7 engaging: pleasant **8** solemnity: seriousness **9** execrate sb.: condemn sb.
10 constrained (adj): *aufgesetzt* **11** adduce sth.: *etw. anführen*

proof of her guilt, she worked up her mind to an appearance of courage. When she entered the court she threw her eyes round it and quickly discovered where we were seated. A tear seemed to dim her eye when she saw us, but she quickly recovered herself, and a look of sorrowful affection seemed to attest her utter guiltlessness.

The trial began, and after the advocate[1] against her had stated the charge, several witnesses were called. Several strange facts combined against her, which might have staggered[2] anyone who had not such proof of her innocence as I had. She had been out the whole of the night on which the murder had been committed and towards morning had been perceived by a market-woman not far from the spot where the body of the murdered child had been afterwards found. The woman asked her what she did there, but she looked very strangely and only returned a confused and unintelligible[3] answer. She returned to the house about eight o'clock, and when one inquired where she had passed the night, she replied that she had been looking for the child and demanded earnestly if anything had been heard concerning him. When shown the body, she fell into violent hysterics and kept her bed for several days. The picture was then produced[4] which the servant had found in her pocket; and when Elizabeth, in a faltering[5] voice, proved that it was the same which, an hour before the child had been missed, she had placed round his neck, a murmur of horror and indignation[6] filled the court.

Justine was called on for her defence. As the trial had proceeded, her countenance had altered. Surprise, horror, and misery were strongly expressed. Sometimes she struggled with her tears, but when she was desired to plead, she collected her powers and spoke in an audible although variable voice.

'God knows,' she said, 'how entirely I am innocent. But I do not pretend that my protestations[7] should acquit me; I rest my innocence on a plain and simple explanation of the facts which have

1 advocate: lawyer **2** stagger sb.: (here) make sb. insecure **3** unintelligible: impossible to understand **4** produce sth.: *(hier) etw. hervorholen* **5** faltering: weak **6** indignation: anger **7** protestation: *Beteuerung*

been adduced against me, and I hope the character I have always borne[1] will incline[2] my judges to a favourable interpretation where any circumstance appears doubtful or suspicious.'

She then related that, by the permission of Elizabeth, she had passed the evening of the night on which the murder had been committed at the house of an aunt at Chêne, a village situated at about a league from Geneva. On her return, at about nine o'clock, she met a man who asked her if she had seen anything of the child who was lost. She was alarmed by this account and passed several hours in looking for him, when the gates of Geneva were shut, and she was forced to remain several hours of the night in a barn belonging to a cottage, being unwilling to call up the inhabitants, to whom she was well known. Most of the night she spent here watching; towards morning she believed that she slept for a few minutes; some steps disturbed her, and she awoke. It was dawn, and she quitted her asylum, that she might again endeavour to find my brother. If she had gone near the spot where his body lay, it was without her knowledge. That she had been bewildered[3] when questioned by the market-woman was not surprising, since she had passed a sleepless night and the fate of poor William was yet uncertain. Concerning the picture she could give no account.

'I know,' continued the unhappy victim, 'how heavily and fatally this one circumstance weighs against me, but I have no power of explaining it; and when I have expressed my utter ignorance, I am only left to conjecture concerning the probabilities by which it might have been placed in my pocket. But here also I am checked[4]. I believe that I have no enemy on earth, and none surely would have been so wicked as to destroy me wantonly[5]. Did the murderer place it there? I know of no opportunity afforded him for so doing; or, if I had, why should he have stolen the jewel, to part with it again so soon?

1 bear sth.: *(hier) etw. an den Tag legen* **2** incline sb.: *jdn. geneigt machen*
3 bewildered [bɪˈwɪldəd]: confused **4** be checked: (here) be brought to a stop
5 wanton: reckless

'I commit my cause to the justice of my judges, yet I see no room for hope. I beg permission to have a few witnesses examined concerning my character, and if their testimony[1] shall not overweigh my supposed guilt, I must be condemned, although I would pledge my salvation[2] on my innocence.'

Several witnesses were called who had known her for many years, and they spoke well of her; but fear and hatred of the crime of which they supposed her guilty rendered them timorous[3] and unwilling to come forward. Elizabeth saw even this last resource, her excellent dispositions and irreproachable[4] conduct, about to fail the accused, when, although violently agitated, she desired permission to address the court.

'I am,' said she, 'the cousin of the unhappy child who was murdered, or rather his sister, for I was educated by and have lived with his parents ever since and even long before his birth. It may therefore be judged indecent[5] in me to come forward on this occasion, but when I see a fellow creature about to perish[6] through the cowardice of her pretended friends, I wish to be allowed to speak, that I may say what I know of her character. I am well acquainted with the accused. I have lived in the same house with her, at one time for five and at another for nearly two years. During all that period she appeared to me the most amiable and benevolent of human creatures. She nursed Madame Frankenstein, my aunt, in her last illness, with the greatest affection and care and afterwards attended her own mother during a tedious illness, in a manner that excited the admiration of all who knew her, after which she again lived in my uncle's house, where she was beloved by all the family. She was warmly attached to the child who is now dead and acted towards him like a most affectionate mother. For my own part, I do not hesitate to say that, notwithstanding all the evidence produced against her, I believe and rely on her perfect innocence. She had no tempta-

1 testimony: statement in a court session **2** pledge my salvation: *mein Seelenheil verpfänden* **3** timorous: shy and fearful **4** irreproachable: perfect **5** indecent [ɪnˈdiːsnt]: inappropriate **6** perish: (here) be ruined

tion for such an action; as to the bauble[1] on which the chief proof rests, if she had earnestly desired it, I should have willingly given it to her, so much do I esteem[2] and value her.'

A murmur of approbation followed Elizabeth's simple and powerful appeal, but it was excited by her generous interference, and not in favour of poor Justine, on whom the public indignation was turned with renewed violence, charging her with the blackest ingratitude. She herself wept as Elizabeth spoke, but she did not answer. My own agitation and anguish was extreme during the whole trial. I believed in her innocence; I knew it. Could the daemon who had (I did not for a minute doubt) murdered my brother also in his hellish sport[3] have betrayed the innocent to death and ignominy? I could not sustain the horror of my situation, and when I perceived that the popular voice and the countenances of the judges had already condemned my unhappy victim, I rushed out of the court in agony. The tortures of the accused did not equal mine; she was sustained by innocence, but the fangs[4] of remorse tore my bosom and would not forgo[5] their hold.

I passed a night of unmingled wretchedness. In the morning I went to the court; my lips and throat were parched[6]. I dared not ask the fatal question, but I was known, and the officer guessed the cause of my visit. The ballots[7] had been thrown; they were all black, and Justine was condemned.

I cannot pretend to describe what I then felt. I had before experienced sensations of horror, and I have endeavoured to bestow upon them adequate expressions, but words cannot convey an idea of the heart-sickening despair that I then endured. The person to whom I addressed myself added that Justine had already confessed her guilt. 'That evidence,' he observed, 'was hardly required in so glaring[8] a case, but I am glad of it, and, indeed, none of our judges like

1 bauble: piece of jewellery **2** esteem sb.: regard sb. highly **3** sport: (here) game **4** fang: long and sharp tooth of an animal **5** forgo sth.: (here) let go of sth. **6** parched: extremely dry **7** ballot: (here) small ball used in secret voting **8** glaring: obvious

to condemn a criminal upon circumstantial evidence, be it ever so decisive.'

This was strange and unexpected intelligence; what could it mean? Had my eyes deceived me? And was I really as mad as the whole world would believe me to be if I disclosed the object of my suspicions? I hastened to return home, and Elizabeth eagerly demanded the result.

'My cousin,' replied I, 'it is decided as you may have expected; all judges had rather that ten innocent should suffer than that one guilty should escape. But she has confessed.'

This was a dire[1] blow to poor Elizabeth, who had relied with firmness upon Justine's innocence. 'Alas!' said she. 'How shall I ever again believe in human goodness? Justine, whom I loved and esteemed as my sister, how could she put on those smiles of innocence only to betray? Her mild eyes seemed incapable of any severity[2] or guile[3], and yet she has committed a murder.'

Soon after we heard that the poor victim had expressed a desire to see my cousin. My father wished her not to go but said that he left it to her own judgment and feelings to decide. 'Yes,' said Elizabeth, 'I will go, although she is guilty; and you, Victor, shall accompany me; I cannot go alone.' The idea of this visit was torture to me, yet I could not refuse.

We entered the gloomy prison chamber and beheld Justine sitting on some straw at the farther end; her hands were manacled[4], and her head rested on her knees. She rose on seeing us enter; and when we were left alone with her, she threw herself at the feet of Elizabeth, weeping bitterly. My cousin wept also.

'Oh, Justine!' said she. 'Why did you rob me of my last consolation? I relied on your innocence, and although I was then very wretched, I was not so miserable as I am now.'

1 dire: very serious **2** severity: hardness **3** guile [gaɪl]: *Arglist* **4** manacle sb./sth.: put handcuffs on sb./sth.

'And do you also believe that I am so very, very wicked? Do you also join with my enemies to crush me, to condemn me as a murderer?' Her voice was suffocated with sobs.

'Rise, my poor girl,' said Elizabeth; 'why do you kneel, if you are innocent? I am not one of your enemies, I believed you guiltless, notwithstanding every evidence, until I heard that you had yourself declared your guilt. That report, you say, is false; and be assured, dear Justine, that nothing can shake my confidence in you for a moment, but your own confession.'

'I did confess, but I confessed a lie. I confessed, that I might obtain absolution[1]; but now that falsehood lies heavier at my heart than all my other sins. The God of heaven forgive me! Ever since I was condemned, my confessor has besieged[2] me; he threatened and menaced, until I almost began to think that I was the monster that he said I was. He threatened excommunication[3] and hell fire in my last moments if I continued obdurate[4]. Dear lady, I had none to support me; all looked on me as a wretch doomed to ignominy and perdition[5]. What could I do? In an evil hour I subscribed[6] to a lie; and now only am I truly miserable.'

She paused, weeping, and then continued, 'I thought with horror, my sweet lady, that you should believe your Justine, whom your blessed aunt had so highly honoured, and whom you loved, was a creature capable of a crime which none but the devil himself could have perpetrated[7]. Dear William! dearest blessed child! I soon shall see you again in heaven, where we shall all be happy; and that consoles me, going as I am to suffer ignominy and death.'

'Oh, Justine! Forgive me for having for one moment distrusted you. Why did you confess? But do not mourn, dear girl. Do not fear. I will proclaim, I will prove your innocence. I will melt the stony hearts of your enemies by my tears and prayers. You shall not die!

1 absolution: (here) forgiveness of sb.'s mortal sins in order to be spared punishment in hell (in Roman Catholisism) **2** besiege sb. [bɪˈsiːdʒ]: (here) pressurize sb. **3** excommunication: exclusion from the Roman Catholic Church
4 obdurate: stubborn **5** perdition: eternal damnation, hell **6** subscribe to sth.: (here) agree to sth. **7** perpetrate: commit

You, my playfellow, my companion, my sister, perish on the scaffold[1]! No! No! I never could survive so horrible a misfortune.'

Justine shook her head mournfully. 'I do not fear to die,' she said; 'that pang is past. God raises my weakness and gives me courage to endure the worst. I leave a sad and bitter world; and if you remember me and think of me as of one unjustly condemned, I am resigned to the fate awaiting me. Learn from me, dear lady, to submit[2] in patience to the will of heaven!'

During this conversation I had retired to a corner of the prison room, where I could conceal the horrid anguish that possessed me. Despair! Who dared talk of that? The poor victim, who on the morrow was to pass the awful boundary between life and death, felt not, as I did, such deep and bitter agony. I gnashed my teeth and ground[3] them together, uttering[4] a groan that came from my inmost soul. Justine started. When she saw who it was, she approached me and said, 'Dear sir, you are very kind to visit me; you, I hope, do not believe that I am guilty?'

I could not answer. 'No, Justine,' said Elizabeth; 'he is more convinced of your innocence than I was, for even when he heard that you had confessed, he did not credit it.'

'I truly thank him. In these last moments I feel the sincerest gratitude towards those who think of me with kindness. How sweet is the affection of others to such a wretch as I am! It removes more than half my misfortune, and I feel as if I could die in peace now that my innocence is acknowledged by you, dear lady, and your cousin.'

Thus the poor sufferer tried to comfort others and herself. She indeed gained the resignation[5] she desired. But I, the true murderer, felt the never-dying worm alive in my bosom, which allowed of no hope or consolation. Elizabeth also wept and was unhappy, but hers also was the misery of innocence, which, like a cloud that passes

1 scaffold: place of execution (*Schafott*) **2** submit to sth.: accept sth. **3** grind sth. (ground – ground): move sth. with a lot of force against a hard surface
4 utter sth.: produce sth. (sound or words) **5** gain the resignation: accept the fate

over the fair moon, for a while hides but cannot tarnish[1] its brightness. Anguish and despair had penetrated into the core of my heart; I bore a hell within me which nothing could extinguish. We stayed several hours with Justine, and it was with great difficulty that Elizabeth could tear herself away. 'I wish,' cried she, 'that I were to die with you; I cannot live in this world of misery.'

Justine assumed[2] an air of cheerfulness, while she with difficulty repressed her bitter tears. She embraced Elizabeth and said in a voice of half-suppressed emotion, 'Farewell, sweet lady, dearest Elizabeth, my beloved and only friend; may heaven, in its bounty[3], bless and preserve you; may this be the last misfortune that you will ever suffer! Live, and be happy, and make others so.'

And on the morrow Justine died. Elizabeth's heart-rending eloquence failed to move the judges from their settled conviction in the criminality of the saintly sufferer. My passionate and indignant[4] appeals were lost upon them. And when I received their cold answers and heard the harsh, unfeeling reasoning of these men, my purposed[5] avowal[6] died away on my lips. Thus I might proclaim myself a madman, but not revoke the sentence passed upon my wretched victim. She perished on the scaffold as a murderess!

From the tortures of my own heart, I turned to contemplate the deep and voiceless grief of my Elizabeth. This also was my doing! And my father's woe, and the desolation of that late so smiling home all was the work of my thrice-accursed[7] hands! Ye[8] weep, unhappy ones, but these are not your last tears! Again shall you raise the funeral wail[9], and the sound of your lamentations[10] shall again and again be heard! Frankenstein, your son, your kinsman[11], your early, much-loved friend; he who would spend each vital drop of blood for your sakes, who has no thought nor sense of joy except as it is mirrored also in your dear countenances, who would fill the air with

1 tarnish sth.: spoil sth. **2** assume sth.: (here) take on sth. **3** bounty: generosity **4** indignant: angry **5** purposed: intended **6** avowal: declaration **7** thrice-accursed: *dreifach verflucht* **8** ye (poetic, old use): you **9** wail (n): moaning **10** lamentation: *Wehklage* **11** kinsman: relative

blessings and spend his life in serving you – he bids[1] you weep, to shed[2] countless tears; happy beyond his hopes, if thus inexorable fate be satisfied, and if the destruction pause[3] before the peace of the grave have succeeded to your sad torments!

Thus spoke my prophetic soul, as, torn by remorse, horror, and despair, I beheld those I loved spend vain sorrow upon the graves of William and Justine, the first hapless[4] victims to my unhallowed arts.

1 bid sb. (to) do sth. (poetic): request sb. to do sth. **2** shed tears: *Tränen vergießen* **3** pause (v): stop **4** hapless: unfortunate

Chapter 9

Nothing is more painful to the human mind than, after the feelings have been worked up by a quick succession of events, the dead calmness of inaction and certainty which follows and deprives the soul both of hope and fear. Justine died, she rested, and I was alive. The blood flowed freely in my veins, but a weight of despair and remorse pressed on my heart which nothing could remove. Sleep fled from my eyes; I wandered like an evil spirit, for I had committed deeds of mischief[1] beyond description horrible, and more, much more (I persuaded myself) was yet behind[2]. Yet my heart overflowed with kindness and the love of virtue. I had begun life with benevolent intentions and thirsted for the moment when I should put them in practice and make myself useful to my fellow beings. Now all was blasted; instead of that serenity of conscience which allowed me to look back upon the past with self-satisfaction, and from thence to gather promise of new hopes, I was seized by remorse and the sense of guilt, which hurried me away to a hell of intense tortures such as no language can describe.

This state of mind preyed[3] upon my health, which had perhaps never entirely recovered from the first shock it had sustained. I shunned the face of man; all sound of joy or complacency[4] was torture to me; solitude was my only consolation – deep, dark, deathlike solitude.

My father observed with pain the alteration perceptible in my disposition and habits and endeavoured by arguments deduced from the feelings of his serene conscience and guiltless life to inspire me with fortitude and awaken in me the courage to dispel the dark

1 mischief [ˈmɪstʃɪf]: harmful behaviour **2** was yet behind: lay yet before me
3 prey upon sth.: attack sth. (like a hunting animal) **4** complacency: self-satisfaction

cloud which brooded[1] over me. 'Do you think, Victor,' said he, 'that I do not suffer also? No one could love a child more than I loved your brother' – tears came into his eyes as he spoke – 'but is it not a duty to the survivors that we should refrain from augmenting[2] their unhappiness by an appearance of immoderate[3] grief? It is also a duty owed to yourself, for excessive sorrow prevents improvement or enjoyment, or even the discharge[4] of daily usefulness, without which no man is fit for society.'

This advice, although good, was totally inapplicable[5] to my case; I should have been the first to hide my grief and console my friends if remorse had not mingled its bitterness, and terror its alarm, with my other sensations. Now I could only answer my father with a look of despair and endeavour to hide myself from his view.

About this time we retired to our house at Belrive. This change was particularly agreeable to me. The shutting of the gates regularly at ten o'clock and the impossibility of remaining on the lake after that hour had rendered our residence within the walls of Geneva very irksome to me. I was now free. Often, after the rest of the family had retired for the night, I took the boat and passed many hours upon the water. Sometimes, with my sails set, I was carried by the wind; and sometimes, after rowing into the middle of the lake, I left the boat to pursue its own course and gave way to my own miserable reflections. I was often tempted, when all was at peace around me, and I the only unquiet thing that wandered restless in a scene so beautiful and heavenly – if I except some bat, or the frogs, whose harsh and interrupted croaking was heard only when I approached the shore – often, I say, I was tempted to plunge[6] into the silent lake, that the waters might close over me and my calamities[7] forever. But I was restrained, when I thought of the heroic and suffering Elizabeth, whom I tenderly loved, and whose existence was bound up in mine. I thought also of my father and surviving brother; should I

1 brood (v): (here) hover oppressively **2** augment sth.: make sth. greater **3** immoderate: excessive **4** discharge (n): (here) fulfillment **5** inapplicable: unfitting **6** plunge into sth.: throw yourself into sth. **7** calamity: misfortune

by my base[1] desertion leave them exposed and unprotected to the malice[2] of the fiend whom I had let loose among them?

At these moments I wept bitterly and wished that peace would revisit my mind only that I might afford them consolation and happiness. But that could not be. Remorse extinguished every hope. I had been the author of unalterable evils, and I lived in daily fear lest[3] the monster whom I had created should perpetrate some new wickedness. I had an obscure feeling that all was not over and that he would still commit some signal[4] crime, which by its enormity should almost efface[5] the recollection of the past. There was always scope for fear so long as anything I loved remained behind. My abhorrence[6] of this fiend cannot be conceived. When I thought of him I gnashed my teeth, my eyes became inflamed[7], and I ardently wished to extinguish that life which I had so thoughtlessly bestowed. When I reflected on his crimes and malice, my hatred and revenge burst all bounds of moderation. I would have made a pilgrimage[8] to the highest peak of the Andes[9], could I when there have precipitated[10] him to their base. I wished to see him again, that I might wreak[11] the utmost[12] extent of abhorrence on his head and avenge[13] the deaths of William and Justine.

Our house was the house of mourning. My father's health was deeply shaken by the horror of the recent events. Elizabeth was sad and desponding[14]; she no longer took delight in her ordinary occupations; all pleasure seemed to her sacrilege toward the dead; eternal woe and tears she then thought was the just tribute she should pay to innocence so blasted and destroyed. She was no longer that happy creature who in earlier youth wandered with me on the banks of the lake and talked with ecstasy of our future prospects. The first

1 base (adj): mean and dishonourable **2** malice: meanness, evil **3** lest: *(hier) dass* **4** signal (adj): serious **5** efface sth.: make sth. disappear **6** abhorrence: strong feeling of dislike and fear **7** become inflamed: (here) start to ache **8** pilgrimage: journey to a holy place **9** Andes: mountain system in South America **10** precipitate sb. [prɪˈsɪpɪteɪt]: throw sb. down **11** wreak sth. on sb.: *etw. an jdm. auslassen* **12** utmost: most extreme **13** avenge sth.: take revenge for sth. **14** despond: lose all hope

of those sorrows which are sent to wean[1] us from the earth had visited her, and its dimming influence quenched her dearest smiles.

'When I reflect, my dear cousin,' said she, 'on the miserable death of Justine Moritz, I no longer see the world and its works as they before appeared to me. Before, I looked upon the accounts of vice and injustice that I read in books or heard from others as tales of ancient days or imaginary evils; at least they were remote and more familiar to reason[2] than to the imagination; but now misery has come home, and men appear to me as monsters thirsting for each other's blood. Yet I am certainly unjust. Everybody believed that poor girl to be guilty; and if she could have committed the crime for which she suffered, assuredly[3] she would have been the most depraved of human creatures. For the sake of a few jewels, to have murdered the son of her benefactor and friend, a child whom she had nursed from its birth, and appeared to love as if it had been her own! I could not consent to the death of any human being, but certainly I should have thought such a creature unfit to remain in the society of men. But she was innocent. I know, I feel she was innocent; you are of the same opinion, and that confirms me. Alas! Victor, when falsehood can look so like the truth, who can assure themselves of certain happiness? I feel as if I were walking on the edge of a precipice, towards which thousands are crowding and endeavouring to plunge me into the abyss[4]. William and Justine were assassinated, and the murderer escapes; he walks about the world free, and perhaps respected. But even if I were condemned to suffer on the scaffold for the same crimes, I would not change places with such a wretch.'

I listened to this discourse[5] with the extremest agony. I, not in deed, but in effect, was the true murderer. Elizabeth read my anguish in my countenance, and kindly taking my hand, said, 'My dearest friend, you must calm yourself. These events have affected me, God knows how deeply; but I am not so wretched as you are.

1 wean sb. from sth.: *(hier) jdn. von etw. entfremden* **2** reason (n): *(hier) Vernunft*
3 assuredly: surely **4** abyss: *Abgrund* **5** discourse: (here) conversation

There is an expression of despair, and sometimes of revenge, in your countenance that makes me tremble. Dear Victor, banish these dark passions. Remember the friends around you, who centre all their hopes in you. Have we lost the power of rendering you happy? Ah! While we love, while we are true to each other, here in this land of peace and beauty, your native country, we may reap[1] every tranquil blessing – what can disturb our peace?'

And could not such words from her whom I fondly prized[2] before every other gift of fortune suffice[3] to chase away the fiend that lurked[4] in my heart? Even as she spoke I drew near to her, as if in terror, lest at that very moment the destroyer had been near to rob me of her.

Thus not the tenderness of friendship, nor the beauty of earth, nor of heaven, could redeem[5] my soul from woe; the very accents[6] of love were ineffectual. I was encompassed by a cloud which no beneficial influence could penetrate. The wounded deer dragging its fainting limbs to some untrodden[7] brake[8], there to gaze upon the arrow which had pierced it, and to die, was but a type of me.

Sometimes I could cope with the sullen despair that overwhelmed me, but sometimes the whirlwind passions of my soul drove me to seek, by bodily exercise and by change of place, some relief from my intolerable sensations. It was during an access[9] of this kind that I suddenly left my home, and bending my steps towards the near Alpine valleys, sought in the magnificence, the eternity of such scenes, to forget myself and my ephemeral[10], because human, sorrows. My wanderings were directed towards the valley of Chamounix[11]. I had visited it frequently during my boyhood. Six years had passed since then: I was a wreck, but nought[12] had changed in those savage and enduring[13] scenes.

1 reap sth.: (here) receive sth. **2** prize sth./sb.: appreciate sb./sth. **3** suffice: be enough **4** lurk: lie in wait before an attack **5** redeem sth./sb.: (here) save sth./sb. **6** accent: (here) word **7** untrodden: lonely **8** brake: *Unterholz* **9** access: (here) moment **10** ephemeral: short-lived **11** Chamounix: alpine town in France (now Chamonix) **12** nought: nothing **13** enduring: lasting

I performed the first part of my journey on horseback. I afterwards hired a mule[1], as the more sure-footed and least liable[2] to receive injury on these rugged roads. The weather was fine; it was about the middle of the month of August, nearly two months after the death of Justine, that miserable epoch from which I dated all my woe. The weight upon my spirit was sensibly lightened as I plunged yet deeper in the ravine[3] of Arve[4]. The immense mountains and precipices that overhung me on every side, the sound of the river raging among the rocks, and the dashing of the waterfalls around spoke of a power mighty as Omnipotence – and I ceased to fear or to bend before any being less almighty than that which had created and ruled the elements, here displayed in their most terrific guise[5]. Still, as I ascended higher, the valley assumed a more magnificent and astonishing character. Ruined castles hanging on the precipices of piny[6] mountains, the impetuous[7] Arve, and cottages every here and there peeping forth from among the trees formed a scene of singular beauty. But it was augmented and rendered sublime by the mighty Alps, whose white and shining pyramids and domes[8] towered above all, as belonging to another earth, the habitations of another race of beings.

I passed the bridge of Pélissier, where the ravine, which the river forms, opened before me, and I began to ascend the mountain that overhangs it. Soon after, I entered the valley of Chamounix. This valley is more wonderful and sublime, but not so beautiful and picturesque as that of Servox[9], through which I had just passed. The high and snowy mountains were its immediate boundaries, but I saw no more ruined castles and fertile fields. Immense glaciers[10] approached the road; I heard the rumbling thunder of the falling avalanche[11] and marked the smoke of its passage. Mont Blanc, the

1 mule: *Maultier* **2** liable: likely to be affected **3** ravine [rəˈviːn]: narrow valley **4** Arve: river in the Mont Blanc region **5** guise: appearance **6** piny: covered with pines *(Kiefern)* **7** impetuous: wild **8** dome: *Kuppel* **9** Servox: village on the Arve **10** glacier: large mass of ice that moves slowly **11** avalanche: large amount of snow and ice that suddenly falls down a mountain

supreme and magnificent Mont Blanc, raised itself from the surrounding *aiguilles*[1], and its tremendous *dôme* overlooked the valley.

A tingling long-lost sense of pleasure often came across me during this journey. Some turn in the road, some new object suddenly perceived and recognised, reminded me of days gone by, and were associated with the lighthearted gaiety of boyhood. The very winds whispered in soothing accents, and maternal[2] Nature bade me weep no more. Then again the kindly influence ceased to act – I found myself fettered[3] again to grief and indulging[4] in all the misery of reflection. Then I spurred[5] on my animal, striving so to forget the world, my fears, and more than all, myself – or, in a more desperate fashion, I alighted and threw myself on the grass, weighed down by horror and despair.

At length I arrived at the village of Chamounix. Exhaustion succeeded to the extreme fatigue both of body and of mind which I had endured. For a short space of time I remained at the window watching the pallid[6] lightnings that played above Mont Blanc and listening to the rushing of the Arve, which pursued its noisy way beneath. The same lulling[7] sounds acted as a lullaby[8] to my too keen sensations; when I placed my head upon my pillow, sleep crept over me; I felt it as it came and blest[9] the giver of oblivion.

1 aiguelles (Fr.): peaks **2** maternal: motherly **3** fetter sb.: put chains on sb.'s feet **4** indulge in sth.: *(hier) sich etw. hingeben* **5** spur on: *die Sporen geben* **6** pallid: pale, colourless **7** lull (v): cause to sleep or rest **8** lullaby: *Wiegenlied* **9** blest: blessed

Chapter 10

I spent the following day roaming[1] through the valley. I stood beside the sources of the Arveiron[2], which take their rise in a glacier, that with slow pace is advancing down from the summit of the hills to barricade the valley. The abrupt sides of vast mountains were before me; the icy wall of the glacier overhung me; a few shattered pines were scattered[3] around; and the solemn[4] silence of this glorious presence-chamber[5] of imperial nature was broken only by the brawling[6] waves or the fall of some vast fragment, the thunder sound of the avalanche or the cracking, reverberated[7] along the mountains, of the accumulated ice, which, through the silent working of immutable laws, was ever and anon[8] rent and torn, as if it had been but a plaything in their hands. These sublime and magnificent scenes afforded me the greatest consolation that I was capable of receiving. They elevated me from all littleness of feeling, and although they did not remove my grief, they subdued and tranquillised it. In some degree, also, they diverted my mind from the thoughts over which it had brooded for the last month. I retired to rest at night; my slumbers[9], as it were[10], waited[11] on and ministered to by the assemblance[12] of grand shapes which I had contemplated during the day. They congregated[13] round me; the unstained[14] snowy mountaintop, the glittering pinnacle[15], the woods, and ragged[16] bare ravine, the eagle,

1 roam: wander without fixed aim **2** Arveiron: river that springs from the Mer de Glace glacier **3** scattered: spread **4** solemn: serious **5** presence-chamber: reception room in castles and mansions **6** brawl (v): produce a loud noise **7** reverberate: echo **8** ever and anon (old use): from time to time **9** slumber: light sleep **10** as it were: *sozusagen* **11** wait on sb.: (here) take care of sb. **12** assemblance (old use): assembly **13** congregate: gather **14** unstained: spotless **15** pinnacle: peak **16** ragged: *zerklüftet*

soaring[1] amidst the clouds – they all gathered round me and bade me be at peace.

Where had they fled when the next morning I awoke? All of soul-inspiriting fled with sleep, and dark melancholy clouded every thought. The rain was pouring in torrents, and thick mists hid the summits of the mountains, so that I even saw not the faces of those mighty friends. Still I would penetrate their misty veil[2] and seek them in their cloudy retreats. What were rain and storm to me? My mule was brought to the door, and I resolved to ascend to the summit of Montanvert[3]. I remembered the effect that the view of the tremendous and ever-moving glacier had produced upon my mind when I first saw it. It had then filled me with a sublime ecstasy that gave wings to the soul and allowed it to soar from the obscure world to light and joy. The sight of the awful[4] and majestic in nature had indeed always the effect of solemnising[5] my mind and causing me to forget the passing cares of life. I determined to go without a guide, for I was well acquainted with the path, and the presence of another would destroy the solitary grandeur of the scene.

The ascent is precipitous[6], but the path is cut into continual and short windings[7], which enable you to surmount the perpendicularity of the mountain. It is a scene terrifically desolate. In a thousand spots the traces of the winter avalanche may be perceived, where trees lie broken and strewed[8] on the ground, some entirely destroyed, others bent, leaning upon the jutting[9] rocks of the mountain or transversely[10] upon other trees. The path, as you ascend nigher, is intersected[11] by ravines of snow, down which stones continually roll from above; one of them is particularly dangerous, as the slightest sound, such as even speaking in a loud voice, produces

1 soar (v): fly high in the sky **2** veil (n): piece of cloth worn to conceal (part of) a woman's head and face **3** Montanvert: area of what is now known as the Mer de Glace glacier **4** awful: (here) awe-inspiring, commanding respect
5 solemnise sth./sb.: give sth./sb. a ceremonial quality **6** precipitous: very steep
7 winding (n): curve **8** strew sth. (strewed – strewed/strewn): scatter sth.
9 jut (v): extend out **10** transversely: across **11** intersect sth.: cross sth.

a concussion[1] of air sufficient to draw destruction upon the head of the speaker. The pines are not tall or luxuriant, but they are sombre[2] and add an air of severity to the scene. I looked on the valley beneath; vast mists were rising from the rivers which ran through it and curling in thick wreaths[3] around the opposite mountains, whose summits were hid in the uniform clouds, while rain poured from the dark sky and added to the melancholy impression I received from the objects around me. Alas! why does man boast of sensibilities superior to those apparent in the brute; it only renders them more necessary beings[4]. If our impulses were confined to hunger, thirst, and desire, we might be nearly free; but now we are moved by every wind that blows and a chance word or scene that that word may convey to us.

We rest[5]; a dream has power to poison sleep.
We rise; one wand'ring thought pollutes the day.
We feel, conceive, or reason; laugh or weep,
Embrace fond woe, or cast our cares away;
It is the same: for, be it joy or sorrow,
The path of its departure still is free.
Man's yesterday may ne'er be like his morrow;
Nought may endure[6] but mutability[7]!

It was nearly noon when I arrived at the top of the ascent. For some time I sat upon the rock that overlooks the sea of ice. A mist covered both that and the surrounding mountains. Presently a breeze dissipated the cloud, and I descended upon the glacier. The surface is very uneven, rising like the waves of a troubled sea, descending low, and interspersed[8] by rifts[9] that sink deep. The field of ice is almost a league in width, but I spent nearly two hours in

1 concussion: (here) shaking **2** sombre: dark and gloomy **3** wreath [ri:θ] (n): *Kranz* **4** it only renders them more necessary beings: *diese unterwerfen ihn nur weiterer Unfreiheit* **5** We rest ...: closing lines of P. B. Shelley's poem 'Mutability' (1816) **6** endure: (here) last **7** mutability: change **8** intersperse sth.: insert sth. in various places **9** rift (n): deep and narrow crack in glacier or rock

crossing it. The opposite mountain is a bare perpendicular rock. From the side where I now stood Montanvert was exactly opposite, at the distance of a league; and above it rose Mont Blanc, in awful majesty. I remained in a recess[1] of the rock, gazing on this wonderful and stupendous scene. The sea, or rather the vast river of ice, wound[2] among its dependent mountains, whose aerial summits hung over its recesses. Their icy and glittering peaks shone in the sunlight over the clouds. My heart, which was before sorrowful, now swelled with something like joy; I exclaimed, 'Wandering spirits, if indeed ye wander, and do not rest in your narrow beds, allow me this faint happiness, or take me, as your companion, away from the joys of life.'

As I said this I suddenly beheld the figure of a man, at some distance, advancing towards me with superhuman speed. He bounded over the crevices[3] in the ice, among which I had walked with caution; his stature, also, as he approached, seemed to exceed that of man. I was troubled; a mist came over my eyes, and I felt a faintness[4] seize me, but I was quickly restored by the cold gale of the mountains. I perceived, as the shape came nearer (sight tremendous and abhorred!) that it was the wretch whom I had created. I trembled with rage and horror, resolving to wait his approach and then close with him in mortal combat[5]. He approached; his countenance bespoke[6] bitter anguish, combined with disdain and malignity, while its unearthly ugliness rendered it almost too horrible for human eyes. But I scarcely observed this; rage and hatred had at first deprived me of utterance, and I recovered only to overwhelm him with words expressive of furious detestation[7] and contempt.

'Devil,' I exclaimed, 'do you dare approach me? And do not you fear the fierce vengeance of my arm wreaked on your miserable head? Begone[8], vile[9] insect! Or rather, stay, that I may trample you

1 recess: (here) cave-like indention **2** wind (wound – wound) [waınd]: follow a curving course **3** crevice: crack **4** faintness: weakness **5** combat (n): fight **6** bespeak sth. (bespoke – bespoken): reveal sth. **7** detestation: hatred, disgust **8** begone: go away **9** vile: disgusting

to dust! and, oh! that I could, with the extinction of your miserable existence, restore those victims whom you have so diabolically murdered!'

'I expected this reception,' said the daemon. 'All men hate the wretched; how, then, must I be hated, who am miserable beyond all living things! Yet you, my creator, detest and spurn[1] me, thy creature, to whom thou art[2] bound by ties only dissoluble[3] by the annihilation of one of us. You purpose to kill me. How dare you sport[4] thus with life? Do your duty towards me, and I will do mine towards you and the rest of mankind. If you will comply with my conditions, I will leave them and you at peace; but if you refuse, I will glut[5] the maw[6] of death, until it be satiated with the blood of your remaining friends.'

'Abhorred monster! Fiend that thou art! The tortures of hell are too mild a vengeance for thy crimes. Wretched devil! You reproach me with your creation, come on, then, that I may extinguish the spark which I so negligently[7] bestowed.'

My rage was without bounds; I sprang on him, impelled by all the feelings which can arm[8] one being against the existence of another.

He easily eluded me and said –

'Be calm! I entreat you to hear me before you give vent[9] to your hatred on my devoted[10] head. Have I not suffered enough, that you seek to increase my misery? Life, although it may only be an accumulation of anguish, is dear to me, and I will defend it. Remember, thou hast made me more powerful than thyself; my height is superior to thine[11], my joints more supple[12]. But I will not be tempted to set myself in opposition to thee. I am thy creature, and I will be even mild and docile to my natural lord and king if thou wilt[13] also perform thy part, the which thou owest[14] me. Oh, Frankenstein, be not

1 spurn sb.: reject sb. **2** art (v, old use): (you) are **3** dissoluble: (here) that can be untied **4** sport (v): play **5** glut sth.: (here) completely fill sth. **6** maw: mouth **7** negligently: carelessly **8** arm sb.: equip sb. with weapons **9** give vent to sth.: express sth. **10** devoted: loyal **11** thine (old use): yours **12** supple: flexible **13** wilt (old use): (you) will **14** owest (old use): (you) owe

equitable[1] to every other and trample upon me alone, to whom thy justice, and even thy clemency[2] and affection, is most due[3]. Remember that I am thy creature; I ought to be thy Adam, but I am rather the fallen angel, whom thou drivest from joy for no misdeed[4]. Everywhere I see bliss[5], from which I alone am irrevocably excluded. I was benevolent and good; misery made me a fiend. Make me happy, and I shall again be virtuous.'

'Begone! I will not hear you. There can be no community between you and me; we are enemies. Begone, or let us try our strength in a fight, in which one must fall.'

'How can I move thee? Will no entreaties cause thee to turn a favourable eye upon thy creature, who implores[6] thy goodness and compassion? Believe me, Frankenstein, I was benevolent; my soul glowed with love and humanity; but am I not alone, miserably alone? You, my creator, abhor me; what hope can I gather from your fellow creatures, who owe me nothing? They spurn and hate me. The desert mountains and dreary glaciers are my refuge. I have wandered here many days; the caves of ice, which I only do not fear, are a dwelling[7] to me, and the only one which man does not grudge[8]. These bleak skies I hail[9], for they are kinder to me than your fellow beings. If the multitude of mankind knew of my existence, they would do as you do, and arm themselves for my destruction. Shall I not then hate them who abhor me? I will keep no terms[10] with my enemies. I am miserable, and they shall share my wretchedness. Yet it is in your power to recompense me, and deliver[11] them from an evil which it only remains for you to make so great, that not only you and your family, but thousands of others, shall be swallowed up in the whirlwinds of its rage. Let your compassion be moved, and do not disdain me. Listen to my tale; when you have heard that,

1 equitable: fair **2** clemency: mercy **3** due: owed **4** misdeed: crime **5** bliss: happiness **6** implore sb.: ask sb. in a very emotional way **7** dwelling: home **8** grudge (sb.) sth.: *jdm. etw. missgönnen* **9** hail sb./sth.: praise sb./sth. **10** keep terms with sb.: (here) be friends with sb. **11** deliver sb. from sth.: rescue sb. from sth.

abandon or commiserate[1] me, as you shall judge that I deserve. But hear me. The guilty are allowed, by human laws, bloody as they are, to speak in their own defence before they are condemned. Listen to me, Frankenstein. You accuse me of murder, and yet you would, with a satisfied conscience, destroy your own creature. Oh, praise the eternal justice of man! Yet I ask you not to spare me; listen to me, and then, if you can, and if you will, destroy the work of your hands.'

'Why do you call to my remembrance,' I rejoined, 'circumstances of which I shudder[2] to reflect, that I have been the miserable origin and author? Cursed be the day, abhorred devil, in which you first saw light! Cursed (although I curse myself) be the hands that formed you! You have made me wretched beyond expression. You have left me no power to consider whether I am just to you or not. Begone! Relieve[3] me from the sight of your detested form.'

'Thus I relieve thee, my creator,' he said, and placed his hated hands before my eyes, which I flung from me with violence; 'thus I take from thee a sight which you abhor. Still thou canst listen to me and grant me thy compassion. By the virtues that I once possessed, I demand this from you. Hear my tale; it is long and strange, and the temperature of this place is not fitting to your fine sensations; come to the hut upon the mountain. The sun is yet high in the heavens; before it descends to hide itself behind your snowy precipices and illuminate another world, you will have heard my story and can decide. On you it rests, whether I quit forever the neighbourhood of man and lead a harmless life, or become the scourge[4] of your fellow creatures and the author of your own speedy ruin.'

As he said this he led the way across the ice; I followed. My heart was full, and I did not answer him, but as I proceeded, I weighed the various arguments that he had used and determined at least to listen to his tale. I was partly urged by curiosity, and compassion confirmed my resolution. I had hitherto supposed him to be the murderer of my brother, and I eagerly sought a confirmation or

1 commiserate sb.: feel and express sorrow for sb. **2** shudder (v): *erschauern*
3 relieve sb.: free sb. **4** scourge [skɜːdʒ] (n): whip, punishment

denial of this opinion. For the first time, also, I felt what the duties of a creator towards his creature were, and that I ought to render him happy before I complained of his wickedness. These motives urged me to comply with his demand. We crossed the ice, therefore, and ascended the opposite rock. The air was cold, and the rain again began to descend; we entered the hut, the fiend with an air of exultation, I with a heavy heart and depressed spirits. But I consented to listen, and seating myself by the fire which my odious companion had lighted, he thus began his tale.

Chapter 11

'It is with considerable difficulty that I remember the original era of my being; all the events of that period appear confused and indistinct. A strange multiplicity of sensations seized me, and I saw, felt, heard, and smelt at the same time; and it was, indeed, a long time before I learned to distinguish between the operations of my various senses. By degrees, I remember, a stronger light pressed upon my nerves, so that I was obliged to shut my eyes. Darkness then came over me and troubled me, but hardly had I felt this when, by opening my eyes, as I now suppose, the light poured in upon me again. I walked and, I believe, descended, but I presently found a great alteration in my sensations. Before, dark and opaque[1] bodies had surrounded me, impervious[2] to my touch or sight; but I now found that I could wander on at liberty, with no obstacles which I could not either surmount or avoid. The light became more and more oppressive to me, and the heat wearying[3] me as I walked, I sought a place where I could receive shade. This was the forest near Ingolstadt; and here I lay by the side of a brook[4] resting from my fatigue, until I felt tormented by hunger and thirst. This roused[5] me from my nearly dormant[6] state, and I ate some berries which I found hanging on the trees or lying on the ground. I slaked[7] my thirst at the brook, and then lying down, was overcome by sleep.

'It was dark when I awoke; I felt cold also, and half frightened, as it were, instinctively, finding myself so desolate. Before I had quitted your apartment, on a sensation of cold, I had covered myself with some clothes, but these were insufficient[8] to secure me from the

1 opaque: impossible to see through **2** impervious to sth.: *(hier) unzugänglich für etw.* **3** weary sb.: make sb. tired **4** brook: small river **5** rouse sb.: wake sb. up **6** dormant (adj): sleeping **7** slake sth.: satisfy sth. **8** insufficient: not enough

dews of night. I was a poor, helpless, miserable wretch; I knew, and could distinguish, nothing; but feeling pain invade me on all sides, I sat down and wept.

'Soon a gentle light stole over the heavens and gave me a sensation of pleasure. I started up and beheld a radiant form rise from among the trees.* I gazed with a kind of wonder. It moved slowly, but it enlightened my path, and I again went out in search of berries. I was still cold when under one of the trees I found a huge cloak[1], with which I covered myself, and sat down upon the ground. No distinct ideas occupied my mind; all was confused. I felt light, and hunger, and thirst, and darkness; innumerable[2] sounds rang in my ears, and on all sides various scents[3] saluted[4] me; the only object that I could distinguish was the bright moon, and I fixed my eyes on that with pleasure.

'Several changes of day and night passed, and the orb[5] of night had greatly lessened, when I began to distinguish my sensations from each other. I gradually saw plainly the clear stream that supplied me with drink and the trees that shaded me with their foliage[6]. I was delighted when I first discovered that a pleasant sound, which often saluted my ears, proceeded[7] from the throats of the little winged animals who had often intercepted[8] the light from my eyes. I began also to observe, with greater accuracy, the forms that surrounded me and to perceive the boundaries of the radiant roof of light which canopied[9] me. Sometimes I tried to imitate the pleasant songs of the birds but was unable. Sometimes I wished to express my sensations in my own mode, but the uncouth and inarticulate sounds which broke from me frightened me into silence again.

'The moon had disappeared from the night, and again, with a lessened form, showed itself, while I still remained in the forest. My sensations had by this time become distinct, and my mind received

* The moon [author's footnote]. **1** cloak: coat **2** innumerable: countless
3 scent (n): smell **4** salute sb.: greet sb. **5** orb: round shape, (here) moon
6 foliage: leaves **7** proceed from: (here) come from **8** intercept sth.: catch sth.
9 canopy sth.: form a curved roof above sth.

every day additional ideas. My eyes became accustomed to the light and to perceive objects in their right forms; I distinguished the insect from the herb[1], and by degrees, one herb from another. I found that the sparrow[2] uttered none but harsh notes, whilst those of the blackbird[3] and thrush[4] were sweet and enticing.

'One day, when I was oppressed by cold, I found a fire which had been left by some wandering beggars, and was overcome with delight at the warmth I experienced from it. In my joy I thrust my hand into the live embers[5], but quickly drew it out again with a cry of pain. How strange, I thought, that the same cause should produce such opposite effects! I examined the materials of the fire, and to my joy found it to be composed of wood. I quickly collected some branches, but they were wet and would not burn. I was pained at this and sat still watching the operation of the fire. The wet wood which I had placed near the heat dried and itself became inflamed. I reflected on this, and by touching the various branches, I discovered the cause and busied myself in collecting a great quantity of wood, that I might dry it and have a plentiful supply of fire. When night came on and brought sleep with it, I was in the greatest fear lest my fire should be extinguished. I covered it carefully with dry wood and leaves and placed wet branches upon it; and then, spreading my cloak, I lay on the ground and sank into sleep.

'It was morning when I awoke, and my first care was to visit the fire. I uncovered it, and a gentle breeze quickly fanned it into a flame. I observed this also and contrived a fan of branches, which roused the embers when they were nearly extinguished. When night came again I found, with pleasure, that the fire gave light as well as heat and that the discovery of this element was useful to me in my food, for I found some of the offals[6] that the travellers had left had been roasted, and tasted much more savoury[7] than the berries I gath-

1 herb: *(hier) Kraut* **2** sparrow: *Spatz* **3** blackbird: *Amsel* **4** thrush: *Drossel* **5** live embers: *heiße Glut* **6** offals: leftover meat **7** savoury: having a salty or spicy taste

ered from the trees. I tried, therefore, to dress[1] my food in the same manner, placing it on the live embers. I found that the berries were spoiled by this operation, and the nuts and roots much improved.

'Food, however, became scarce, and I often spent the whole day searching in vain for a few acorns[2] to assuage[3] the pangs of hunger. When I found this, I resolved to quit the place that I had hitherto inhabited, to seek for one where the few wants I experienced would be more easily satisfied. In this emigration I exceedingly lamented the loss of the fire which I had obtained through accident and knew not how to reproduce it. I gave several hours to the serious consideration of this difficulty, but I was obliged to relinquish all attempt to supply it, and wrapping myself up in my cloak, I struck[4] across the wood towards the setting sun. I passed three days in these rambles and at length discovered the open country. A great fall of snow had taken place the night before, and the fields were of one uniform white; the appearance was disconsolate, and I found my feet chilled by the cold damp substance that covered the ground.

'It was about seven in the morning, and I longed to obtain food and shelter; at length I perceived a small hut, on a rising ground, which had doubtless been built for the convenience of some shepherd. This was a new sight to me, and I examined the structure with great curiosity. Finding the door open, I entered. An old man sat in it, near a fire, over which he was preparing his breakfast. He turned on hearing a noise, and perceiving me, shrieked loudly, and quitting the hut, ran across the fields with a speed of which his debilitated[5] form hardly appeared capable. His appearance, different from any I had ever before seen, and his flight somewhat surprised me. But I was enchanted by the appearance of the hut; here the snow and rain could not penetrate; the ground was dry; and it presented to me then as exquisite and divine a retreat as Pandemonium[6] appeared

1 dress sth.: (here) prepare sth. **2** acorn: *Eichel* **3** assuage sth. [əˈsweɪdʒ]: lessen the intensity of sth. **4** strike (struck – struck/stricken): (here) go **5** debilitated: weakened **6** Pandemonium: spacious and impressive place in hell where demons reside (as described in Milton's *Paradise Lost*)

to the demons of hell after their sufferings in the lake of fire. I greedily devoured[1] the remnants[2] of the shepherd's breakfast, which consisted of bread, cheese, milk, and wine; the latter, however, I did not like. Then, overcome by fatigue, I lay down among some straw and fell asleep.

'It was noon when I awoke, and allured[3] by the warmth of the sun, which shone brightly on the white ground, I determined to recommence my travels; and, depositing the remains of the peasant's breakfast in a wallet[4] I found, I proceeded across the fields for several hours, until at sunset I arrived at a village. How miraculous did this appear! the huts, the neater cottages, and stately[5] houses engaged my admiration by turns. The vegetables in the gardens, the milk and cheese that I saw placed at the windows of some of the cottages, allured my appetite. One of the best of these I entered, but I had hardly placed my foot within the door before the children shrieked, and one of the women fainted. The whole village was roused; some fled, some attacked me, until, grievously[6] bruised[7] by stones and many other kinds of missile weapons[8], I escaped to the open country and fearfully took refuge in a low hovel[9], quite bare, and making a wretched appearance after the palaces I had beheld in the village. This hovel, however, joined a cottage of a neat and pleasant appearance, but after my late dearly bought experience, I dared not enter it. My place of refuge was constructed of wood, but so low that I could with difficulty sit upright in it. No wood, however, was placed on the earth, which formed the floor, but it was dry; and although the wind entered it by innumerable chinks[10], I found it an agreeable asylum from the snow and rain.

'Here, then, I retreated and lay down happy to have found a shelter, however miserable, from the inclemency of the season, and still more from the barbarity of man.

1 devour sth.: eat sth. hastily and with great appetite **2** remnant: leftover
3 allure sb.: attract sb. **4** wallet: (here) small bag **5** stately: impressive
6 grievously: severely **7** bruised: injured **8** missile weapon: *Wurfgeschoss*
9 hovel: shed **10** chink: small crack

As soon as morning dawned I crept from my kennel[1], that I might view the adjacent[2] cottage and discover if I could remain in the habitation I had found. It was situated against the back of the cottage and surrounded on the sides which were exposed by a pig-sty[3] and a clear pool of water. One part was open, and by that I had crept in; but now I covered every crevice by which I might be perceived with stones and wood, yet in such a manner that I might move them on occasion to pass out; all the light I enjoyed came through the sty, and that was sufficient for me.

'Having thus arranged my dwelling and carpeted it with clean straw, I retired, for I saw the figure of a man at a distance, and I remembered too well my treatment the night before to trust myself in his power. I had first, however, provided for my sustenance for that day by a loaf of coarse bread, which I purloined[4], and a cup with which I could drink more conveniently than from my hand of the pure water which flowed by my retreat. The floor was a little raised, so that it was kept perfectly dry, and by its vicinity[5] to the chimney of the cottage it was tolerably warm.

'Being thus provided, I resolved to reside in this hovel until something should occur which might alter my determination. It was indeed a paradise compared to the bleak forest, my former residence, the rain-dropping branches, and dank[6] earth. I ate my breakfast with pleasure and was about to remove a plank[7] to procure myself a little water when I heard a step, and looking through a small chink, I beheld a young creature, with a pail[8] on her head, passing before my hovel. The girl was young and of gentle demeanour[9], unlike what I have since found cottagers and farmhouse servants to be. Yet she was meanly[10] dressed, a coarse blue petticoat[11] and a linen jacket being her only garb; her fair hair was plaited[12] but

1 kennel: small building where a dog sleeps **2** adjacent: neighbouring
3 pig-sty: place to keep pigs **4** purloin sth.: steal sth. **5** vicinity: closeness
6 dank: moist **7** plank (n): wooden board **8** pail: bucket **9** demeanour: behaviour **10** meanly: poorly **11** petticoat: skirt-like undergarment
12 plaited: *geflochten*

not adorned[1]: she looked patient yet sad. I lost sight of her, and in about a quarter of an hour she returned bearing the pail, which was now partly filled with milk. As she walked along, seemingly incommoded[2] by the burden, a young man met her, whose countenance expressed a deeper despondence. Uttering a few sounds with an air of melancholy, he took the pail from her head and bore it to the cottage himself. She followed, and they disappeared. Presently I saw the young man again, with some tools in his hand, cross the field behind the cottage; and the girl was also busied, sometimes in the house and sometimes in the yard.

'On examining my dwelling, I found that one of the windows of the cottage had formerly occupied a part of it, but the panes had been filled up with wood. In one of these was a small and almost imperceptible chink through which the eye could just penetrate. Through this crevice a small room was visible, whitewashed[3] and clean but very bare of furniture. In one corner, near a small fire, sat an old man, leaning his head on his hands in a disconsolate attitude. The young girl was occupied in arranging the cottage; but presently she took something out of a drawer, which employed her hands, and she sat down beside the old man, who, taking up an instrument, began to play and to produce sounds sweeter than the voice of the thrush or the nightingale[4]. It was a lovely sight, even to me, poor wretch who had never beheld aught beautiful before. The silver hair and benevolent countenance of the aged cottager won my reverence, while the gentle manners of the girl enticed my love. He played a sweet mournful air[5] which I perceived drew tears from the eyes of his amiable companion, of which the old man took no notice, until she sobbed audibly; he then pronounced a few sounds, and the fair creature, leaving her work, knelt[6] at his feet. He raised her and smiled with such kindness and affection that I felt sensations of a peculiar and overpowering nature; they were a mixture of pain and

1 adorned: decorated **2** incommode sb.: give distress to sb., disturb sb.
3 whitewashed: painted white **4** nightingale: *Nachtigall* **5** air: (here) song
6 kneel (knelt – knelt): have one or two knees on the ground

pleasure, such as I had never before experienced, either from hunger or cold, warmth or food; and I withdrew from the window, unable to bear these emotions.

'Soon after this the young man returned, bearing on his shoulders a load of wood. The girl met him at the door, helped to relieve him of his burden, and taking some of the fuel into the cottage, placed it on the fire; then she and the youth went apart into a nook[1] of the cottage, and he showed her a large loaf and a piece of cheese. She seemed pleased and went into the garden for some roots and plants, which she placed in water, and then upon the fire. She afterwards continued her work, whilst the young man went into the garden and appeared busily employed in digging and pulling up roots. After he had been employed thus about an hour, the young woman joined him and they entered the cottage together.

'The old man had, in the meantime, been pensive[2], but on the appearance of his companions he assumed a more cheerful air, and they sat down to eat. The meal was quickly despatched[3]. The young woman was again occupied in arranging the cottage, the old man walked before the cottage in the sun for a few minutes, leaning on the arm of the youth. Nothing could exceed in beauty the contrast between these two excellent creatures. One was old, with silver hairs and a countenance beaming with benevolence and love; the younger was slight and graceful in his figure, and his features were moulded with the finest symmetry, yet his eyes and attitude expressed the utmost sadness and despondency. The old man returned to the cottage, and the youth, with tools different from those he had used in the morning, directed his steps across the fields.

'Night quickly shut in, but to my extreme wonder, I found that the cottagers had a means of prolonging light by the use of tapers[4], and was delighted to find that the setting of the sun did not put an end to the pleasure I experienced in watching my human neighbours. In the evening the young girl and her companion were employed in

1 nook: small section of a larger room **2** pensive: sadly thoughtful **3** despatch sth.: (here) eat up sth. quickly **4** taper: candle

various occupations which I did not understand; and the old man again took up the instrument which produced the divine sounds that had enchanted me in the morning. So soon as he had finished, the youth began, not to play, but to utter sounds that were monotonous, and neither resembling the harmony of the old man's instrument nor the songs of the birds; I since found that he read aloud, but at that time I knew nothing of the science of words or letters.

'The family, after having been thus occupied for a short time, extinguished their lights and retired, as I conjectured, to rest.'

Chapter 12

'I lay on my straw, but I could not sleep. I thought of the occurrences of the day. What chiefly struck me was the gentle manners of these people, and I longed to join them, but dared not. I remembered too well the treatment I had suffered the night before from the barbarous villagers, and resolved, whatever course of conduct I might hereafter think it right to pursue, that for the present I would remain quietly in my hovel, watching and endeavouring to discover the motives which influenced their actions.

'The cottagers arose the next morning before the sun. The young woman arranged the cottage and prepared the food, and the youth departed after the first meal.

'This day was passed in the same routine as that which preceded it. The young man was constantly employed out of doors, and the girl in various laborious[1] occupations within. The old man, whom I soon perceived to be blind, employed his leisure hours on his instrument or in contemplation. Nothing could exceed the love and respect which the younger cottagers exhibited towards their venerable companion. They performed towards him every little office[2] of affection and duty with gentleness, and he rewarded them by his benevolent smiles.

'They were not entirely happy. The young man and his companion often went apart and appeared to weep. I saw no cause for their unhappiness, but I was deeply affected by it. If such lovely creatures were miserable, it was less strange that I, an imperfect and solitary being, should be wretched. Yet why were these gentle beings unhappy? They possessed a delightful house (for such it was in my eyes) and every luxury; they had a fire to warm them when chill,

1 laborious: long, difficult and boring **2** office: (here) service

and delicious viands[1] when hungry; they were dressed in excellent clothes; and, still more, they enjoyed one another's company and speech, interchanging each day looks of affection and kindness. What did their tears imply? Did they really express pain? I was at first unable to solve these questions, but perpetual attention and time explained to me many appearances which were at first enigmatic[2].

'A considerable period elapsed before I discovered one of the causes of the uneasiness of this amiable family: it was poverty, and they suffered that evil in a very distressing degree. Their nourishment[3] consisted entirely of the vegetables of their garden and the milk of one cow, which gave very little during the winter, when its masters could scarcely procure food to support it. They often, I believe, suffered the pangs of hunger very poignantly, especially the two younger cottagers, for several times they placed food before the old man when they reserved none for themselves.

'This trait of kindness moved me sensibly. I had been accustomed, during the night, to steal a part of their store for my own consumption, but when I found that in doing this I inflicted pain on the cottagers, I abstained[4] and satisfied myself with berries, nuts, and roots which I gathered from a neighbouring wood.

'I discovered also another means through which I was enabled to assist their labours. I found that the youth spent a great part of each day in collecting wood for the family fire, and during the night I often took his tools, the use of which I quickly discovered, and brought home firing[5] sufficient for the consumption of several days.

'I remember, the first time that I did this, the young woman, when she opened the door in the morning, appeared greatly astonished on seeing a great pile of wood on the outside. She uttered some words in a loud voice, and the youth joined her, who also expressed surprise. I observed, with pleasure, that he did not go to

1 viand ['vīənd]: food **2** enigmatic: mysterious **3** nourishment: food
4 abstain from sth.: avoid doing sth. that is enjoyable **5** firing: *(hier) Brennholz*

the forest that day, but spent it in repairing the cottage and cultivating the garden.

'By degrees I made a discovery of still greater moment[1]. I found that these people possessed a method of communicating their experience and feelings to one another by articulate[2] sounds. I perceived that the words they spoke sometimes produced pleasure or pain, smiles or sadness, in the minds and countenances of the hearers. This was indeed a godlike science, and I ardently desired to become acquainted with it. But I was baffled[3] in every attempt I made for this purpose. Their pronunciation was quick, and the words they uttered, not having any apparent connection with visible objects, I was unable to discover any clue by which I could unravel[4] the mystery of their reference. By great application, however, and after having remained during the space of several revolutions[5] of the moon in my hovel, I discovered the names that were given to some of the most familiar objects of discourse; I learned and applied the words, "fire", "milk", "bread", and "wood". I learned also the names of the cottagers themselves. The youth and his companion had each of them several names, but the old man had only one, which was "father". The girl was called "sister" or "Agatha", and the youth "Felix", "brother", or "son". I cannot describe the delight I felt when I learned the ideas appropriated[6] to each of these sounds and was able to pronounce them. I distinguished several other words without being able as yet to understand or apply them, such as "good", "dearest", "unhappy".

'I spent the winter in this manner. The gentle manners and beauty of the cottagers greatly endeared[7] them to me; when they were unhappy, I felt depressed; when they rejoiced, I sympathised in their joys. I saw few human beings besides them, and if any other happened to enter the cottage, their harsh manners and rude gait[8]

1 moment: (here) importance **2** articulate: (here) clearly understandable
3 baffle sb.: hinder sb. **4** unravel sth.: solve sth. **5** revolution: (here) circulation around the earth **6** appropriate sth. to sth.: link sth. to sth. **7** endear sth./sb. to sb.: make sb. like sth./sb. **8** gait: way of walking

only enhanced[1] to me the superior accomplishments of my friends. The old man, I could perceive, often endeavoured to encourage his children, as sometimes I found that he called them, to cast off their melancholy. He would talk in a cheerful accent, with an expression of goodness that bestowed pleasure even upon me. Agatha listened with respect, her eyes sometimes filled with tears, which she endeavoured to wipe away unperceived; but I generally found that her countenance and tone were more cheerful after having listened to the exhortations[2] of her father. It was not thus with Felix. He was always the saddest of the group, and even to my unpractised senses, he appeared to have suffered more deeply than his friends. But if his countenance was more sorrowful, his voice was more cheerful than that of his sister, especially when he addressed the old man.

'I could mention innumerable instances which, although slight, marked the dispositions of these amiable cottagers. In the midst of poverty and want, Felix carried with pleasure to his sister the first little white flower that peeped out from beneath the snowy ground. Early in the morning, before she had risen, he cleared away the snow that obstructed[3] her path to the milk-house, drew water from the well, and brought the wood from the out-house[4], where, to his perpetual astonishment, he found his store always replenished[5] by an invisible hand. In the day, I believe, he worked sometimes for a neighbouring farmer, because he often went forth and did not return until dinner, yet brought no wood with him. At other times he worked in the garden, but as there was little to do in the frosty season, he read to the old man and Agatha.

'This reading had puzzled[6] me extremely at first, but by degrees I discovered that he uttered many of the same sounds when he read as when he talked. I conjectured, therefore, that he found on the paper signs for speech which he understood, and I ardently longed to comprehend these also; but how was that possible when I did

1 enhance sth.: make sth. more attractive or valuable **2** exhortation: strict advice or warning **3** obstruct sth.: block the way of sth. **4** out-house: small, neighbouring building **5** replenish sth.: fill sth. up **6** puzzle sb.: confuse sb.

not even understand the sounds for which they stood as signs? I improved, however, sensibly in this science, but not sufficiently to follow up any kind of conversation, although I applied my whole mind to the endeavour, for I easily perceived that, although I eagerly longed to discover[1] myself to the cottagers, I ought not to make the attempt until I had first become master of their language, which knowledge might enable me to make them overlook the deformity of my figure, for with this also the contrast perpetually presented to my eyes had made me acquainted.

'I had admired the perfect forms of my cottagers – their grace, beauty, and delicate[2] complexions; but how was I terrified when I viewed myself in a transparent pool! At first I started back, unable to believe that it was indeed I who was reflected in the mirror; and when I became fully convinced that I was in reality the monster that I am, I was filled with the bitterest sensations of despondence and mortification[3]. Alas! I did not yet entirely know the fatal effects of this miserable deformity.

'As the sun became warmer and the light of day longer, the snow vanished, and I beheld the bare trees and the black earth. From this time Felix was more employed, and the heart-moving indications of impending[4] famine disappeared. Their food, as I afterwards found, was coarse, but it was wholesome[5]; and they procured a sufficiency of it. Several new kinds of plants sprang up in the garden, which they dressed; and these signs of comfort increased daily as the season advanced.

'The old man, leaning on his son, walked each day at noon, when it did not rain, as I found it was called when the heavens poured forth[6] its waters. This frequently took place, but a high[7] wind quickly dried the earth, and the season became far more pleasant than it had been.

1 discover yourself to sb.: show yourself to sb. by coming out of hiding
2 delicate: (here) pleasant **3** mortification: humiliation **4** impending: upcoming **5** wholesome: healthy **6** pour sth. forth: *etw. ausgießen* **7** high: (here) strong

'My mode of life in my hovel was uniform. During the morning I attended the motions of the cottagers, and when they were dispersed in various occupations, I slept; the remainder of the day was spent in observing my friends. When they had retired to rest, if there was any moon or the night was star-light, I went into the woods and collected my own food and fuel for the cottage. When I returned, as often as it was necessary, I cleared their path from the snow and performed those offices that I had seen done by Felix. I afterwards found that these labours, performed by an invisible hand, greatly astonished them; and once or twice I heard them, on these occasions, utter the words "good spirit", "wonderful"; but I did not then understand the signification[1] of these terms.

'My thoughts now became more active, and I longed to discover the motives and feelings of these lovely creatures; I was inquisitive to know why Felix appeared so miserable and Agatha so sad. I thought (foolish wretch!) that it might be in my power to restore happiness to these deserving people. When I slept or was absent, the forms of the venerable blind father, the gentle Agatha, and the excellent Felix flitted[2] before me. I looked upon them as superior beings who would be the arbiters[3] of my future destiny. I formed in my imagination a thousand pictures of presenting myself to them, and their reception of me. I imagined that they would be disgusted, until, by my gentle demeanour and conciliating words, I should first win their favour and afterwards their love.

'These thoughts exhilarated[4] me and led me to apply with fresh ardour to the acquiring the art of language. My organs were indeed harsh, but supple; and although my voice was very unlike the soft music of their tones, yet I pronounced such words as I understood with tolerable ease. It was as the ass and the lap-dog[5]; yet surely the gentle ass whose intentions were affectionate, although his man-

1 signification: meaning **2** flit: move quickly **3** arbiter [ˈɑːbɪtə(r)]: (here) master, judge **4** exhilarate sb.: cheer sb. up **5** The ass and the lap-dog: fable by Greek writer Aesop (620–564 BC) in which an ass, i.e. a donkey, gets beaten after clumsily imitating a lap-dog's flattering behaviour towards its human master

ners were rude, deserved better treatment than blows and execration[1].

'The pleasant showers and genial warmth of spring greatly altered the aspect of the earth. Men who before this change seemed to have been hid in caves dispersed themselves and were employed in various arts of cultivation. The birds sang in more cheerful notes, and the leaves began to bud forth on the trees. Happy, happy earth! Fit habitation for gods, which, so short a time before, was bleak, damp, and unwholesome. My spirits were elevated by the enchanting appearance of nature; the past was blotted[2] from my memory, the present was tranquil, and the future gilded[3] by bright rays of hope and anticipations of joy.'

1 execration: cursing **2** blot sth.: delete sth., erase sth. **3** gilded: covered in gold

Chapter 13

'I now hasten to the more moving part of my story. I shall relate events that impressed me with feelings which, from what I had been, have made me what I am.

'Spring advanced rapidly; the weather became fine and the skies cloudless. It surprised me that what before was desert and gloomy should now bloom with the most beautiful flowers and verdure[1]. My senses were gratified and refreshed by a thousand scents of delight and a thousand sights of beauty.

'It was on one of these days, when my cottagers periodically rested from labour – the old man played on his guitar, and the children listened to him – that I observed the countenance of Felix was melancholy beyond expression; he sighed frequently, and once his father paused in his music, and I conjectured by his manner that he inquired the cause of his son's sorrow. Felix replied in a cheerful accent, and the old man was recommencing his music when someone tapped at the door.

'It was a lady on horseback, accompanied by a countryman as a guide. The lady was dressed in a dark suit and covered with a thick black veil. Agatha asked a question, to which the stranger only replied by pronouncing, in a sweet accent, the name of Felix. Her voice was musical but unlike that of either of my friends. On hearing this word, Felix came up hastily to the lady, who, when she saw him, threw up her veil, and I beheld a countenance of angelic beauty and expression. Her hair of a shining raven black, and curiously braided[2]; her eyes were dark, but gentle, although animated; her features of a regular proportion, and her complexion wondrously fair, each cheek tinged with a lovely pink.

1 verdure: greenness **2** braided: *geflochten*

'Felix seemed ravished[1] with delight when he saw her, every trait of sorrow vanished from his face, and it instantly expressed a degree of ecstatic joy, of which I could hardly have believed it capable; his eyes sparkled[2], as his cheek flushed with pleasure; and at that moment I thought him as beautiful as the stranger. She appeared affected by different feelings; wiping a few tears from her lovely eyes, she held out her hand to Felix, who kissed it rapturously[3] and called her, as well as I could distinguish, his sweet Arabian. She did not appear to understand him, but smiled. He assisted her to dismount[4], and dismissing her guide, conducted her into the cottage. Some conversation took place between him and his father, and the young stranger knelt at the old man's feet and would have kissed his hand, but he raised her and embraced her affectionately.

'I soon perceived that although the stranger uttered articulate sounds and appeared to have a language of her own, she was neither understood by nor herself understood the cottagers. They made many signs which I did not comprehend, but I saw that her presence diffused gladness through the cottage, dispelling their sorrow as the sun dissipates the morning mists. Felix seemed peculiarly happy and with smiles of delight welcomed his Arabian. Agatha, the ever-gentle Agatha, kissed the hands of the lovely stranger, and pointing to her brother, made signs which appeared to me to mean that he had been sorrowful until she came. Some hours passed thus, while they, by their countenances, expressed joy, the cause of which I did not comprehend. Presently I found, by the frequent recurrence of some sound which the stranger repeated after them, that she was endeavouring to learn their language; and the idea instantly occurred to me that I should make use of the same instructions to the same end. The stranger learned about twenty words at the first lesson; most of them, indeed, were those which I had before understood, but I profited by the others.

1 ravished with sth.: overcome by sth. **2** sparkle: *funkeln* **3** rapturously: overcome by emotion **4** dismount sth.: get off sth. (e.g. a horse)

'As night came on, Agatha and the Arabian retired early. When they separated Felix kissed the hand of the stranger and said, "Good night sweet Safie." He sat up much longer, conversing with his father, and by the frequent repetition of her name I conjectured that their lovely guest was the subject of their conversation. I ardently desired to understand them, and bent every faculty towards that purpose, but found it utterly impossible.

'The next morning Felix went out to his work, and after the usual occupations of Agatha were finished, the Arabian sat at the feet of the old man, and taking his guitar, played some airs so entrancingly[1] beautiful that they at once drew tears of sorrow and delight from my eyes. She sang, and her voice flowed in a rich cadence[2], swelling or dying away like a nightingale of the woods.

'When she had finished, she gave the guitar to Agatha, who at first declined it. She played a simple air, and her voice accompanied it in sweet accents, but unlike the wondrous strain of the stranger. The old man appeared enraptured[3] and said some words which Agatha endeavoured to explain to Safie, and by which he appeared to wish to express that she bestowed on him the greatest delight by her music.

'The days now passed as peaceably as before, with the sole alteration that joy had taken place of sadness in the countenances of my friends. Safie was always gay and happy; she and I improved rapidly in the knowledge of language, so that in two months I began to comprehend most of the words uttered by my protectors.

'In the meanwhile also the black ground was covered with herbage, and the green banks[4] interspersed with innumerable flowers, sweet to the scent and the eyes, stars of pale radiance among the moonlight woods; the sun became warmer, the nights clear and balmy[5]; and my nocturnal[6] rambles were an extreme pleasure to me, although they were considerably shortened by the late setting and

1 entrancingly: *hinreißend* **2** cadence: *Tonfülle* **3** enraptured (adj): overcome by emotion **4** bank: *(hier) Hang* **5** balmy: (here) mild **6** nocturnal: at night

early rising of the sun, for I never ventured abroad[1] during daylight, fearful of meeting with the same treatment I had formerly endured in the first village which I entered.

'My days were spent in close attention, that I might more speedily master the language; and I may boast that I improved more rapidly than the Arabian, who understood very little and conversed in broken accents, whilst I comprehended and could imitate almost every word that was spoken.

'While I improved in speech, I also learned the science of letters as it was taught to the stranger, and this opened before me a wide field for wonder and delight.

'The book from which Felix instructed Safie was Volney's *Ruins of Empires*[2]. I should not have understood the purport[3] of this book had not Felix, in reading it, given very minute explanations. He had chosen this work, he said, because the declamatory[4] style was framed[5] in imitation of the Eastern authors. Through this work I obtained a cursory knowledge of history and a view of the several empires at present existing in the world; it gave me an insight into the manners, governments, and religions of the different nations of the earth. I heard of the slothful[6] Asiatics, of the stupendous genius and mental activity of the Grecians, of the wars and wonderful virtue of the early Romans – of their subsequent degenerating – of the decline of that mighty empire, of chivalry, Christianity, and kings. I heard of the discovery of the American hemisphere and wept with Safie over the hapless fate of its original inhabitants.

'These wonderful narrations inspired me with strange feelings. Was man, indeed, at once so powerful, so virtuous and magnificent,

1 abroad: (here) outside **2** *Ruins of Empires*: historico-philosophical work by French author Comte de Volney (1757–1820) published in 1791 which had considerable impact on the Romantic poets and other freethinkers. It seeks to explain and criticize the world religions and treats such subjects as wealth, rank and property. Against this background, it analyses the fall of ancient civilisations. **3** purport (n): meaning **4** declamatory: pompous, flowery **5** frame sth.: (here) give a form to sth. **6** slothful: lazy

yet so vicious[1] and base? He appeared at one time a mere scion[2] of the evil principle and at another as all that can be conceived of noble and godlike. To be a great and virtuous man appeared the highest honour that can befall a sensitive being; to be base and vicious, as many on record have been, appeared the lowest degradation, a condition more abject[3] than that of the blind mole[4] or harmless worm. For a long time I could not conceive how one man could go forth to murder his fellow, or even why there were laws and governments; but when I heard details of vice and bloodshed, my wonder ceased and I turned away with disgust and loathing.

'Every conversation of the cottagers now opened new wonders to me. While I listened to the instructions which Felix bestowed upon the Arabian, the strange system of human society was explained to me. I heard of the division of property, of immense wealth and squalid[5] poverty, of rank, descent[6], and noble blood.

'The words induced me to turn towards myself. I learned that the possessions most esteemed by your fellow creatures were high and unsullied[7] descent united with riches. A man might be respected with only one of these advantages, but without either he was considered, except in very rare instances, as a vagabond and a slave, doomed to waste his powers for the profits of the chosen few! And what was I? Of my creation and creator I was absolutely ignorant, but I knew that I possessed no money, no friends, no kind of property. I was, besides, endued with a figure hideously deformed and loathsome; I was not even of the same nature as man. I was more agile than they and could subsist[8] upon coarser diet; I bore the extremes of heat and cold with less injury to my frame; my stature far exceeded theirs. When I looked around I saw and heard of none like me. Was I, then, a monster, a blot[9] upon the earth, from which all men fled and whom all men disowned[10]?

1 vicious: evil **2** scion ['saɪən]: child, descendant **3** abject: miserable **4** mole: *Maulwurf* **5** squalid: pitiful **6** descent [dɪ'sent]: family origin **7** unsullied: pure **8** subsist upon sth.: exist on sth. **9** blot (n): *Schandfleck* **10** disown sb.: reject sb.

'I cannot describe to you the agony that these reflections inflicted upon me; I tried to dispel them, but sorrow only increased with knowledge. Oh, that I had forever remained in my native wood, nor known nor felt beyond the sensations of hunger, thirst, and heat!

'Of what a strange nature is knowledge! It clings to the mind when it has once seized on it like a lichen[1] on the rock. I wished sometimes to shake off all thought and feeling, but I learned that there was but one means to overcome the sensation of pain, and that was death – a state which I feared yet did not understand. I admired virtue and good feelings and loved the gentle manners and amiable qualities of my cottagers, but I was shut out from intercourse with them, except through means which I obtained by stealth[2], when I was unseen and unknown, and which rather increased than satisfied the desire I had of becoming one among my fellows. The gentle words of Agatha and the animated smiles of the charming Arabian were not for me. The mild exhortations of the old man and the lively conversation of the loved Felix were not for me. Miserable, unhappy wretch!

'Other lessons were impressed upon me even more deeply. I heard of the difference of sexes, and the birth and growth of children, how the father doted[3] on the smiles of the infant, and the lively sallies[4] of the older child, how all the life and cares of the mother were wrapped up in the precious charge, how the mind of youth expanded and gained knowledge, of brother, sister, and all the various relationships which bind one human being to another in mutual bonds.

'But where were my friends and relations? No father had watched my infant days, no mother had blessed me with smiles and caresses; or if they had, all my past life was now a blot, a blind vacancy in which I distinguished nothing. From my earliest remembrance I had been as I then was in height and proportion. I had never yet seen a being resembling me or who claimed any intercourse with me.

1 lichen ['laɪkən]: Flechte **2** by stealth: secretly **3** dote on sb.: love sb. excessively without seeing their faults **4** sally: joke

What was I? The question again recurred, to be answered only with groans.

'I will soon explain to what these feelings tended[1], but allow me now to return to the cottagers, whose story excited in me such various feelings of indignation, delight, and wonder, but which all terminated in additional love and reverence for my protectors (for so I loved, in an innocent, half-painful self-deceit[2], to call them).'

1 tend to sth.: (here) lead up to sth. **2** self-deceit: state of mind in which you make yourself believe sth. good that is not true

Chapter 14

'Some time elapsed before I learned the history of my friends. It was one which could not fail to impress itself deeply on my mind, unfolding as it did a number of circumstances, each interesting and wonderful to one so utterly inexperienced as I was.

'The name of the old man was De Lacey. He was descended from a good family in France, where he had lived for many years in affluence[1], respected by his superiors[2] and beloved by his equals. His son was bred[3] in the service[4] of his country, and Agatha had ranked with ladies of the highest distinction. A few months before my arrival they had lived in a large and luxurious city called Paris, surrounded by friends and possessed of every enjoyment which virtue, refinement of intellect, or taste, accompanied by a moderate fortune, could afford.

'The father of Safie had been the cause of their ruin. He was a Turkish merchant and had inhabited Paris for many years, when, for some reason which I could not learn, he became obnoxious[5] to the government. He was seized and cast into prison the very day that Safie arrived from Constantinople[6] to join him. He was tried[7] and condemned to death. The injustice of his sentence was very flagrant[8]; all Paris was indignant; and it was judged that his religion and wealth rather than the crime alleged against him had been the cause of his condemnation.

'Felix had accidentally been present at the trial; his horror and indignation were uncontrollable when he heard the decision of the court. He made, at that moment, a solemn vow[9] to deliver him and

1 affluence: wealth **2** superior (n): person who is above another in rank **3** be bred in sth.: be trained in sth. **4** service (n): (here) military **5** obnoxious: unpleasant **6** Constantinople: city in western Turkey, today's Istanbul **7** try sb.: put sb. on trial **8** flagrant: obviously wrong **9** vow (n): promise

then looked around for the means. After many fruitless attempts to gain admittance to the prison, he found a strongly grated[1] window in an unguarded part of the building, which lighted the dungeon of the unfortunate Mahometan[2], who, loaded with chains, waited in despair the execution of the barbarous sentence. Felix visited the grate at night and made known to the prisoner his intentions in his favour. The Turk, amazed and delighted, endeavoured to kindle[3] the zeal of his deliverer by promises of reward and wealth. Felix rejected his offers with contempt, yet when he saw the lovely Safie, who was allowed to visit her father and who by her gestures expressed her lively gratitude, the youth could not help owning[4] to his own mind that the captive[5] possessed a treasure which would fully reward his toil and hazard[6].

'The Turk quickly perceived the impression that his daughter had made on the heart of Felix and endeavoured to secure him more entirely in his interests by the promise of her hand in marriage so soon as he should be conveyed to a place of safety. Felix was too delicate[7] to accept this offer, yet he looked forward to the probability of the event as to the consummation of his happiness.

'During the ensuing days, while the preparations were going forward for the escape of the merchant, the zeal of Felix was warmed by several letters that he received from this lovely girl, who found means to express her thoughts in the language of her lover by the aid of an old man, a servant of her father who understood French. She thanked him in the most ardent terms for his intended services towards her parent, and at the same time she gently deplored her own fate.

'I have copies of these letters, for I found means, during my residence in the hovel, to procure the implements[8] of writing; and the letters were often in the hands of Felix or Agatha. Before I depart I will give them to you; they will prove the truth of my tale; but at

1 grated (adj): *vergittert* **2** Mahometan: Muslim **3** kindle sth.: (here) encourage sth. **4** own sth.: (here) admit sth. **5** captive (n): prisoner **6** hazard (n): risk **7** delicate: (here) decent **8** implement (n): tool

present, as the sun is already far declined, I shall only have time to repeat the substance of them to you.

'Safie related that her mother was a Christian Arab, seized and made a slave by the Turks; recommended by her beauty, she had won the heart of the father of Safie, who married her. The young girl spoke in high and enthusiastic terms of her mother, who, born in freedom, spurned the bondage[1] to which she was now reduced. She instructed her daughter in the tenets[2] of her religion and taught her to aspire to higher powers of intellect and an independence of spirit forbidden to the female followers of Mahomet. This lady died, but her lessons were indelibly impressed on the mind of Safie, who sickened at the prospect of again returning to Asia and being immured within the walls of a harem, allowed only to occupy herself with infantile amusements, ill-suited to the temper of her soul, now accustomed to grand ideas and a noble emulation[3] for virtue. The prospect of marrying a Christian and remaining in a country where women were allowed to take a rank in society was enchanting to her.

'The day for the execution of the Turk was fixed, but on the night previous to it he quitted his prison and before morning was distant many leagues from Paris. Felix had procured passports in the name of his father, sister, and himself. He had previously communicated his plan to the former, who aided the deceit by quitting his house, under the pretence of a journey and concealed himself, with his daughter, in an obscure part of Paris.

'Felix conducted the fugitives[4] through France to Lyons and across Mont Cenis[5] to Leghorn[6], where the merchant had decided to wait a favourable opportunity of passing into some part of the Turkish dominions[7].

1 bondage: (here) captivity, slavery **2** tenet: principle, belief **3** emulation: (here) ambition **4** fugitive: escapee **5** Mont Cenis: mountain pass to Italy in Savoy Alps in south-eastern France **6** Leghorn: traditional English name of Livorno, a port in Tuscany (northern Italy) **7** dominion: territory

'Safie resolved to remain with her father until the moment of his departure, before which time the Turk renewed his promise that she should be united to his deliverer; and Felix remained with them in expectation of that event; and in the meantime he enjoyed the society of the Arabian, who exhibited towards him the simplest and tenderest affection. They conversed with one another through the means of an interpreter, and sometimes with the interpretation of looks; and Safie sang to him the divine airs of her native country.

'The Turk allowed this intimacy[1] to take place and encouraged the hopes of the youthful lovers, while in his heart he had formed far other plans. He loathed the idea that his daughter should be united to a Christian, but he feared the resentment[2] of Felix if he should appear lukewarm[3], for he knew that he was still in the power of his deliverer if he should choose to betray him to the Italian state which they inhabited. He revolved a thousand plans by which he should be enabled to prolong the deceit until it might be no longer necessary, and secretly to take his daughter with him when he departed. His plans were facilitated[4] by the news which arrived from Paris.

'The government of France were greatly enraged at the escape of their victim and spared no pains[5] to detect and punish his deliverer. The plot of Felix was quickly discovered, and DeLacey and Agatha were thrown into prison. The news reached Felix and roused him from his dream of pleasure. His blind and aged father and his gentle sister lay in a noisome[6] dungeon while he enjoyed the free air and the society of her whom he loved. This idea was torture to him. He quickly arranged with the Turk that if the latter should find a favourable opportunity for escape before Felix could return to Italy, Safie should remain as a boarder[7] at a convent[8] at Leghorn; and then, quitting the lovely Arabian, he hastened to Paris and delivered him-

1 intimacy: (here) closeness **2** resentment: displeasure **3** lukewarm: (here) half-hearted **4** faciliate sth.: make sth. simpler **5** spare no pains: make every effort **6** noisome: unhealthy **7** boarder: guest **8** convent: monastery

self up to the vengeance of the law, hoping to free De Lacey and Agatha by this proceeding[1].

'He did not succeed. They remained confined for five months before the trial took place, the result of which deprived them of their fortune and condemned them to a perpetual exile from their native country.

'They found a miserable asylum in the cottage in Germany, where I discovered them. Felix soon learned that the treacherous[2] Turk, for whom he and his family endured such unheard-of oppression[3], on discovering that his deliverer was thus reduced to poverty and ruin, became a traitor[4] to good feeling and honour and had quitted Italy with his daughter, insultingly sending Felix a pittance of money to aid him, as he said, in some plan of future maintenance[5].

'Such were the events that preyed on the heart of Felix and rendered him, when I first saw him, the most miserable of his family. He could have endured poverty, and while this distress had been the meed[6] of his virtue, he gloried[7] in it; but the ingratitude of the Turk and the loss of his beloved Safie were misfortunes more bitter and irreparable. The arrival of the Arabian now infused[8] new life into his soul.

'When the news reached Leghorn that Felix was deprived of his wealth and rank, the merchant commanded his daughter to think no more of her lover, but to prepare to return to her native country. The generous nature of Safie was outraged by this command; she attempted to expostulate[9] with her father, but he left her angrily, reiterating[10] his tyrannical mandate[11].

'A few days after, the Turk entered his daughter's apartment and told her hastily that he had reason to believe that his residence at Leghorn had been divulged[12] and that he should speedily be deliv-

1 proceeding (n): course of action **2** treacherous: betraying trust, disloyal **3** oppression: (here) misery **4** traitor: treacherous person **5** maintenance: (here) money to pay for daily needs **6** meed: reward **7** glory in sth.: be joyful about sth. **8** infuse sth.: *etw. einflößen* **9** expostulate: protest, express strong disagreement **10** reiterate sth.: repeat sth. **11** mandate: command **12** divulge sth.: make known sth. that was previously kept secret

ered up to the French government; he had consequently hired a vessel to convey him to Constantinople, for which city he should sail in a few hours. He intended to leave his daughter under the care of a confidential servant, to follow at her leisure[1] with the greater part of his property, which had not yet arrived at Leghorn.

'When alone, Safie resolved in her own mind the plan of conduct that it would become[2] her to pursue in this emergency. A residence in Turkey was abhorrent to her; her religion and her feelings were alike averse to it. By some papers of her father which fell into her hands she heard of the exile of her lover and learnt the name of the spot where he then resided. She hesitated some time, but at length she formed her determination. Taking with her some jewels that belonged to her and a sum of money, she quitted Italy with an attendant[3], a native of Leghorn, but who understood the common language of Turkey, and departed for Germany.

'She arrived in safety at a town about twenty leagues from the cottage of De Lacey, when her attendant fell dangerously ill. Safie nursed her with the most devoted affection, but the poor girl died, and the Arabian was left alone, unacquainted with the language of the country and utterly ignorant of the customs of the world. She fell, however, into good hands. The Italian had mentioned the name of the spot for which they were bound, and after her death the woman of the house in which they had lived took care that Safie should arrive in safety at the cottage of her lover.'

1 at her leisure: letting her decide on the point of time herself **2** become sb.: be appropriate for sb. **3** attendant (n): servant

Chapter 15

'Such was the history of my beloved cottagers. It impressed me deeply. I learned, from the views of social life which it developed, to admire their virtues and to deprecate[1] the vices of mankind.

'As yet I looked upon crime as a distant evil, benevolence and generosity were ever present before me, inciting within me a desire to become an actor in the busy scene where so many admirable qualities were called forth and displayed. But in giving an account of the progress of my intellect, I must not omit a circumstance which occurred in the beginning of the month of August of the same year.

'One night during my accustomed visit to the neighbouring wood where I collected my own food and brought home firing for my protectors, I found on the ground a leathern portmanteau[2] containing several articles of dress and some books. I eagerly seized the prize[3] and returned with it to my hovel. Fortunately the books were written in the language, the elements of which I had acquired at the cottage; they consisted of *Paradise Lost*, a volume of Plutarch's *Lives*[4], and the *Sorrows of Werter*[5]. The possession of these treasures gave me extreme delight; I now continually studied and exercised my mind upon these histories, whilst my friends were employed in their ordinary occupations.

'I can hardly describe to you the effect of these books. They produced in me an infinity of new images and feelings, that some-

1 deprecate sth.: disapprove of sth. **2** portmanteau: suitcase **3** prize (n): (here) finding **4** Plutarch's *Lives*: series of biographies by Roman author Plutarch (45–125 AD) in which he compares famous Roman and Greek personalities for the purpose of revealing their common moral virtues or failings
5 *Sorrows of Werter*: full German title: *Die Leiden des jungen Werthers* (1774); novel by Johann Wolfgang von Goethe (1749–1832) in which the protagonist's thoughts and feelings of unhappy and unrequited love are expressed in a series of his letters

times raised me to ecstasy, but more frequently sunk me into the lowest dejection. In the *Sorrows of Werter*, besides the interest of its simple and affecting story, so many opinions are canvassed[1] and so many lights thrown upon what had hitherto been to me obscure subjects that I found in it a never-ending source of speculation and astonishment. The gentle and domestic manners it described, combined with lofty[2] sentiments and feelings, which had for their object something out of self, accorded[3] well with my experience among my protectors and with the wants which were forever alive in my own bosom. But I thought Werter himself a more divine being than I had ever beheld or imagined; his character contained no pretension[4], but it sank deep. The disquisitions[5] upon death and suicide were calculated to fill me with wonder. I did not pretend to enter into the merits of the case[6], yet I inclined[7] towards the opinions of the hero, whose extinction[8] I wept, without precisely understanding it.

'As I read, however, I applied much personally to my own feelings and condition. I found myself similar yet at the same time strangely unlike to the beings concerning whom I read and to whose conversation I was a listener. I sympathised with and partly understood them, but I was unformed in mind; I was dependent on none and related to none. "The path of my departure was free,"[9] and there was none to lament my annihilation. My person was hideous and my stature gigantic. What did this mean? Who was I? What was I? Whence did I come? What was my destination? These questions continually recurred, but I was unable to solve them.

'The volume of Plutarch's *Lives* which I possessed contained the histories of the first founders of the ancient republics. This book had a far different effect upon me from the *Sorrows of Werter*. I learned from Werter's imaginations despondency and gloom, but Plutarch

1 canvas sth.: describe sth., explain sth. **2** lofty: refined, elegant **3** accord with sth. (v): harmonize with sth. **4** pretension: *Anmaßung* **5** disquisition: exploration, study **6** enter into the merits of the case: try to understand the argument thoroughly **7** incline towards sth.: have a tendency toward sth. **8** extinction: (here) death **9** 'The path of my departure was free': line from P. B. Shelley's poem 'Mutability' (1816)

taught me high thoughts; he elevated me above the wretched sphere of my own reflections, to admire and love the heroes of past ages. Many things I read surpassed my understanding and experience. I had a very confused knowledge of kingdoms, wide extents of country, mighty rivers, and boundless seas. But I was perfectly unacquainted with towns and large assemblages[1] of men. The cottage of my protectors had been the only school in which I had studied human nature, but this book developed new and mightier scenes of action. I read of men concerned in public affairs, governing or massacring their species. I felt the greatest ardour for virtue rise within me, and abhorrence for vice, as far as I understood the signification of those terms, relative as they were, as I applied them, to pleasure and pain alone. Induced by these feelings, I was of course led to admire peaceable lawgivers, Numa, Solon, and Lycurgus, in preference to Romulus and Theseus[2]. The patriarchal[3] lives of my protectors caused these impressions to take a firm hold on my mind; perhaps, if my first introduction to humanity had been made by a young soldier, burning for glory and slaughter[4], I should have been imbued with different sensations.

'But *Paradise Lost* excited different and far deeper emotions. I read it, as I had read the other volumes which had fallen into my hands, as a true history. It moved every feeling of wonder and awe[5] that the picture of an omnipotent God warring with his creatures was capable of exciting. I often referred the several situations, as their similarity struck me, to my own. Like Adam, I was apparently united by no link to any other being in existence; but his state was far different from mine in every other respect. He had come forth from the hands of God a perfect creature, happy and prosperous, guarded by the especial care of his Creator; he was allowed to converse with and acquire knowledge from beings of a superior nature, but I was

1 assemblage: gathering **2** Numa ... Theseus: personalities featured in Plutarch's *Lives* **3** patriarchal (adj): referring to patriarchy ('rule of the father'), i.e. the dominant role of men in family and society; (here) obedient to the decisions of an older (calmer and wiser) man **4** slaughter (n): killing (usu. of animals) **5** awe: amazement

wretched, helpless, and alone. Many times I considered Satan as the fitter emblem of my condition, for often, like him, when I viewed the bliss of my protectors, the bitter gall[1] of envy rose within me.

'Another circumstance strengthened and confirmed these feelings. Soon after my arrival in the hovel I discovered some papers in the pocket of the dress which I had taken from your laboratory. At first I had neglected them, but now that I was able to decipher the characters in which they were written, I began to study them with diligence. It was your journal[2] of the four months that preceded my creation. You minutely described in these papers every step you took in the progress of your work; this history was mingled with accounts of domestic occurrences. You doubtless recollect these papers. Here they are. Everything is related in them which bears reference to my accursed origin; the whole detail of that series of disgusting circumstances which produced it is set in view; the minutest description of my odious and loathsome person is given, in language which painted your own horrors and rendered mine indelible. I sickened as I read. "Hateful day when I received life!" I exclaimed in agony. "Accursed creator! Why did you form a monster so hideous that even *you* turned from me in disgust? God, in pity, made man beautiful and alluring, after his own image; but my form is a filthy type of yours, more horrid even from the very resemblance. Satan had his companions, fellow devils, to admire and encourage him, but I am solitary and abhorred."

'These were the reflections of my hours of despondency and solitude; but when I contemplated the virtues of the cottagers, their amiable and benevolent dispositions, I persuaded myself that when they should become acquainted with my admiration of their virtues they would compassionate[3] me and overlook my personal deformity. Could they turn from their door one, however monstrous, who solicited their compassion and friendship? I resolved, at least, not to despair, but in every way to fit myself for an interview[4] with them

1 gall: *Galle*; (here fig.) bitterness **2** journal: (here) diary **3** compassionate sb.: feel pity for sb. **4** interview: (here) conversation

which would decide my fate. I postponed[1] this attempt for some months longer, for the importance attached to its success inspired me with a dread lest I should fail. Besides, I found that my understanding improved so much with every day's experience that I was unwilling to commence this undertaking until a few more months should have added to my sagacity[2].

'Several changes, in the mean time, took place in the cottage. The presence of Safie diffused happiness among its inhabitants, and I also found that a greater degree of plenty[3] reigned[4] there. Felix and Agatha spent more time in amusement and conversation, and were assisted in their labours by servants. They did not appear rich, but they were contented and happy; their feelings were serene and peaceful, while mine became every day more tumultuous[5]. Increase of knowledge only discovered to me more clearly what a wretched outcast I was. I cherished hope[6], it is true, but it vanished when I beheld my person reflected in water or my shadow in the moonshine, even as that frail[7] image and that inconstant shade.

'I endeavoured to crush these fears and to fortify[8] myself for the trial which in a few months I resolved to undergo; and sometimes I allowed my thoughts, unchecked by reason, to ramble in the fields of Paradise, and dared to fancy amiable and lovely creatures sympathising with my feelings and cheering my gloom; their angelic countenances breathed[9] smiles of consolation. But it was all a dream; no Eve soothed my sorrows nor shared my thoughts; I was alone. I remembered Adam's supplication[10] to his Creator. But where was mine? He had abandoned me, and in the bitterness of my heart I cursed him.

'Autumn passed thus. I saw, with surprise and grief, the leaves decay and fall, and nature again assume the barren[11] and bleak appearance it had worn when I first beheld the woods and the lovely

1 postpone sth.: decide that sth. will be done at a later time **2** sagacity: wisdom, insight **3** plenty (n): wealth **4** reign (v): *(vor)herrschen* **5** tumultuous: agitated **6** cherish hope: allow hope to take over **7** frail: weak **8** fortify sth./sb.: make sth./sb. strong **9** breathe sth.: (here) spread sth. **10** supplication: emotional request for help to sb. in authority **11** barren: devoid of life

moon. Yet I did not heed[1] the bleakness of the weather; I was better fitted by my conformation for the endurance of cold than heat. But my chief delights were the sight of the flowers, the birds, and all the gay apparel of summer; when those deserted me, I turned with more attention towards the cottagers. Their happiness was not decreased by the absence of summer. They loved and sympathised with one another; and their joys, depending on each other, were not interrupted by the casualties[2] that took place around them. The more I saw of them, the greater became my desire to claim their protection and kindness; my heart yearned[3] to be known and loved by these amiable creatures; to see their sweet looks directed towards me with affection was the utmost limit of my ambition. I dared not think that they would turn them from me with disdain and horror. The poor that stopped at their door were never driven away. I asked, it is true, for greater treasures than a little food or rest: I required kindness and sympathy; but I did not believe myself utterly unworthy of it.

'The winter advanced, and an entire revolution of the seasons had taken place since I awoke into life. My attention at this time was solely directed towards my plan of introducing myself into the cottage of my protectors. I revolved many projects, but that on which I finally fixed was to enter the dwelling when the blind old man should be alone. I had sagacity enough to discover that the unnatural hideousness of my person was the chief object of horror with those who had formerly beheld me. My voice, although harsh, had nothing terrible in it; I thought, therefore, that if in the absence of his children I could gain the good will and mediation of the old De Lacey, I might by his means be tolerated by my younger protectors.

'One day, when the sun shone on the red leaves that strewed the ground and diffused cheerfulness, although it denied warmth, Safie, Agatha, and Felix departed on a long country walk, and the old man, at his own desire, was left alone in the cottage. When his children

1 heed sth.: mind sth. **2** casualty: (here) sth. that happens by chance and without your involvement **3** yearn to do sth.: have a strong desire to do sth.

had departed, he took up his guitar and played several mournful but sweet airs, more sweet and mournful than I had ever heard him play before. At first his countenance was illuminated with pleasure, but as he continued, thoughtfulness and sadness succeeded; at length, laying aside the instrument, he sat absorbed[1] in reflection.

'My heart beat quick; this was the hour and moment of trial, which would decide my hopes or realise[2] my fears. The servants were gone to a neighbouring fair[3]. All was silent in and around the cottage; it was an excellent opportunity; yet, when I proceeded to execute my plan, my limbs failed me and I sank to the ground. Again I rose, and exerting all the firmness of which I was master, removed the planks which I had placed before my hovel to conceal my retreat. The fresh air revived me, and with renewed determination I approached the door of their cottage.

'I knocked. "Who is there?" said the old man – "Come in."

'I entered; "Pardon this intrusion", said I; "I am a traveller in want of a little rest; you would greatly oblige[4] me if you would allow me to remain a few minutes before the fire."

'"Enter," said De Lacey, "and I will try in what manner I can to relieve your wants; but, unfortunately, my children are from home, and as I am blind, I am afraid I shall find it difficult to procure food for you."

'"Do not trouble yourself, my kind host; I have food; it is warmth and rest only that I need."

'I sat down, and a silence ensued. I knew that every minute was precious to me, yet I remained irresolute[5] in what manner to commence the interview, when the old man addressed me. "By your language, stranger, I suppose you are my countryman; – are you French?"

'"No; but I was educated by a French family and understand that language only. I am now going to claim the protection of some

1 be absorbed in sth.: *in etw. versunken sein* **2** realise sth.: (here) make sth. become real **3** fair (n): *Jahrmarkt, Rummel* **4** oblige sb.: *jdm. einen Gefallen erweisen* **5** irresolute: uncertain how to act

friends, whom I sincerely love, and of whose favour I have some hopes."

'"Are they Germans?"

'"No, they are French. But let us change the subject. I am an unfortunate and deserted creature, I look around and I have no relation or friend upon earth. These amiable people to whom I go have never seen me and know little of me. I am full of fears, for if I fail there, I am an outcast in the world forever."

'"Do not despair. To be friendless is indeed to be unfortunate, but the hearts of men, when unprejudiced by any obvious self-interest, are full of brotherly love and charity. Rely, therefore, on your hopes; and if these friends are good and amiable, do not despair."

'"They are kind – they are the most excellent creatures in the world; but, unfortunately, they are prejudiced against me. I have good dispositions; my life has been hitherto harmless and in some degree beneficial; but a fatal prejudice clouds their eyes, and where they ought to see a feeling and kind friend, they behold only a detestable monster."

'"That is indeed unfortunate; but if you are really blameless, cannot you undeceive[1] them?"

'"I am about to undertake that task; and it is on that account that I feel so many overwhelming terrors. I tenderly love these friends; I have, unknown to them, been for many months in the habits of daily kindness towards them; but they believe that I wish to injure them, and it is that prejudice which I wish to overcome."

'"Where do these friends reside?"

'"Near this spot."

'The old man paused and then continued, "If you will unreservedly[2] confide to me the particulars of your tale, I perhaps may be of use in undeceiving them. I am blind and cannot judge of your countenance, but there is something in your words which persuades me

1 undeceive sb.: free sb. from wrong beliefs **2** unreservedly: completely, without reservations

that you are sincere. I am poor and an exile, but it will afford me true pleasure to be in any way serviceable[1] to a human creature."

'"Excellent man! I thank you and accept your generous offer. You raise me from the dust by this kindness; and I trust that, by your aid, I shall not be driven from the society and sympathy of your fellow creatures."

'"Heaven forbid! Even if you were really criminal, for that can only drive you to desperation, and not instigate[2] you to virtue. I also am unfortunate; I and my family have been condemned, although innocent; judge, therefore, if I do not feel for your misfortunes."

'"How can I thank you, my best and only benefactor? From your lips first have I heard the voice of kindness directed towards me; I shall be forever grateful; and your present humanity assures me of success with those friends whom I am on the point of meeting."

'"May I know the names and residence of those friends?"

'I paused. This, I thought, was the moment of decision, which was to rob me of or bestow happiness on me forever. I struggled vainly for firmness sufficient to answer him, but the effort destroyed all my remaining strength; I sank on the chair and sobbed aloud. At that moment I heard the steps of my younger protectors. I had not a moment to lose, but seizing the hand of the old man, I cried, "Now is the time! Save and protect me! You and your family are the friends whom I seek. Do not you desert me in the hour of trial!"

'"Great God!" exclaimed the old man. "Who are you?"

'At that instant the cottage door was opened, and Felix, Safie, and Agatha entered. Who can describe their horror and consternation[3] on beholding me? Agatha fainted, and Safie, unable to attend to her friend, rushed out of the cottage. Felix darted forward, and with supernatural force tore me from his father, to whose knees I clung, in a transport[4] of fury, he dashed[5] me to the ground and struck me violently with a stick. I could have torn him limb from limb, as the

1 serviceable: helpful **2** instigate sb. to (do) sth.: motivate sb. to (do) sth. **3** consternation: astonishment, alarm **4** transport of fury: *Wutanfall* **5** dash sb./sth.: thrust sb./sth. violently

lion rends[1] the antelope. But my heart sank within me as with bitter sickness, and I refrained. I saw him on the point of repeating his blow, when, overcome by pain and anguish, I quitted the cottage, and in the general tumult escaped unperceived to my hovel.'

1 rend sb./sth.: tear sb./sth. apart

Chapter 16

'Cursed, cursed creator! Why did I live? Why, in that instant, did I not extinguish the spark of existence which you had so wantonly bestowed? I know not; despair had not yet taken possession of me; my feelings were those of rage and revenge. I could with pleasure have destroyed the cottage and its inhabitants and have glutted[1] myself with their shrieks and misery.

'When night came I quitted my retreat and wandered in the wood; and now, no longer restrained by the fear of discovery, I gave vent to my anguish in fearful howlings[2]. I was like a wild beast that had broken the toils[3], destroying the objects that obstructed me and ranging[4] through the wood with a staglike[5] swiftness. Oh! what a miserable night I passed! The cold stars shone in mockery, and the bare trees waved their branches above me; now and then the sweet voice of a bird burst forth amidst the universal stillness. All, save[6] I, were at rest or in enjoyment; I, like the arch-fiend[7], bore a hell within me, and finding myself unsympathised with, wished to tear up the trees, spread havoc[8] and destruction around me, and then to have sat down and enjoyed the ruin.

'But this was a luxury of sensation that could not endure; I became fatigued with excess of bodily exertion and sank on the damp grass in the sick impotence[9] of despair. There was none among the myriads[10] of men that existed who would pity or assist me; and should I feel kindness towards my enemies? No; from that moment I declared everlasting war against the species, and more

1 glut yourself with sth.: enjoy sth. **2** howling (n): long sound made by wolves and dogs **3** break the toils: break the trap to escape **4** range through sth.: *etw. durchstreifen* **5** staglike: like a deer **6** save (prep): except **7** arch-fiend: devil **8** spread havoc: cause chaos **9** impotence: (here) powerlessness **10** myriad: great number

than all, against him who had formed me and sent me forth to this insupportable misery.

'The sun rose; I heard the voices of men and knew that it was impossible to return to my retreat during that day. Accordingly I hid myself in some thick underwood, determining to devote the ensuing hours to reflection on my situation.

'The pleasant sunshine and the pure air of day restored me to some degree of tranquillity; and when I considered what had passed at the cottage, I could not help believing that I had been too hasty in my conclusions. I had certainly acted imprudently. It was apparent that my conversation had interested the father in my behalf, and I was a fool in having exposed my person to the horror of his children. I ought to have familiarised the old De Lacey to me, and by degrees to have discovered myself to the rest of his family, when they should have been prepared for my approach. But I did not believe my errors to be irretrievable[1], and after much consideration I resolved to return to the cottage, seek the old man, and by my representations[2] win him to my party.

'These thoughts calmed me, and in the afternoon I sank into a profound[3] sleep; but the fever of my blood did not allow me to be visited by peaceful dreams. The horrible scene of the preceding day was forever acting before my eyes; the females were flying and the enraged Felix tearing me from his father's feet. I awoke exhausted, and finding that it was already night, I crept forth from my hiding-place, and went in search of food.

'When my hunger was appeased[4], I directed my steps towards the well-known path that conducted to the cottage. All there was at peace. I crept into my hovel and remained in silent expectation of the accustomed hour when the family arose. That hour passed, the sun mounted high in the heavens, but the cottagers did not appear. I trembled violently, apprehending[5] some dreadful misfortune. The

1 irretrievable: irreversable **2** representation: (here) explanation **3** profound: deep **4** appeased: calmed **5** apprehend sth.: (here) fear sth.

inside of the cottage was dark, and I heard no motion; I cannot describe the agony of this suspense.

'Presently two countrymen passed by, but pausing near the cottage, they entered into conversation, using violent gesticulations; but I did not understand what they said, as they spoke the language of the country, which differed from that of my protectors. Soon after, however, Felix approached with another man; I was surprised, as I knew that he had not quitted the cottage that morning, and waited anxiously to discover from his discourse the meaning of these unusual appearances.

'"Do you consider," said his companion to him, "that you will be obliged to pay three months' rent and to lose the produce[1] of your garden? I do not wish to take any unfair advantage, and I beg therefore that you will take some days to consider[2] of your determination."

'"It is utterly useless," replied Felix; "we can never again inhabit your cottage. The life of my father is in the greatest danger, owing to the dreadful circumstance that I have related. My wife and my sister will never recover from their horror. I entreat you not to reason[3] with me any more. Take possession of your tenement[4] and let me fly from this place."

'Felix trembled violently as he said this. He and his companion entered the cottage, in which they remained for a few minutes, and then departed. I never saw any of the family of De Lacey more.

'I continued for the remainder of the day in my hovel in a state of utter and stupid[5] despair. My protectors had departed and had broken the only link that held me to the world. For the first time the feelings of revenge and hatred filled my bosom, and I did not strive to control them, but allowing myself to be borne away by the stream, I bent my mind towards injury and death. When I thought of my friends, of the mild voice of De Lacey, the gentle eyes of Agatha, and

1 produce [ˈprɒdjuːs] (n): fruits and vegetables **2** consider of sth.: think sth. over **3** reason with sb.: argue with sb. **4** tenement: building **5** stupid: *(hier) benommen*

the exquisite beauty of the Arabian, these thoughts vanished and a gush of tears somewhat soothed me. But again when I reflected that they had spurned and deserted me, anger returned, a rage of anger, and unable to injure anything human, I turned my fury towards inanimate objects. As night advanced I placed a variety of combustibles[1] around the cottage, and after having destroyed every vestige[2] of cultivation in the garden, I waited with forced impatience until the moon had sunk to commence my operations.

'As the night advanced, a fierce wind arose from the woods and quickly dispersed the clouds that had loitered[3] in the heavens; the blast[4] tore along[5] like a mighty avalanche and produced a kind of insanity in my spirits that burst all bounds of reason and reflection. I lighted the dry branch of a tree and danced with fury around the devoted[6] cottage, my eyes still fixed on the western horizon, the edge of which the moon nearly touched. A part of its orb was at length hid, and I waved my brand[7]; it sank, and with a loud scream I fired the straw, and heath[8], and bushes, which I had collected. The wind fanned the fire, and the cottage was quickly enveloped by the flames, which clung to it and licked it with their forked and destroying tongues.

'As soon as I was convinced that no assistance could save any part of the habitation, I quitted the scene and sought for refuge in the woods.

'And now, with the world before me, whither should I bend my steps? I resolved to fly far from the scene of my misfortunes; but to me, hated and despised, every country must be equally horrible. At length the thought of you crossed my mind. I learned from your papers that you were my father, my creator; and to whom could I apply[9] with more fitness[10] than to him who had given me life? Among the lessons that Felix had bestowed upon Safie, geography had not

1 combustible (n): burnable material **2** vestige: trace **3** loiter: stay somewhere without moving around much **4** blast (n): (thunder)storm **5** tear along: speed by with great force **6** devoted: (here) beloved **7** brand (n): (here) torch **8** heath: *Heide* **9** apply to sb.: turn to sb. **10** with fitness: (here) rightfully

been omitted; I had learned from these the relative situations of the different countries of the earth. You had mentioned Geneva as the name of your native town, and towards this place I resolved to proceed.

'But how was I to direct myself? I knew that I must travel in a southwesterly direction to reach my destination, but the sun was my only guide. I did not know the names of the towns that I was to pass through, nor could I ask information from a single human being; but I did not despair. From you only could I hope for succour[1], although towards you I felt no sentiment but that of hatred. Unfeeling, heartless creator! You had endowed me with perceptions and passions and then cast me abroad an object for the scorn[2] and horror of mankind. But on you only had I any claim for pity and redress[3], and from you I determined to seek that justice which I vainly attempted to gain from any other being that wore the human form.

'My travels were long and the sufferings I endured intense. It was late in autumn when I quitted the district where I had so long resided. I travelled only at night, fearful of encountering the visage of a human being. Nature decayed around me, and the sun became heatless; rain and snow poured around me; mighty rivers were frozen; the surface of the earth was hard and chill, and bare, and I found no shelter. Oh, earth! How often did I imprecate[4] curses on the cause of my being! The mildness of my nature had fled, and all within me was turned to gall and bitterness. The nearer I approached to your habitation, the more deeply did I feel the spirit of revenge enkindled[5] in my heart. Snow fell, and the waters were hardened, but I rested not. A few incidents now and then directed me, and I possessed a map of the country; but I often wandered wide from my path. The agony of my feelings allowed me no respite; no incident occurred from which my rage and misery could not extract[6] its food; but a

1 succour: support **2** scorn (n): disrespect, contempt **3** redress (n): *Wiedergutmachung* **4** imprecate curses on sth.: put curses on sth. **5** enkindle sth.: set sth. on fire, (here) evoke sth. **6** extract sth. from sth.: draw sth. out of sth.

circumstance that happened when I arrived on the confines[1] of Switzerland, when the sun had recovered its warmth and the earth again began to look green, confirmed in an especial manner the bitterness and horror of my feelings.

'I generally rested during the day and travelled only when I was secured by night from the view of man. One morning, however, finding that my path lay through a deep wood, I ventured to continue my journey after the sun had risen; the day, which was one of the first of spring, cheered even me by the loveliness of its sunshine and the balminess of the air. I felt emotions of gentleness and pleasure, that had long appeared dead, revive within me. Half surprised by the novelty of these sensations, I allowed myself to be borne away by them, and forgetting my solitude and deformity, dared to be happy. Soft tears again bedewed[2] my cheeks, and I even raised my humid eyes with thankfulness towards the blessed sun, which bestowed such joy upon me.

'I continued to wind among the paths of the wood, until I came to its boundary, which was skirted[3] by a deep and rapid river, into which many of the trees bent their branches, now budding with the fresh spring. Here I paused, not exactly knowing what path to pursue, when I heard the sound of voices, that induced me to conceal myself under the shade of a cypress. I was scarcely hid when a young girl came running towards the spot where I was concealed, laughing, as if she ran from someone in sport. She continued her course along the precipitous sides of the river, when suddenly her foot slipped, and she fell into the rapid stream. I rushed from my hiding-place and with extreme labour, from the force of the current, saved her and dragged her to shore. She was senseless, and I endeavoured by every means in my power to restore animation, when I was suddenly interrupted by the approach of a rustic[4], who was probably the person from whom she had playfully fled. On seeing me, he darted towards me, and tearing the girl from my arms, hastened

1 confines (n, pl): borders **2** bedew sth.: moisten sth. **3** skirt sth.: (here) run along sth. **4** rustic (n): simple rural person

towards the deeper parts of the wood. I followed speedily, I hardly knew why; but when the man saw me draw near, he aimed a gun, which he carried, at my body and fired. I sank to the ground, and my injurer, with increased swiftness, escaped into the wood.

'This was then the reward of my benevolence! I had saved a human being from destruction, and as a recompense I now writhed under the miserable pain of a wound which shattered the flesh and bone. The feelings of kindness and gentleness which I had entertained but a few moments before gave place to hellish rage and gnashing of teeth. Inflamed by pain, I vowed eternal hatred and vengeance to all mankind. But the agony of my wound overcame me; my pulses paused, and I fainted.

'For some weeks I led a miserable life in the woods, endeavouring to cure the wound which I had received. The ball had entered my shoulder, and I knew not whether it had remained there or passed through; at any rate I had no means of extracting it. My sufferings were augmented also by the oppressive sense of the injustice and ingratitude of their infliction[1]. My daily vows rose for revenge – a deep and deadly revenge, such as would alone compensate for the outrages and anguish I had endured.

'After some weeks my wound healed, and I continued my journey. The labours I endured were no longer to be alleviated by the bright sun or gentle breezes of spring; all joy was but a mockery which insulted my desolate state and made me feel more painfully that I was not made for the enjoyment of pleasure.

'But my toils now drew near a close[2], and in two months from this time I reached the environs of Geneva.

'It was evening when I arrived, and I retired to a hiding-place among the fields that surround it to meditate in what manner I should apply to you. I was oppressed by fatigue and hunger and far too unhappy to enjoy the gentle breezes of evening or the prospect of the sun setting behind the stupendous mountains of Jura.

1 infliction: sth. unpleasant that sb. does to you **2** draw near a close: come to an end

'At this time a slight sleep relieved me from the pain of reflection, which was disturbed by the approach of a beautiful child, who came running into the recess I had chosen, with all the sportiveness[1] of infancy[2]. Suddenly, as I gazed on him, an idea seized me that this little creature was unprejudiced and had lived too short a time to have imbibed a horror of deformity. If, therefore, I could seize him and educate him as my companion and friend, I should not be so desolate in this peopled earth.

'Urged by this impulse, I seized on the boy as he passed and drew him towards me. As soon as he beheld my form, he placed his hands before his eyes and uttered a shrill scream; I drew his hand forcibly from his face and said, "Child, what is the meaning of this? I do not intend to hurt you; listen to me."

'He struggled violently. "Let me go," he cried; "monster! Ugly wretch! You wish to eat me and tear me to pieces. You are an ogre[3]. Let me go, or I will tell my papa."

'"Boy, you will never see your father again; you must come with me."

'"Hideous monster! Let me go. My papa is a syndic – he is M. Frankenstein – he will punish you. You dare not keep me."

'"Frankenstein! you belong then to my enemy – to him towards whom I have sworn eternal revenge; you shall be my first victim."

'The child still struggled and loaded me with epithets[4] which carried despair to my heart; I grasped his throat to silence him, and in a moment he lay dead at my feet.

'I gazed on my victim, and my heart swelled with exultation and hellish triumph; clapping my hands, I exclaimed, "I too can create desolation; my enemy is not invulnerable; this death will carry despair to him, and a thousand other miseries shall torment and destroy him."

'As I fixed my eyes on the child, I saw something glittering on his breast. I took it; it was a portrait of a most lovely woman. In spite

1 sportiveness: playfulness **2** infancy: childhood **3** ogre: large, frightening and cruel figure in children's stories **4** epithet: (here) swear word

of my malignity, it softened and attracted me. For a few moments I gazed with delight on her dark eyes, fringed by deep lashes, and her lovely lips; but presently my rage returned; I remembered that I was forever deprived of the delights that such beautiful creatures could bestow and that she whose resemblance I contemplated would, in regarding me, have changed that air of divine benignity to one expressive of disgust and affright[1].

'Can you wonder that such thoughts transported[2] me with rage? I only wonder that at that moment, instead of venting[3] my sensations in exclamations and agony, I did not rush among mankind and perish in the attempt to destroy them.

'While I was overcome by these feelings, I left the spot where I had committed the murder, and seeking a more secluded hiding-place, I entered a barn which had appeared to me to be empty. A woman was sleeping on some straw; she was young, not indeed so beautiful as her whose portrait I held, but of an agreeable aspect and blooming in the loveliness of youth and health. Here, I thought, is one of those whose joy-imparting[4] smiles are bestowed on all but me. And then I bent over her and whispered, "Awake, fairest, thy lover is near – he who would give his life but to obtain one look of affection from thine eyes; my beloved, awake!"

'The sleeper stirred; a thrill of terror ran through me. Should she indeed awake, and see me, and curse me, and denounce[5] the murderer? Thus would she assuredly act if her darkened eyes opened and she beheld me. The thought was madness; it stirred the fiend within me – not I, but she, shall suffer; the murder I have committed because I am forever robbed of all that she could give me, she shall atone[6]. The crime had its source in her; be hers the punishment! Thanks to the lessons of Felix and the sanguinary[7] laws of man, I had learned now to work mischief. I bent over her and placed the

1 affright (old use): great fear **2** transport sb. with sth.: (here) fill sb. with sth. **3** vent sth.: express sth. **4** impart sth.: give sth. **5** denounce sb.: (here) betray sb. **6** atone (for sth.): make up (for sth.), suffer (for sth.) **7** sanguinary ['sæŋgwɪnəri]: bloodthirsty, violent

portrait securely in one of the folds of her dress. She moved again, and I fled.

'For some days I haunted[1] the spot where these scenes had taken place, sometimes wishing to see you, sometimes resolved to quit the world and its miseries forever. At length I wandered towards these mountains, and have ranged through their immense recesses, consumed by a burning passion which you alone can gratify. We may not part until you have promised to comply with my requisition[2]. I am alone and miserable; man will not associate with me; but one as deformed and horrible as myself would not deny herself to me. My companion must be of the same species and have the same defects. This being you must create.'

1 haunt sth.: (here) keep on coming back to sth. **2** requisition (n): demand

Chapter 17

The being finished speaking and fixed his looks upon me in the expectation of a reply. But I was bewildered, perplexed, and unable to arrange my ideas sufficiently to understand the full extent of his proposition. He continued.

'You must create a female for me with whom I can live in the interchange of those sympathies necessary for my being. This you alone can do, and I demand it of you as a right which you must not refuse to concede[1].'

The latter part of his tale had kindled anew in me the anger that had died away while he narrated his peaceful life among the cottagers, and as he said this I could no longer suppress the rage that burned within me.

'I do refuse it,' I replied; 'and no torture shall ever extort[2] a consent from me. You may render me the most miserable of men, but you shall never make me base in my own eyes. Shall I create another like yourself, whose joint[3] wickedness might desolate the world. Begone! I have answered you; you may torture me, but I will never consent.'

'You are in the wrong,' replied the fiend; 'and instead of threatening, I am content to reason with you. I am malicious[4] because I am miserable. Am I not shunned and hated by all mankind? You, my creator, would tear me to pieces and triumph; remember that, and tell me why I should pity man more than he pities me? You would not call it murder if you could precipitate me into one of those ice-rifts and destroy my frame, the work of your own hands. Shall I respect man when he contemns[5] me? Let him live with me in the

1 concede sth.: *etw. zugestehen* **2** extort sth. from sb.: obtain sth. from sb. by force **3** joint (adj): combined **4** malicious: showing a desire to cause harm to sb. **5** contemn sb. (old use): condemn sb.

interchange of kindness, and instead of injury I would bestow every benefit upon him with tears of gratitude at his acceptance. But that cannot be; the human senses are insurmountable[1] barriers to our union. Yet mine shall not be the submission of abject slavery. I will revenge my injuries; if I cannot inspire love, I will cause fear, and chiefly towards you my arch-enemy, because my creator, do I swear inextinguishable hatred. Have a care[2]; I will work at your destruction, nor finish until I desolate your heart, so that you shall curse the hour of your birth.'

A fiendish rage animated him as he said this; his face was wrinkled into contortions[3] too horrible for human eyes to behold; but presently he calmed himself and proceeded.

'I intended to reason. This passion is detrimental[4] to me, for you do not reflect that *you* are the cause of its excess. If any being felt emotions of benevolence towards me, I should return them a hundred and a hundredfold; for that one creature's sake I would make peace with the whole kind! But I now indulge in dreams of bliss that cannot be realised. What I ask of you is reasonable and moderate; I demand a creature of another sex, but as hideous as myself; the gratification is small, but it is all that I can receive, and it shall content me. It is true, we shall be monsters, cut off from all the world; but on that account we shall be more attached to one another. Our lives will not be happy, but they will be harmless and free from the misery I now feel. Oh! my creator, make me happy; let me feel gratitude towards you for one benefit! Let me see that I excite the sympathy of some existing thing; do not deny me my request!'

I was moved. I shuddered when I thought of the possible consequences of my consent, but I felt that there was some justice in his argument. His tale and the feelings he now expressed proved him to be a creature of fine sensations, and did I not as his maker owe him all the portion of happiness that it was in my power to bestow? He saw my change of feeling and continued.

1 insurmountable: impossible to be overcome **2** have a care: be careful
3 contortion: *(hier) Verzerrung, Grimasse* **4** detrimental: harmful

'If you consent, neither you nor any other human being shall ever see us again; I will go to the vast wilds of South America. My food is not that of man; I do not destroy the lamb and the kid to glut my appetite; acorns and berries afford me sufficient nourishment. My companion will be of the same nature as myself and will be content with the same fare. We shall make our bed of dried leaves; the sun will shine on us as on man and will ripen our food. The picture I present to you is peaceful and human, and you must feel that you could deny it only in the wantonness of power and cruelty. Pitiless as you have been towards me, I now see compassion in your eyes; let me seize the favourable moment and persuade you to promise what I so ardently desire.'

'You propose,' replied I, 'to fly from the habitations of man, to dwell in those wilds where the beasts of the field will be your only companions. How can you, who long for the love and sympathy of man, persevere[1] in this exile? You will return and again seek their kindness, and you will meet with their detestation; your evil passions will be renewed, and you will then have a companion to aid you in the task of destruction. This may not be; cease to argue the point, for I cannot consent.'

'How inconstant are your feelings! But a moment ago you were moved by my representations, and why do you again harden yourself to my complaints? I swear to you, by the earth which I inhabit, and by you that made me, that with the companion you bestow I will quit the neighbourhood of man and dwell, as it may chance[2], in the most savage of places. My evil passions will have fled, for I shall meet with sympathy! my life will flow quietly away, and in my dying moments I shall not curse my maker.'

His words had a strange effect upon me. I compassionated him and sometimes felt a wish to console him, but when I looked upon him, when I saw the filthy mass that moved and talked, my heart sickened and my feelings were altered to those of horror and hatred.

1 persevere: *durchhalten* **2** as it may chance: as fate may determine

I tried to stifle[1] these sensations; I thought that as I could not sympathise with him, I had no right to withhold[2] from him the small portion of happiness which was yet in my power to bestow.

'You swear,' I said, 'to be harmless; but have you not already shown a degree of malice that should reasonably make me distrust you? May not even this be a feint[3] that will increase your triumph by affording a wider scope for your revenge?'

'How is this? I must not be trifled[4] with, and I demand an answer. If I have no ties and no affections, hatred and vice must be my portion[5]; the love of another will destroy the cause of my crimes, and I shall become a thing of whose existence everyone will be ignorant. My vices are the children of a forced solitude that I abhor, and my virtues will necessarily arise when I live in communion[6] with an equal. I shall feel the affections of a sensitive being and become linked to the chain of existence and events, from which I am now excluded.'

I paused some time to reflect on all he had related and the various arguments which he had employed. I thought of the promise of virtues which he had displayed on the opening of his existence and the subsequent blight[7] of all kindly feeling by the loathing and scorn which his protectors had manifested towards him. His power and threats were not omitted in my calculations; a creature who could exist in the ice caves of the glaciers and hide himself from pursuit among the ridges[8] of inaccessible precipices was a being possessing faculties it would be vain to cope with. After a long pause of reflection I concluded that the justice due both to him and my fellow creatures demanded of me that I should comply with his request. Turning to him, therefore, I said –

'I consent to your demand, on your solemn oath[9] to quit Europe forever, and every other place in the neighbourhood of man, as soon

1 stifle sth.: suppress sth. **2** withhold sth. from sb.: deliberately not give sth. to sb. **3** feint (n): bluff, trick **4** trifle with sb.: talk in a joking way with sb. **5** portion (n): (here) fate **6** in communion: together **7** blight (n): (here) destruction **8** ridge: *(Berg-)Rücken* **9** oath: *Eid*

as I shall deliver into your hands a female who will accompany you in your exile.'

'I swear,' he cried, 'by the sun, and by the blue sky of heaven, and by the fire of love that burns my heart, that if you grant my prayer, while they exist you shall never behold me again. Depart to your home and commence your labours; I shall watch their progress with unutterable[1] anxiety; and fear not but that when you are ready I shall appear.'

Saying this, he suddenly quitted me, fearful, perhaps, of any change in my sentiments. I saw him descend the mountain with greater speed than the flight of an eagle, and quickly lost among the undulations[2] of the sea of ice.

His tale had occupied the whole day, and the sun was upon the verge[3] of the horizon when he departed. I knew that I ought to hasten my descent towards the valley, as I should soon be encompassed in darkness; but my heart was heavy, and my steps slow. The labour of winding among the little paths of the mountain and fixing my feet firmly as I advanced perplexed me, occupied as I was by the emotions which the occurrences of the day had produced. Night was far advanced when I came to the halfway resting-place and seated myself beside the fountain. The stars shone at intervals as the clouds passed from over them; the dark pines rose before me, and every here and there a broken tree lay on the ground; it was a scene of wonderful solemnity and stirred strange thoughts within me. I wept bitterly, and clasping my hands in agony, I exclaimed, 'Oh! stars and clouds and winds, ye are all about to mock me; if ye really pity me, crush sensation and memory; let me become as nought; but if not, depart, depart, and leave me in darkness.'

These were wild and miserable thoughts, but I cannot describe to you how the eternal twinkling[4] of the stars weighed upon me and how I listened to every blast of wind as if it were a dull ugly siroc[5] on its way to consume me. Morning dawned before I arrived at the

1 unutterable: inexpressable **2** undulation: pattern of waves **3** verge: edge
4 twinkle (v): flicker, blink **5** siroc: sirocco: warm, dry wind from North Africa

village of Chamounix; I took no rest, but returned immediately to Geneva. Even in my own heart I could give no expression to my sensations – they weighed on me with a mountain's weight and their excess destroyed my agony beneath them. Thus I returned home, and entering the house, presented myself to the family. My haggard[1] and wild appearance awoke intense alarm, but I answered no question, scarcely did I speak. I felt as if I were placed under a ban[2] – as if I had no right to claim their sympathies – as if never more might I enjoy companionship with them. Yet even thus I loved them to adoration[3]; and to save them, I resolved to dedicate myself to my most abhorred task. The prospect of such an occupation made every other circumstance of existence pass before me like a dream, and that thought only had to me the reality of life.

1 haggard: undernourished, wasted **2** ban (n): (here) curse **3** adoration: great admiration

Chapter 18

Day after day, week after week, passed away on my return to Geneva; and I could not collect the courage to recommence my work. I feared the vengeance of the disappointed fiend, yet I was unable to overcome my repugnance to the task which was enjoined[1] me. I found that I could not compose a female without again devoting several months to profound study and laborious disquisition. I had heard of some discoveries having been made by an English philosopher, the knowledge of which was material to my success, and I sometimes thought of obtaining my father's consent to visit England for this purpose; but I clung to every pretence of delay and shrank from taking the first step in an undertaking whose immediate necessity began to appear less absolute to me. A change indeed had taken place in me; my health, which had hitherto declined, was now much restored; and my spirits, when unchecked by the memory of my unhappy promise, rose proportionably. My father saw this change with pleasure, and he turned his thoughts towards the best method of eradicating[2] the remains of my melancholy, which every now and then would return by fits[3], and with a devouring blackness overcast the approaching sunshine. At these moments I took refuge in the most perfect solitude. I passed whole days on the lake alone in a little boat, watching the clouds and listening to the rippling of the waves, silent and listless[4]. But the fresh air and bright sun seldom failed to restore me to some degree of composure, and on my return I met the salutations[5] of my friends with a readier smile and a more cheerful heart.

It was after my return from one of these rambles that my father, calling me aside, thus addressed me –

1 enjoin sb. to do sth.: order sb. to do sth. **2** eradicate sth.: destroy sth. **3** fit (n): *Anfall* **4** listless: lacking interest and energy **5** salutation: greeting

'I am happy to remark, my dear son, that you have resumed[1] your former pleasures and seem to be returning to yourself. And yet you are still unhappy and still avoid our society. For some time I was lost in conjecture as to the cause of this, but yesterday an idea struck me, and if it is well founded, I conjure[2] you to avow it. Reserve[3] on such a point would be not only useless, but draw down treble[4] misery on us all.'

I trembled violently at his exordium[5], and my father continued –

'I confess, my son, that I have always looked forward to your marriage with our dear Elizabeth as the tie of our domestic comfort and the stay[6] of my declining years. You were attached to each other from your earliest infancy; you studied together, and appeared, in dispositions and tastes, entirely suited to one another. But so blind is the experience of man that what I conceived to be the best assistants to my plan may have entirely destroyed it. You, perhaps, regard her as your sister, without any wish that she might become your wife. Nay, you may have met with another whom you may love; and considering yourself as bound in honour to Elizabeth, this struggle may occasion[7] the poignant misery which you appear to feel.'

'My dear father, reassure yourself. I love my cousin tenderly and sincerely. I never saw any woman who excited, as Elizabeth does, my warmest admiration and affection. My future hopes and prospects are entirely bound up in the expectation of our union.'

'The expression of your sentiments of this subject, my dear Victor, gives me more pleasure than I have for some time experienced. If you feel thus, we shall assuredly be happy, however present events may cast a gloom over us. But it is this gloom which appears to have taken so strong a hold of your mind that I wish to dissipate. Tell me, therefore, whether you object to an immediate solemnisation of the marriage. We have been unfortunate, and recent events

1 resume sth.: begin sth. again **2** conjure sb. to do sth.: ask sb. vehemently to do sth. **3** reserve (n): *Zurückhaltung* **4** treble: three times **5** exordium: opening of a speech **6** stay (n): (here) support **7** occasion sth.: cause sth., bring about sth.

have drawn us from that everyday tranquillity befitting my years and infirmities[1]. You are younger; yet I do not suppose, possessed as you are of a competent[2] fortune, that an early marriage would at all interfere with any future plans of honour and utility[3] that you may have formed. Do not suppose, however, that I wish to dictate happiness to you or that a delay on your part would cause me any serious uneasiness. Interpret my words with candour and answer me, I conjure you, with confidence and sincerity.'

I listened to my father in silence and remained for some time incapable of offering any reply. I revolved rapidly in my mind a multitude of thoughts and endeavoured to arrive at some conclusion. Alas! To me the idea of an immediate union with my Elizabeth was one of horror and dismay. I was bound by a solemn promise which I had not yet fulfilled and dared not break, or if I did, what manifold[4] miseries might not impend over me and my devoted family! Could I enter into a festival with this deadly weight yet hanging round my neck and bowing me to the ground? I must perform my engagement[5] and let the monster depart with his mate before I allowed myself to enjoy the delight of a union from which I expected peace.

I remembered also the necessity imposed upon me of either journeying to England or entering into a long correspondence with those philosophers of that country whose knowledge and discoveries were of indispensable[6] use to me in my present undertaking. The latter method of obtaining the desired intelligence was dilatory[7] and unsatisfactory; besides, I had an insurmountable aversion[8] to the idea of engaging myself in my loathsome task in my father's house while in habits of familiar intercourse with those I loved. I knew that a thousand fearful accidents might occur, the slightest of which would disclose a tale to thrill all connected with me with horror. I was aware also that I should often lose all self-command,

1 infirmity: bad health **2** competent: (here) sufficient **3** utility: usefulness **4** manifold: many **5** perform your engagement: fulfil your promise **6** indispensable: absolutely necessary **7** dilatory: causing delay **8** aversion: disgust, repulsion

all capacity of hiding the harrowing sensations that would possess me during the progress of my unearthly occupation. I must absent myself from all I loved while thus employed. Once commenced, it would quickly be achieved, and I might be restored to my family in peace and happiness. My promise fulfilled, the monster would depart forever. Or (so my fond fancy imaged) some accident might meanwhile occur to destroy him and put an end to my slavery forever.

These feelings dictated my answer to my father. I expressed a wish to visit England, but concealing the true reasons of this request, I clothed my desires under a guise which excited no suspicion, while I urged my desire with an earnestness that easily induced my father to comply. After so long a period of an absorbing melancholy that resembled madness in its intensity and effects, he was glad to find that I was capable of taking pleasure in the idea of such a journey, and he hoped that change of scene and varied amusement would, before my return, have restored me entirely to myself.

The duration of my absence was left to my own choice; a few months, or at most a year, was the period contemplated. One paternal kind precaution he had taken to ensure my having a companion. Without previously communicating with me, he had, in concert with Elizabeth, arranged that Clerval should join me at Strasbourg[1]. This interfered with the solitude I coveted[2] for the prosecution of my task; yet at the commencement of my journey the presence of my friend could in no way be an impediment, and truly I rejoiced that thus I should be saved many hours of lonely, maddening reflection. Nay, Henry might stand between me and the intrusion of my foe. If I were alone, would he not at times force his abhorred presence on me to remind me of my task or to contemplate its progress?

To England, therefore, I was bound, and it was understood that my union with Elizabeth should take place immediately on my return. My father's age rendered him extremely averse to delay. For

1 Strasbourg: town in eastern France, close to the Swiss and German borders
2 covet sth.: long for sth.

myself, there was one reward I promised myself from my detested toils – one consolation for my unparalleled sufferings; it was the prospect of that day when, enfranchised[1] from my miserable slavery, I might claim Elizabeth and forget the past in my union with her.

I now made arrangements for my journey, but one feeling haunted me which filled me with fear and agitation. During my absence I should leave my friends unconscious[2] of the existence of their enemy and unprotected from his attacks, exasperated[3] as he might be by my departure. But he had promised to follow me wherever I might go, and would he not accompany me to England? This imagination was dreadful in itself, but soothing inasmuch as it supposed the safety of my friends. I was agonised with the idea of the possibility that the reverse of this might happen. But through the whole period during which I was the slave of my creature I allowed myself to be governed by the impulses of the moment; and my present sensations strongly intimated[4] that the fiend would follow me and exempt my family from the danger of his machinations[5].

It was in the latter end of September that I again quitted my native country. My journey had been my own suggestion, and Elizabeth therefore acquiesced[6], but she was filled with disquiet at the idea of my suffering, away from her, the inroads[7] of misery and grief. It had been her care which provided me a companion in Clerval – and yet a man is blind to a thousand minute circumstances which call forth a woman's sedulous[8] attention. She longed to bid me hasten my return; a thousand conflicting emotions rendered her mute[9] as she bade me a tearful, silent farewell.

I threw myself into the carriage that was to convey me away, hardly knowing whither I was going, and careless of what was passing around. I remembered only, and it was with a bitter anguish that I reflected on it, to order that my chemical instruments should

1 enfranchise sb.: set sb. free **2** unconscious: (here) unaware **3** exasperated: irritated, angry **4** intimate sth. [ˈɪntɪmeɪt]: suggest sth. **5** machination: *Machenschaft* **6** acquiesce [ˌækwiˈes]: agree **7** inroad: attack **8** sedulous: *eifrig* **9** mute: unable to speak

be packed to go with me. Filled with dreary imaginations, I passed through many beautiful and majestic scenes, but my eyes were fixed and unobserving. I could only think of the bourne[1] of my travels and the work which was to occupy me whilst they endured.

After some days spent in listless indolence[2], during which I traversed many leagues, I arrived at Strasbourg, where I waited two days for Clerval. He came. Alas, how great was the contrast between us! He was alive to every new scene, joyful when he saw the beauties of the setting sun, and more happy when he beheld it rise and recommence a new day. He pointed out to me the shifting colours of the landscape and the appearances of the sky. 'This is what it is to live,' he cried; 'how I enjoy existence! But you, my dear Frankenstein, wherefore are you desponding and sorrowful!' In truth, I was occupied by gloomy thoughts and neither saw the descent of the evening star, nor the golden sunrise reflected in the Rhine. – And you, my friend, would be far more amused with the journal of Clerval, who observed the scenery with an eye of feeling and delight, than in listening to my reflections. I, a miserable wretch, haunted by a curse that shut up every avenue to enjoyment.

We had agreed to descend the Rhine in a boat from Strasbourg to Rotterdam[3], whence we might take shipping for London. During this voyage we passed many willowy[4] islands and saw several beautiful towns. We stayed a day at Mannheim, and on the fifth from our departure from Strasbourg, arrived at Mayence[5]. The course of the Rhine below Mainz becomes much more picturesque. The river descends rapidly, and winds between hills, not high, but steep, and of beautiful forms. We saw many ruined castles standing on the edges of precipices, surrounded by black woods, high and inaccessible. This part of the Rhine, indeed, presents a singularly variegated[6] landscape. In one spot you view rugged hills, ruined castles overlooking tremendous precipices, with the dark Rhine rushing

1 bourne (old use): aim **2** indolence: apathy **3** Rotterdam: port in the Netherlands **4** willowy: *mit Weidenbäumen bestanden* **5** Mayence (Fr.): *Mainz* **6** variegated: colourful

beneath; and on the sudden turn of a promontory, flourishing[1] vineyards[2] with green sloping banks and a meandering[3] river and populous towns occupy the scene.

We travelled at the time of the vintage and heard the song of the labourers as we glided down the stream. Even I, depressed in mind, and my spirits continually agitated by gloomy feelings, even I was pleased. I lay at the bottom of the boat, and as I gazed on the cloudless blue sky, I seemed to drink in a tranquillity to which I had long been a stranger. And if these were my sensations, who can describe those of Henry? He felt as if he had been transported to Fairy-land and enjoyed a happiness seldom tasted by man. 'I have seen,' he said, 'the most beautiful scenes of my own country; I have visited the lakes of Lucerne and Uri[4], where the snowy mountains descend almost perpendicularly to the water, casting black and impenetrable shades, which would cause a gloomy and mournful appearance were it not for the most verdant islands that relieve the eye by their gay appearance; I have seen this lake agitated by a tempest, when the wind tore up whirlwinds of water and gave you an idea of what the water-spout[5] must be on the great ocean; and the waves dash with fury the base of the mountain, where the priest and his mistress were overwhelmed by an avalanche and where their dying voices are still said to be heard amid the pauses of the nightly wind; I have seen the mountains of La Valais, and the Pays de Vaud[6]; but this country, Victor, pleases me more than all those wonders. The mountains of Switzerland are more majestic and strange, but there is a charm in the banks of this divine river that I never before saw equalled. Look at that castle which overhangs yon[7] precipice; and that also on the island, almost concealed amongst the foliage of those lovely trees; and now that group of labourers coming

1 flourishing: prosperous **2** vineyard ['vɪnjəd]: piece of land where grapes are grown for wine production **3** meander: follow a course of many turns and curves **4** lakes of Lucerne and Uri: two lakes in central Switzerland *(Vierwaldstätter See, Urnersee)* **5** water-spout: (here) column of rotating wind and spray over water surface **6** La Valais / Pays de Vaud (Fr.): two cantons in Switzerland *(das Wallis / die Waadt)* **7** yon (poetic): this one ... over there

from among their vines; and that village half hid in the recess of the mountain. Oh, surely the spirit that inhabits and guards this place has a soul more in harmony with man than those who pile[1] the glacier or retire to the inaccessible peaks of the mountains of our own country.'

Clerval! Beloved friend! Even now it delights me to record your words and to dwell on the praise of which you are so eminently deserving. He was a being formed in the 'very poetry of nature'.[2] His wild and enthusiastic imagination was chastened[3] by the sensibility of his heart. His soul overflowed with ardent affections, and his friendship was of that devoted and wondrous nature that the world-minded teach us to look for only in the imagination. But even human sympathies were not sufficient to satisfy his eager mind. The scenery of external nature, which others regard only with admiration, he loved with ardour: –

The sounding cataract[4]
Haunted him like a passion: the tall rock,
The mountain, and the deep and gloomy wood,
Their colours and their forms, were then to him
An appetite; a feeling, and a love,
That had no need of a remoter charm,
By thought supplied, or any interest
Unborrow'd from the eye.*

And where does he now exist? Is this gentle and lovely being lost forever? Has this mind, so replete[5] with ideas, imaginations fanciful and magnificent, which formed a world, whose existence depended on the life of its creator – has this mind perished? Does

1 pile sth.: (here) gather in a place, inhabit a place **2** 'very poetry of nature': quotation from the poem 'Rimini' (1816) by English poet James Henry Leigh Hunt (1784–1859) **3** chasten sth.: (here) control sth. **4** cataract (old use): waterfall * Wordworth's Tintern Abbey [author's footnote]. ['Tintern Abbey' (1798): poem by English Romantic poet William Wordsworth (1770–1850)]
5 replete with sth.: full of sth.

it now only exist in my memory? No, it is not thus; your form so divinely wrought[1], and beaming with beauty, has decayed, but your spirit still visits and consoles your unhappy friend.

Pardon this gush of sorrow; these ineffectual words are but a slight tribute to the unexampled worth of Henry, but they soothe my heart, overflowing with the anguish which his remembrance creates. I will proceed with my tale.

Beyond Cologne[2] we descended to the plains of Holland; and we resolved to post[3] the remainder of our way, for the wind was contrary and the stream of the river was too gentle to aid us.

Our journey here lost the interest arising from beautiful scenery, but we arrived in a few days at Rotterdam, whence we proceeded by sea to England. It was on a clear morning, in the latter days of December, that I first saw the white cliffs of Britain. The banks of the Thames presented a new scene; they were flat but fertile, and almost every town was marked by the remembrance of some story. We saw Tilbury Fort[4], and remembered the Spanish Armada;[5] Gravesend[6], Woolwich, and Greenwich[7] – places which I had heard of even in my country.

At length we saw the numerous steeples of London, St. Paul's towering above all, and the Tower famed in English history.

1 wrought (old use): past participle of work **2** Cologne [kəˈləʊn]: *Köln* **3** post (v): travel by stagecoach (*Postkutsche*) **4** Tilbury Fort: fortification built in the 16th century to protect London against attacks from the sea **5** Spanish Armada: fleet of Spanish warships that was defeated by the English in its attempt to conquer England in 1588 **6** Gravesend: town on the Thames east of London **7** Woolwich [wʊlɪtʃ] / Greenwich [ˈgrenɪtʃ]: districts located in the south east of London

Chapter 19

London was our present point of rest; we determined to remain several months in this wonderful and celebrated city. Clerval desired the intercourse of the men of genius and talent who flourished at this time, but this was with me a secondary object; I was principally occupied with the means of obtaining the information necessary for the completion of my promise and quickly availed[1] myself of the letters of introduction that I had brought with me, addressed to the most distinguished natural philosophers.

If this journey had taken place during my days of study and happiness, it would have afforded me inexpressible pleasure. But a blight had come over my existence, and I only visited these people for the sake of the information they might give me on the subject in which my interest was so terribly profound. Company was irksome to me; when alone, I could fill my mind with the sights of heaven and earth; the voice of Henry soothed me, and I could thus cheat myself into a transitory peace. But busy, uninteresting, joyous faces brought back despair to my heart. I saw an insurmountable barrier placed between me and my fellow-men; this barrier was sealed with the blood of William and Justine, and to reflect on the events connected with those names filled my soul with anguish.

But in Clerval I saw the image of my former self; he was inquisitive and anxious to gain experience and instruction. The difference of manners which he observed was to him an inexhaustible source of instruction and amusement. He was also pursuing an object he had long had in view. His design was to visit India, in the belief that he had in his knowledge of its various languages, and in the views he had taken of its society, the means of materially assisting the progress of European colonisation and trade. In Britain only could he

1 avail yourself of sth.: use sth.

further the execution of his plan. He was forever busy, and the only check[1] to his enjoyments was my sorrowful and dejected mind. I tried to conceal this as much as possible, that I might not debar him from the pleasures natural to one who was entering on a new scene of life, undisturbed by any care or bitter recollection. I often refused to accompany him, alleging another engagement, that I might remain alone. I now also began to collect the materials necessary for my new creation, and this was to me like the torture of single drops of water continually falling on the head. Every thought that was devoted to it was an extreme anguish, and every word that I spoke in allusion to it caused my lips to quiver, and my heart to palpitate.

After passing some months in London, we received a letter from a person in Scotland who had formerly been our visitor at Geneva. He mentioned the beauties of his native country and asked us if those were not sufficient allurements to induce us to prolong our journey as far north as Perth,[2] where he resided. Clerval eagerly desired to accept this invitation, and I, although I abhorred society, wished to view again mountains and streams and all the wondrous works with which Nature adorns her chosen dwelling-places.

We had arrived in England at the beginning of October, and it was now February. We accordingly determined to commence our journey towards the north at the expiration[3] of another month. In this expedition we did not intend to follow the great road to Edinburgh, but to visit Windsor[4], Oxford[5], Matlock[6], and the Cumberland lakes[7], resolving to arrive at the completion of this tour about the end of July. I packed up my chemical instruments and the materials I had collected, resolving to finish my labours in some obscure nook in the northern highlands of Scotland.

1 check (n): *(hier) Beeinträchtigung* **2** Perth: city in central Scotland **3** expiration: end **4** Windsord: town 35 km west of London **5** Oxford: university town in the English midlands **6** Matlock: town in central England **7** Cumberland lakes: lakes at the border to Scotland

We quitted London on the 27th of March and remained a few days at Windsor, rambling in its beautiful forest. This was a new scene to us mountaineers; the majestic oaks, the quantity of game[1], and the herds of stately deer were all novelties to us.

From thence we proceeded to Oxford. As we entered this city our minds were filled with the remembrance of the events that had been transacted[2] there more than a century and a half before. It was here that Charles I[3] had collected his forces. This city had remained faithful to him, after the whole nation had forsaken[4] his cause to join the standard[5] of Parliament and liberty. The memory of that unfortunate king and his companions, the amiable Falkland[6], the insolent[7] Goring[8], his queen, and son, gave a peculiar interest to every part of the city which they might be supposed to have inhabited. The spirit of elder days found a dwelling here, and we delighted to trace its footsteps. If these feelings had not found an imaginary gratification, the appearance of the city had yet in itself sufficient beauty to obtain our admiration. The colleges are ancient and picturesque; the streets are almost magnificent; and the lovely Isis[9], which flows beside it through meadows[10] of exquisite verdure, is spread forth into a placid expanse[11] of waters, which reflects its majestic assemblage of towers, and spires, and domes, embosomed[12] among aged trees.

I enjoyed this scene, and yet my enjoyment was embittered both by the memory of the past and the anticipation of the future. I was formed for peaceful happiness. During my youthful days discontent never visited my mind, and if I was ever overcome by *ennui*[13], the sight of what is beautiful in nature or the study of what is excellent and sublime in the productions of man could always interest my

1 game: wild animals that people hunt **2** transact: (here) happen **3** Charles I: king of England (1600–1649); the English Civil War (1642–1651) took place in his reign **4** foresake sb.'s cause: turn away from sb. **5** standard: (here) flag around which an army gathers **6** Falkland: Lucius Cary, 2nd Viscount Falkland (1610–1643): high-ranking Secretary of State under Charles I **7** insolent: lacking respect, cheeky **8** Goring: George Goring: general under Charles I in the Civil War **9** Isis: alternative name for the River Thames, especially in Oxford area **10** meadow: large, grass-covered area **11** expanse: area **12** embosom sth.: surround sth. closely **13** ennui (Fr.): boredom

heart and communicate elasticity to my spirits[1]. But I am a blasted tree; the bolt[2] has entered my soul; and I felt then that I should survive to exhibit what I shall soon cease to be – a miserable spectacle of wrecked humanity, pitiable to others and intolerable to myself.

We passed a considerable period at Oxford, rambling among its environs and endeavouring to identify every spot which might relate to the most animating epoch of English history. Our little voyages of discovery were often prolonged by the successive objects that presented themselves. We visited the tomb of the illustrious Hampden[3] and the field on which that patriot fell. For a moment my soul was elevated from its debasing[4] and miserable fears to contemplate the divine ideas of liberty and self-sacrifice of which these sights were the monuments and the remembrancers. For an instant I dared to shake off my chains and look around me with a free and lofty spirit, but the iron had eaten into my flesh, and I sank again, trembling and hopeless, into my miserable self.

We left Oxford with regret and proceeded to Matlock, which was our next place of rest. The country in the neighbourhood of this village resembled, to a greater degree, the scenery of Switzerland; but everything is on a lower scale, and the green hills want[5] the crown of distant white Alps which always attend on the piny mountains of my native country. We visited the wondrous cave and the little cabinets[6] of natural history, where the curiosities are disposed[7] in the same manner as in the collections at Servox and Chamounix. The latter name made me tremble when pronounced by Henry, and I hastened to quit Matlock, with which that terrible scene was thus associated.

From Derby[8], still journeying northwards, we passed two months in Cumberland and Westmorland[9]. I could now almost fancy myself

1 communicate elasticity to my spirits: *meinen Geist bewegen* **2** bolt: flash of lightning **3** Hampden: John Hampden (1549–1643): politician who fought for parliamentarism in the English Civil War **4** debasing: humiliating **5** want sth.: (here) lack sth. **6** cabinet: small exhibition room in a museum **7** dispose sth.: (here) arrange sth. **8** Derby: town in the East Midlands **9** Westmorland: county in northwest England

among the Swiss mountains. The little patches of snow which yet lingered on the northern sides of the mountains, the lakes, and the dashing of the rocky streams were all familiar and dear sights to me. Here also we made some acquaintances, who almost contrived to cheat me into happiness. The delight of Clerval was proportionably greater than mine; his mind expanded in the company of men of talent, and he found in his own nature greater capacities and resources than he could have imagined himself to have possessed while he associated with his inferiors. 'I could pass my life here,' said he to me; 'and among these mountains I should scarcely regret Switzerland and the Rhine.'

But he found that a traveller's life is one that includes much pain amidst its enjoyments. His feelings are forever on the stretch[1]; and when he begins to sink into repose, he finds himself obliged to quit that on which he rests in pleasure for something new, which again engages his attention, and which also he forsakes for other novelties.

We had scarcely visited the various lakes of Cumberland and Westmorland and conceived an affection for some of the inhabitants when the period of our appointment with our Scotch friend approached, and we left them to travel on. For my own part I was not sorry. I had now neglected my promise for some time, and I feared the effects of the daemon's disappointment. He might remain in Switzerland and wreak his vengeance on my relatives. This idea pursued me and tormented me at every moment from which I might otherwise have snatched[2] repose and peace. I waited for my letters with feverish impatience; if they were delayed I was miserable and overcome by a thousand fears; and when they arrived and I saw the superscription[3] of Elizabeth or my father, I hardly dared to read and ascertain my fate. Sometimes I thought that the fiend

1 on the stretch: tense **2** snatch sth.: take sth. abruptly **3** superscription: address written on the outside of a letter

followed me and might expedite my remissness[1] by murdering my companion. When these thoughts possessed me, I would not quit Henry for a moment, but followed him as his shadow, to protect him from the fancied[2] rage of his destroyer. I felt as if I had committed some great crime, the consciousness of which haunted me. I was guiltless, but I had indeed drawn down a horrible curse upon my head, as mortal as that of crime.

I visited Edinburgh with languid[3] eyes and mind; and yet that city might have interested the most unfortunate being. Clerval did not like it so well as Oxford, for the antiquity of the latter city was more pleasing to him. But the beauty and regularity of the new town of Edinburgh, its romantic castle and its environs, the most delightful in the world, Arthur's Seat[4], St. Bernard's Well[5], and the Pentland Hills[6] compensated him for the change and filled him with cheerfulness and admiration. But I was impatient to arrive at the termination of my journey.

We left Edinburgh in a week, passing through Coupar, St. Andrew's[7], and along the banks of the Tay, to Perth, where our friend expected us. But I was in no mood to laugh and talk with strangers or enter into their feelings or plans with the good humour expected from a guest; and accordingly I told Clerval that I wished to make the tour of Scotland alone. 'Do you,' said I, 'enjoy yourself, and let this be our rendezvous[8]. I may be absent a month or two; but do not interfere with my motions, I entreat you; leave me to peace and solitude for a short time; and when I return, I hope it will be with a lighter heart, more congenial[9] to your own temper.

1 expedite my remissmess: *meine Nachlässigkeit vertreiben, mich aus meiner Inaktivität reißen* **2** fancied: imagined **3** languid: tired **4** Arthur's Seat: mountain close to Edinburgh's city centre **5** St. Bernard's Well: neo-Roman temple that houses a popular mineral water spring **6** Pentland Hills: range of hills in the south-west vicinity of Edinburgh **7** Coupar / St. Andrew's: medieval coastal towns north of Edinburgh **8** rendezvous: (here) meeting place
9 congenial [kən'dʒiːniəl]: (here) fitting

Henry wished to dissuade[1] me, but seeing me bent[2] on this plan, ceased to remonstrate[3]. He entreated me to write often. 'I had rather be with you,' he said, 'in your solitary rambles, than with these Scotch people, whom I do not know; hasten, then, my dear friend, to return, that I may again feel myself somewhat at home, which I cannot do in your absence.'

Having parted from my friend, I determined to visit some remote spot of Scotland and finish my work in solitude. I did not doubt but that the monster followed me and would discover himself to me when I should have finished, that he might receive his companion.

With this resolution I traversed the northern highlands and fixed on one of the remotest of the Orkneys[4] as the scene of my labours. It was a place fitted for such a work, being hardly more than a rock whose high sides were continually beaten upon by the waves. The soil was barren, scarcely affording pasture[5] for a few miserable cows, and oatmeal[6] for its inhabitants, which consisted of five persons, whose gaunt[7] and scraggy[8] limbs gave tokens of their miserable fare. Vegetables and bread, when they indulged in such luxuries, and even fresh water, was to be procured from the mainland, which was about five miles distant.

On the whole island there were but three miserable huts, and one of these was vacant when I arrived. This I hired. It contained but two rooms, and these exhibited all the squalidness of the most miserable penury. The thatch[9] had fallen in, the walls were unplastered[10], and the door was off its hinges[11]. I ordered it to be repaired, bought some furniture, and took possession[12], an incident which would doubtless have occasioned[13] some surprise had not all the senses of the cottagers been benumbed[14] by want and squalid poverty. As it

1 dissuade sb. from sth.: advise sb. against sth. **2** be bent on sth.: be firmly decided to do sth. **3** remonstrate: criticize **4** Orkneys: group of islands off the north coast of Scotland **5** pasture: meadowland where animals graze **6** oatmeal: *Hafermehl* **7** gaunt: very thin **8** scraggy: uneven **9** thatch (n): straw-covered roof **10** unplastered: *unverputzt* **11** off its hinges: *aus den Angeln* **12** take possession: (here) move in **13** occasion sth.: cause sth. **14** benumbed: *abgestumpft*

was, I lived ungazed at and unmolested[1], hardly thanked for the pittance of food and clothes which I gave, so much does suffering blunt even the coarsest sensations of men.

In this retreat I devoted the morning to labour; but in the evening, when the weather permitted, I walked on the stony beach of the sea to listen to the waves as they roared and dashed at my feet. It was a monotonous yet ever-changing scene. I thought of Switzerland; it was far different from this desolate and appalling landscape. Its hills are covered with vines, and its cottages are scattered thickly[2] in the plains. Its fair lakes reflect a blue and gentle sky, and when troubled by the winds, their tumult is but as the play of a lively infant when compared to the roarings of the giant ocean.

In this manner I distributed my occupations when I first arrived, but as I proceeded in my labour, it became every day more horrible and irksome to me. Sometimes I could not prevail on myself to enter my laboratory for several days, and at other times I toiled day and night in order to complete my work. It was, indeed, a filthy process in which I was engaged. During my first experiment, a kind of enthusiastic frenzy[3] had blinded me to the horror of my employment; my mind was intently fixed on the consummation of my labour, and my eyes were shut to the horror of my proceedings. But now I went to it in cold blood, and my heart often sickened at the work of my hands.

Thus situated, employed in the most detestable occupation, immersed in a solitude where nothing could for an instant call my attention from the actual scene in which I was engaged, my spirits became unequal[4]; I grew restless and nervous. Every moment I feared to meet my persecutor[5]. Sometimes I sat with my eyes fixed on the ground, fearing to raise them lest they should encounter the object which I so much dreaded to behold. I feared to wander from the sight of my fellow creatures lest when alone he should come to claim his companion.

1 unmolested: undisturbed **2** thickly: (here) close to each other **3** frenzy: madness **4** unequal: (here) out of balance **5** persecutor: (here) person chasing after another person

In the mean time I worked on, and my labour was already considerably advanced. I looked towards its completion with a tremulous[1] and eager hope, which I dared not trust myself to question but which was intermixed with obscure forebodings of evil that made my heart sicken in my bosom.

1 tremulous: fearful

Chapter 20

I sat one evening in my laboratory; the sun had set, and the moon was just rising from the sea; I had not sufficient light for my employment, and I remained idle, in a pause of consideration of whether I should leave my labour for the night or hasten its conclusion by an unremitting attention to it. As I sat, a train of reflection occurred to me which led me to consider the effects of what I was now doing. Three years before, I was engaged in the same manner and had created a fiend whose unparalleled barbarity had desolated my heart and filled it forever with the bitterest remorse. I was now about to form another being of whose dispositions I was alike ignorant; she might become ten thousand times more malignant than her mate and delight, for its own sake, in murder and wretchedness. He had sworn to quit the neighbourhood of man and hide himself in deserts, but she had not; and she, who in all probability was to become a thinking and reasoning animal, might refuse to comply with a compact[1] made before her creation. They might even hate each other; the creature who already lived loathed his own deformity, and might he not conceive a greater abhorrence for it when it came before his eyes in the female form? She also might turn with disgust from him to the superior beauty of man; she might quit him, and he be again alone, exasperated by the fresh provocation of being deserted by one of his own species.

Even if they were to leave Europe and inhabit the deserts of the new world, yet one of the first results of those sympathies for which the daemon thirsted would be children, and a race of devils would be propagated[2] upon the earth who might make the very existence of the species of man a condition precarious[3] and full of terror. Had

1 compact (n): agreement **2** propagate sth.: multiply sth., reproduce sth.
3 precarious: uncertain

I right, for my own benefit, to inflict this curse upon everlasting generations? I had before been moved by the sophisms[1] of the being I had created; I had been struck senseless by his fiendish threats; but now, for the first time, the wickedness of my promise burst[2] upon me; I shuddered to think that future ages might curse me as their pest, whose selfishness had not hesitated to buy its own peace at the price, perhaps, of the existence of the whole human race.

I trembled and my heart failed within me, when, on looking up, I saw by the light of the moon the daemon at the casement[3]. A ghastly grin wrinkled his lips as he gazed on me, where I sat fulfilling the task which he had allotted[4] to me. Yes, he had followed me in my travels; he had loitered in forests, hid himself in caves, or taken refuge in wide and desert heaths; and he now came to mark[5] my progress and claim the fulfillment of my promise.

As I looked on him, his countenance expressed the utmost extent of malice and treachery. I thought with a sensation of madness on my promise of creating another like to him, and trembling with passion, tore to pieces the thing on which I was engaged. The wretch saw me destroy the creature on whose future existence he depended for happiness, and with a howl of devilish despair and revenge, withdrew.

I left the room, and locking the door, made a solemn vow in my own heart never to resume my labours; and then, with trembling steps, I sought my own apartment. I was alone; none were near me to dissipate the gloom and relieve me from the sickening oppression of the most terrible reveries.

Several hours passed, and I remained near my window gazing on the sea; it was almost motionless, for the winds were hushed, and all nature reposed under the eye of the quiet moon. A few fishing vessels alone specked[6] the water, and now and then the gentle breeze wafted the sound of voices as the fishermen called to one another. I

1 sophism: argument used to deceive **2** it burst upon me: I realized **3** casement: window **4** allot sth. to sb.: *jdm. etw. zuteilen* **5** mark sth.: (here) check on sth. **6** speck sth.: be visible on sth. like small dots

felt the silence, although I was hardly conscious of its extreme profundity, until my ear was suddenly arrested[1] by the paddling of oars[2] near the shore, and a person landed close to my house.

In a few minutes after, I heard the creaking of my door, as if some one endeavoured to open it softly. I trembled from head to foot; I felt a presentiment[3] of who it was and wished to rouse one of the peasants who dwelt in a cottage not far from mine; but I was overcome by the sensation of helplessness, so often felt in frightful dreams, when you in vain endeavour to fly from an impending danger, and was rooted to the spot.

Presently I heard the sound of footsteps along the passage; the door opened, and the wretch whom I dreaded appeared. Shutting the door, he approached me and said in a smothered[4] voice –

'You have destroyed the work which you began; what is it that you intend? Do you dare to break your promise? I have endured toil and misery; I left Switzerland with you; I crept along the shores of the Rhine, among its willow islands and over the summits of its hills. I have dwelt many months in the heaths of England and among the deserts of Scotland. I have endured incalculable fatigue, and cold, and hunger; do you dare destroy my hopes?'

'Begone! I do break my promise; never will I create another like yourself, equal in deformity and wickedness.'

'Slave, I before reasoned with you, but you have proved yourself unworthy of my condescension[5]. Remember that I have power; you believe yourself miserable, but I can make you so wretched that the light of day will be hateful to you. You are my creator, but I am your master; obey!'

'The hour of my irresolution is past, and the period of your power is arrived. Your threats cannot move me to do an act of wickedness; but they confirm me in a determination of not creating you a companion in vice. Shall I, in cool blood, set loose upon the earth a

1 my ear was arrested: a sound caught my attention **2** oar: *Ruder* **3** presentiment [prɪˈzentɪmənt]: feeling that sth. bad is going to happen **4** smothered: suppressed **5** condescension [ˌkɒndɪˈsenʃn]: *(hier) guter Wille, Entgegenkommen*

daemon whose delight is in death and wretchedness? Begone! I am firm, and your words will only exasperate my rage.'

The monster saw my determination in my face and gnashed his teeth in the impotence of anger. 'Shall each man,' cried he, 'find a wife for his bosom, and each beast have his mate, and I be alone? I had feelings of affection, and they were requited[1] by detestation and scorn. Man! You may hate, but beware! Your hours will pass in dread and misery, and soon the bolt will fall which must ravish[2] from you your happiness forever. Are you to be happy while I grovel[3] in the intensity of my wretchedness? You can blast my other passions, but revenge remains – revenge, henceforth[4] dearer than light or food! I may die, but first you, my tyrant and tormentor, shall curse the sun that gazes on your misery. Beware, for I am fearless and therefore powerful. I will watch with the wiliness[5] of a snake, that I may sting with its venom[6]. Man, you shall repent of the injuries you inflict.'

'Devil, cease; and do not poison the air with these sounds of malice. I have declared my resolution to you, and I am no coward to bend beneath words. Leave me; I am inexorable.'

'It is well. I go; but remember, I shall be with you on your wedding-night.'

I started forward and exclaimed, 'Villain[7]! Before you sign my death-warrant[8], be sure that you are yourself safe.'

I would have seized him, but he eluded me and quitted the house with precipitation[9]. In a few moments I saw him in his boat, which shot across the waters with an arrowy swiftness and was soon lost amidst the waves.

All was again silent, but his words rang in my ears. I burned with rage to pursue the murderer of my peace and precipitate him into the ocean. I walked up and down my room hastily and perturbed[10],

1 requite sth.: *etw. erwidern* **2** ravish sth.: take away sth. by violence **3** grovel: creep with the face to the ground to express inferiority to sb. **4** henceforth: from now on **5** wiliness: *List, Verschlagenheit* **6** venom: poison **7** villain: evil person **8** death-warrant: announcement that sb. is going to be killed **9** with precipitation: hastily **10** perturbed: worried

while my imagination conjured[1] up a thousand images to torment and sting me. Why had I not followed him and closed with him in mortal strife[2]? But I had suffered[3] him to depart, and he had directed his course towards the mainland. I shuddered to think who might be the next victim sacrificed to his insatiate[4] revenge. And then I thought again of his words – *'I will be with you on your wedding-night.'* That, then, was the period fixed for the fulfillment of my destiny. In that hour I should die and at once satisfy and extinguish his malice. The prospect did not move me to fear; yet when I thought of my beloved Elizabeth, of her tears and endless sorrow, when she should find her lover so barbarously snatched from her, tears, the first I had shed for many months, streamed from my eyes, and I resolved not to fall before my enemy without a bitter struggle.

The night passed away, and the sun rose from the ocean; my feelings became calmer, if it may be called calmness when the violence of rage sinks into the depths of despair. I left the house, the horrid scene of the last night's contention[5], and walked on the beach of the sea, which I almost regarded as an insuperable[6] barrier between me and my fellow creatures; nay, a wish that such should prove the fact stole[7] across me. I desired that I might pass my life on that barren rock, wearily[8], it is true, but uninterrupted by any sudden shock of misery. If I returned, it was to be sacrificed or to see those whom I most loved die under the grasp of a daemon whom I had myself created.

I walked about the isle like a restless spectre, separated from all it loved and miserable in the separation. When it became noon, and the sun rose higher, I lay down on the grass and was overpowered by a deep sleep. I had been awake the whole of the preceding night, my nerves were agitated, and my eyes inflamed by watching and misery. The sleep into which I now sank refreshed me; and when

1 conjure up sth.: bring sth. to mind **2** mortal strife: deadly fight **3** suffer sb. to do sth. (old use): permit sb. to so sth. **4** insatiate: never-ending **5** contention: fight, argument **6** insuperable: impossible to be overcome **7** steal across sb.: spread through sb. quickly **8** wearily: (here) bored, taking no pleasure in sth.

I awoke, I again felt as if I belonged to a race of human beings like myself, and I began to reflect upon what had passed with greater composure; yet still the words of the fiend rang in my ears like a death-knell[1]; they appeared like a dream, yet distinct and oppressive as a reality.

The sun had far descended, and I still sat on the shore, satisfying my appetite, which had become ravenous[2], with an oaten[3] cake, when I saw a fishing-boat land close to me, and one of the men brought me a packet; it contained letters from Geneva, and one from Clerval entreating me to join him. He said that he was wearing[4] away his time fruitlessly where he was, that letters from the friends he had formed in London desired his return to complete the negotiation they had entered into for his Indian enterprise. He could not any longer delay his departure; but as his journey to London might be followed, even sooner than he now conjectured, by his longer voyage, he entreated me to bestow as much of my society on him as I could spare[5]. He besought[6] me, therefore, to leave my solitary isle and to meet him at Perth, that we might proceed southwards together. This letter in a degree recalled me to life, and I determined to quit my island at the expiration of two days.

Yet, before I departed, there was a task to perform, on which I shuddered to reflect; I must pack up my chemical instruments, and for that purpose I must enter the room which had been the scene of my odious work, and I must handle those utensils the sight of which was sickening to me. The next morning, at daybreak, I summoned[7] sufficient courage and unlocked the door of my laboratory. The remains of the half-finished creature, whom I had destroyed, lay scattered on the floor, and I almost felt as if I had mangled[8] the living flesh of a human being. I paused to collect myself and then entered the chamber. With trembling hand I conveyed the instruments out

1 death-knell: ringing of a church bell immediately after a death to announce it
2 ravenous: greedy **3** oaten: *Hafer-* **4** wear away time: spend time ineffectively
5 spare sth.: be able to give away sth. **6** beseech sb. to do sth. (besought – besought) (poetic): beg sb. urgently to do sth. **7** summon sth.: (here) find sth.
8 mangle sth.: violently destroy or deform sth.

of the room, but I reflected that I ought not to leave the relics[1] of my work to excite the horror and suspicion of the peasants; and I accordingly put them into a basket, with a great quantity of stones, and laying them up, determined to throw them into the sea that very night; and in the mean time I sat upon the beach, employed in cleaning and arranging my chemical apparatus.

Nothing could be more complete than the alteration that had taken place in my feelings since the night of the appearance of the daemon. I had before regarded my promise with a gloomy despair as a thing that, with whatever consequences, must be fulfilled; but I now felt as if a film had been taken from before my eyes and that I for the first time saw clearly. The idea of renewing my labours did not for one instant occur to me; the threat I had heard weighed on my thoughts, but I did not reflect that a voluntary act of mine could avert it. I had resolved in my own mind that to create another like the fiend I had first made would be an act of the basest and most atrocious[2] selfishness, and I banished from my mind every thought that could lead to a different conclusion.

Between two and three in the morning the moon rose; and I then, putting my basket aboard a little skiff, sailed out about four miles from the shore. The scene was perfectly solitary; a few boats were returning towards land, but I sailed away from them. I felt as if I was about the commission[3] of a dreadful crime and avoided with shuddering anxiety any encounter with my fellow creatures. At one time the moon, which had before been clear, was suddenly overspread by a thick cloud, and I took advantage of the moment of darkness and cast my basket into the sea; I listened to the gurgling sound as it sank and then sailed away from the spot. The sky became clouded, but the air was pure, although chilled by the northeast breeze that was then rising. But it refreshed me and filled me with such agreeable sensations that I resolved to prolong my stay on the water, and fixing the rudder in a direct position, stretched myself at the bottom

1 relics: remains **2** atrocious: evil, cruel **3** commission of sth.: act of committing sth.

of the boat. Clouds hid the moon, everything was obscure, and I heard only the sound of the boat as its keel[1] cut through the waves; the murmur lulled me, and in a short time I slept soundly.

I do not know how long I remained in this situation, but when I awoke I found that the sun had already mounted considerably. The wind was high, and the waves continually threatened the safety of my little skiff. I found that the wind was northeast and must have driven me far from the coast from which I had embarked. I endeavoured to change my course but quickly found that if I again made the attempt the boat would be instantly filled with water.

Thus situated, my only resource was to drive before the wind. I confess that I felt a few sensations of terror. I had no compass with me and was so slenderly[2] acquainted with the geography of this part of the world that the sun was of little benefit to me. I might be driven into the wide Atlantic and feel all the tortures of starvation or be swallowed up in the immeasurable waters that roared and buffeted[3] around me. I had already been out many hours and felt the torment of a burning thirst, a prelude[4] to my other sufferings. I looked on the heavens, which were covered by clouds that flew before the wind, only to be replaced by others; I looked upon the sea; it was to be my grave. 'Fiend,' I exclaimed, 'your task is already fulfilled!' I thought of Elizabeth, of my father, and of Clerval – all left behind, on whom the monster might satisfy his sanguinary and merciless passions. This idea plunged me into a reverie so despairing and frightful that even now, when the scene is on the point of closing before me forever, I shudder to reflect on it.

Some hours passed thus; but by degrees[5], as the sun declined towards the horizon, the wind died away into a gentle breeze and the sea became free from breakers[6]. But these gave place to a heavy swell[7]; I felt sick and hardly able to hold the rudder, when suddenly I saw a line of high land towards the south.

1 keel: *Kiel* **2** slenderly: (here) little **3** buffet [ˈbʌfɪt] (v): push, beat **4** prelude [ˈprelju:d]: *Vorspiel* **5** by degreees: gradually **6** breaker: big wave **7** swell (n): succession of massive waves

Almost spent[1], as I was, by fatigue and the dreadful suspense I endured for several hours, this sudden certainty of life rushed like a flood of warm joy to my heart, and tears gushed from my eyes.

How mutable[2] are our feelings, and how strange is that clinging love we have of life even in the excess of misery! I constructed another sail with a part of my dress and eagerly steered my course towards the land. It had a wild and rocky appearance, but as I approached nearer I easily perceived the traces of cultivation. I saw vessels near the shore and found myself suddenly transported back to the neighbourhood of civilised man. I carefully traced the windings of the land and hailed a steeple which I at length saw issuing from behind a small promontory. As I was in a state of extreme debility[3], I resolved to sail directly towards the town, as a place where I could most easily procure nourishment. Fortunately I had money with me. As I turned the promontory I perceived a small neat town and a good harbour, which I entered, my heart bounding with joy at my unexpected escape.

As I was occupied in fixing the boat and arranging the sails, several people crowded towards the spot. They seemed much surprised at my appearance, but instead of offering me any assistance, whispered together with gestures that at any other time might have produced in me a slight sensation of alarm. As it was, I merely remarked that they spoke English, and I therefore addressed them in that language. 'My good friends,' said I, 'will you be so kind as to tell me the name of this town and inform me where I am?'

'You will know that soon enough,' replied a man with a hoarse[4] voice. 'Maybe you are come to a place that will not prove much to your taste, but you will not be consulted as to your quarters[5], I promise you.'

I was exceedingly surprised on receiving so rude an answer from a stranger, and I was also disconcerted[6] on perceiving the frowning and angry countenances of his companions. 'Why do you answer

1 spent: (here) utterly exhausted **2** mutable: changeable **3** debility: weakness
4 hoarse: *heiser* **5** quarters: accomodation **6** disconcerted: surprised, worried

me so roughly?' I replied. 'Surely it is not the custom of Englishmen to receive strangers so inhospitably.'

'I do not know,' said the man, 'what the custom of the English may be, but it is the custom of the Irish to hate villains.'

While this strange dialogue continued, I perceived the crowd rapidly increase. Their faces expressed a mixture of curiosity and anger, which annoyed and in some degree alarmed me. I inquired the way to the inn, but no one replied. I then moved forward, and a murmuring sound arose from the crowd as they followed and surrounded me, when an ill-looking man approaching tapped me on the shoulder and said, 'Come, sir, you must follow me to Mr. Kirwin's to give an account of yourself.'

'Who is Mr. Kirwin? Why am I to give an account of myself? Is not this a free country?'

'Ay, sir, free enough for honest folks. Mr. Kirwin is a magistrate, and you are to give an account of the death of a gentleman who was found murdered here last night.'

This answer startled me, but I presently recovered myself. I was innocent; that could easily be proved; accordingly I followed my conductor[1] in silence and was led to one of the best houses in the town. I was ready to sink from fatigue and hunger, but being surrounded by a crowd, I thought it politic[2] to rouse all my strength, that no physical debility might be construed[3] into apprehension or conscious guilt. Little did I then expect the calamity that was in a few moments to overwhelm me and extinguish in horror and despair all fear of ignominy or death.

I must pause here, for it requires all my fortitude to recall the memory of the frightful events which I am about to relate, in proper detail, to my recollection.

1 conductor: (here) guide **2** politic: diplomatic **3** construe sth. into sth.: interpret sth. as sth.

Chapter 21

I was soon introduced into the presence of the magistrate, an old benevolent man with calm and mild manners. He looked upon me, however, with some degree of severity, and then, turning towards my conductors, he asked who appeared as witnesses on this occasion.

About half a dozen men came forward; and, one being selected by the magistrate, he deposed[1] that he had been out fishing the night before with his son and brother-in-law, Daniel Nugent, when, about ten o'clock, they observed a strong northerly blast rising, and they accordingly put in for port[2]. It was a very dark night, as the moon had not yet risen; they did not land at the harbour, but, as they had been accustomed, at a creek[3] about two miles below. He walked on first, carrying a part of the fishing tackle[4], and his companions followed him at some distance. As he was proceeding along the sands, he struck his foot against something and fell at his length on the ground. His companions came up to assist him, and by the light of their lantern they found that he had fallen on the body of a man, who was to all appearance dead. Their first supposition was that it was the corpse of some person who had been drowned and was thrown on shore by the waves, but on examination they found that the clothes were not wet and even that the body was not then cold. They instantly carried it to the cottage of an old woman near the spot and endeavoured, but in vain, to restore it to life. It appeared to be a handsome young man, about five and twenty years of age. He had apparently been strangled[5], for there was no sign of any violence except the black mark of fingers on his neck.

1 depose sth.: make a statement under oath in court **2** put in for port: direct the boat to the port **3** creek: *(hier) Flussmündung* **4** tackle (n): equipment, gear **5** strangle sb.: choke sb. to death

The first part of this deposition did not in the least interest me, but when the mark of the fingers was mentioned I remembered the murder of my brother and felt myself extremely agitated; my limbs trembled, and a mist came over my eyes, which obliged me to lean on a chair for support. The magistrate observed me with a keen eye and of course drew an unfavourable augury[1] from my manner.

The son confirmed his father's account, but when Daniel Nugent was called he swore positively that just before the fall of his companion, he saw a boat, with a single man in it, at a short distance from the shore; and as far as he could judge by the light of a few stars, it was the same boat in which I had just landed.

A woman deposed that she lived near the beach and was standing at the door of her cottage, waiting for the return of the fishermen, about an hour before she heard of the discovery of the body, when she saw a boat with only one man in it push off from that part of the shore where the corpse was afterwards found.

Another woman confirmed the account of the fishermen having brought the body into her house; it was not cold. They put it into a bed and rubbed it, and Daniel went to the town for an apothecary, but life was quite gone.

Several other men were examined concerning my landing, and they agreed that, with the strong north wind that had arisen during the night, it was very probable that I had beaten[2] about for many hours and had been obliged to return nearly to the same spot from which I had departed. Besides, they observed that it appeared that I had brought the body from another place, and it was likely that as I did not appear to know the shore, I might have put into the harbour ignorant of the distance of the town of * * * from the place where I had deposited the corpse.

Mr. Kirwin, on hearing this evidence, desired that I should be taken into the room where the body lay for interment, that it might be observed what effect the sight of it would produce upon me.

1 draw an unfavourable augury from sth.: interpret sth. as a sign that reflects negatively on sb. **2** beat about: *(mit dem Schiff) kreuzen*

This idea was probably suggested by the extreme agitation I had exhibited when the mode[1] of the murder had been described. I was accordingly conducted, by the magistrate and several other persons, to the inn. I could not help being struck by the strange coincidences that had taken place during this eventful night; but, knowing that I had been conversing with several persons in the island I had inhabited about the time that the body had been found, I was perfectly tranquil as to the consequences of the affair.

I entered the room where the corpse lay and was led up to the coffin[2]. How can I describe my sensations on beholding it? I feel yet parched with horror, nor can I reflect on that terrible moment without shuddering and agony. The examination, the presence of the magistrate and witnesses, passed like a dream from my memory when I saw the lifeless form of Henry Clerval stretched before me. I gasped for breath, and throwing myself on the body, I exclaimed, 'Have my murderous machinations deprived you also, my dearest Henry, of life? Two I have already destroyed; other victims await their destiny; but you, Clerval, my friend, my benefactor –'

The human frame could no longer support the agonies that I endured, and I was carried out of the room in strong convulsions[3].

A fever succeeded to this. I lay for two months on the point of death; my ravings, as I afterwards heard, were frightful; I called myself the murderer of William, of Justine, and of Clerval. Sometimes I entreated my attendants to assist me in the destruction of the fiend by whom I was tormented; and at others I felt the fingers of the monster already grasping my neck, and screamed aloud with agony and terror. Fortunately, as I spoke my native language, Mr. Kirwin alone understood me; but my gestures and bitter cries were sufficient to affright the other witnesses.

Why did I not die? More miserable than man ever was before, why did I not sink into forgetfulness and rest? Death snatches away many blooming children, the only hopes of their doting parents;

1 mode: way sth. is done **2** coffin: box in which a dead person is buried
3 convulsion: *Krampf*

how many brides and youthful lovers have been one day in the bloom of health and hope, and the next a prey for worms and the decay of the tomb! Of what materials was I made that I could thus resist so many shocks, which, like the turning of the wheel, continually renewed the torture?

But I was doomed to live and in two months found myself as awaking from a dream, in a prison, stretched on a wretched bed, surrounded by jailers, turnkeys[1], bolts[2], and all the miserable apparatus of a dungeon. It was morning, I remember, when I thus awoke to understanding[3]; I had forgotten the particulars of what had happened and only felt as if some great misfortune had suddenly overwhelmed me; but when I looked around and saw the barred[4] windows and the squalidness of the room in which I was, all flashed across my memory and I groaned bitterly.

This sound disturbed an old woman who was sleeping in a chair beside me. She was a hired nurse, the wife of one of the turnkeys, and her countenance expressed all those bad qualities which often characterise that class. The lines of her face were hard and rude, like that of persons accustomed to see without sympathising in sights of misery. Her tone expressed her entire indifference; she addressed me in English, and the voice struck me as one that I had heard during my sufferings.

'Are you better now, sir?' said she.

I replied in the same language, with a feeble voice, 'I believe I am; but if it be all true, if indeed I did not dream, I am sorry that I am still alive to feel this misery and horror.'

'For that matter,' replied the old woman, 'if you mean about the gentleman you murdered, I believe that it were better for you if you were dead, for I fancy it will go hard with you! However, that's none of my business; I am sent to nurse you and get you well; I do my duty with a safe conscience; it were well if everybody did the same.'

1 jailer / turnkey: prison guards **2** bolt: bar used to lock a door **3** awake to understanding: come to full realization **4** barred: *vergittert*

I turned with loathing from the woman who could utter so unfeeling a speech to a person just saved, on the very edge of death; but I felt languid and unable to reflect on all that had passed. The whole series of my life appeared to me as a dream; I sometimes doubted if indeed it were all true, for it never presented itself to my mind with the force of reality.

As the images that floated before me became more distinct, I grew feverish; a darkness pressed around me; no one was near me who soothed me with the gentle voice of love; no dear hand supported me. The physician[1] came and prescribed medicines, and the old woman prepared them for me; but utter carelessness was visible in the first, and the expression of brutality was strongly marked in the visage of the second. Who could be interested in the fate of a murderer but the hangman[2] who would gain his fee?

These were my first reflections, but I soon learned that Mr. Kirwin had shown me extreme kindness. He had caused the best room in the prison to be prepared for me (wretched indeed was the best); and it was he who had provided a physician and a nurse. It is true, he seldom came to see me, for although he ardently desired to relieve the sufferings of every human creature, he did not wish to be present at the agonies and miserable ravings of a murderer. He came, therefore, sometimes to see that I was not neglected, but his visits were short and with long intervals.

One day, while I was gradually recovering, I was seated in a chair, my eyes half open and my cheeks livid like those in death. I was overcome by gloom and misery and often reflected I had better seek death than desire to remain in a world which to me was replete with wretchedness. At one time I considered whether I should not declare myself guilty and suffer the penalty of the law, less innocent than poor Justine had been. Such were my thoughts when the door of my apartment was opened and Mr. Kirwin entered. His countenance expressed sympathy and compassion; he drew a chair close to mine and addressed me in French –

1 physician: doctor **2** hangman: public executioner

'I fear that this place is very shocking to you; can I do anything to make you more comfortable?'

'I thank you, but all that you mention is nothing to me; on the whole earth there is no comfort which I am capable of receiving.'

'I know that the sympathy of a stranger can be but of little relief to one borne[1] down as you are by so strange a misfortune. But you will, I hope, soon quit this melancholy abode, for doubtless evidence can easily be brought to free you from the criminal charge.'

'That is my least concern; I am, by a course of strange events, become the most miserable of mortals. Persecuted and tortured as I am and have been, can death be any evil to me?'

'Nothing indeed could be more unfortunate and agonising than the strange chances that have lately occurred. You were thrown, by some surprising accident, on this shore, renowned for its hospitality[2], seized immediately, and charged with murder. The first sight that was presented to your eyes was the body of your friend, murdered in so unaccountable[3] a manner and placed, as it were, by some fiend across your path.'

As Mr. Kirwin said this, notwithstanding the agitation I endured on this retrospect of my sufferings, I also felt considerable surprise at the knowledge he seemed to possess concerning me. I suppose some astonishment was exhibited in my countenance, for Mr. Kirwin hastened to say –

'Immediately upon your being taken ill, all the papers that were on your person were brought me, and I examined them that I might discover some trace by which I could send to your relations an account of your misfortune and illness. I found several letters, and, among others, one which I discovered from its commencement to be from your father. I instantly wrote to Geneva: nearly two months have elapsed since the departure of my letter: – But you are ill; even now you tremble; you are unfit for agitation of any kind.'

1 borne down: burdened **2** hospitality: friendly behaviour towards visitors and guests **3** unaccountable: inexplicable

'This suspense is a thousand times worse than the most horrible event; tell me what new scene of death has been acted, and whose murder I am now to lament?'

'Your family is perfectly well,' said Mr. Kirwin, with gentleness: 'and someone, a friend, is come to visit you.'

I know not by what chain of thought the idea presented itself, but it instantly darted into my mind that the murderer had come to mock at my misery and taunt[1] me with the death of Clerval, as a new incitement for me to comply with his hellish desires. I put my hand before my eyes, and cried out in agony –

'Oh! Take him away! I cannot see him; for God's sake, do not let him enter!'

Mr. Kirwin regarded me with a troubled countenance. He could not help regarding my exclamation as a presumption of my guilt and said in rather a severe tone –

'I should have thought, young man, that the presence of your father would have been welcome instead of inspiring such violent repugnance.'

'My father!' cried I, while every feature and every muscle was relaxed from anguish to pleasure. 'Is my father indeed come? How kind, how very kind! But where is he, why does he not hasten to me?'

My change of manner surprised and pleased the magistrate; perhaps he thought that my former exclamation was a momentary return of delirium, and now he instantly resumed his former benevolence. He rose and quitted the room with my nurse, and in a moment my father entered it.

Nothing, at this moment, could have given me greater pleasure than the arrival of my father. I stretched out my hand to him and cried –

'Are you, then, safe – and Elizabeth – and Ernest?'

My father calmed me with assurances of their welfare and endeavoured, by dwelling on these subjects so interesting to my heart, to raise my desponding spirits; but he soon felt that a prison

1 taunt sb.: insult sb., ridicule sb.

cannot be the abode of cheerfulness. 'What a place is this that you inhabit, my son!' said he, looking mournfully at the barred windows and wretched appearance of the room. 'You travelled to seek happiness, but a fatality seems to pursue you. And poor Clerval –'

The name of my unfortunate and murdered friend was an agitation too great to be endured in my weak state; I shed tears.

'Alas! Yes, my father,' replied I; 'some destiny of the most horrible kind hangs over me, and I must live to fulfil it, or surely I should have died on the coffin of Henry.'

We were not allowed to converse for any length of time, for the precarious state of my health rendered every precaution necessary that could ensure tranquillity. Mr. Kirwin came in and insisted that my strength should not be exhausted by too much exertion. But the appearance of my father was to me like that of my good angel, and I gradually recovered my health.

As my sickness quitted me, I was absorbed by a gloomy and black melancholy that nothing could dissipate. The image of Clerval was forever before me, ghastly and murdered. More than once the agitation into which these reflections threw me made my friends dread a dangerous relapse. Alas! Why did they preserve so miserable and detested a life? It was surely that I might fulfil my destiny, which is now drawing to a close. Soon, oh, very soon, will death extinguish these throbbings[1] and relieve me from the mighty weight of anguish that bears me to the dust; and, in executing the award of justice[2], I shall also sink to rest. Then the appearance of death was distant, although the wish was ever present to my thoughts; and I often sat for hours motionless and speechless, wishing for some mighty revolution[3] that might bury me and my destroyer in its ruins.

The season of the assizes[4] approached. I had already been three months in prison, and although I was still weak and in continual danger of a relapse, I was obliged to travel nearly a hundred miles

1 throbbing: beating **2** award of justice: *Urteilsspruch* **3** revolution: *(hier) Umwälzung, Erdbeben* **4** season of the assizes: trial sessions held periodically (at least once a year) in every county of the UK

to the country town where the court was held. Mr. Kirwin charged[1] himself with every care of collecting witnesses and arranging my defence. I was spared the disgrace of appearing publicly as a criminal, as the case was not brought before the court that decides on life and death. The grand jury[2] rejected the bill[3], on its being proved that I was on the Orkney Islands at the hour the body of my friend was found; and a fortnight after my removal I was liberated from prison.

My father was enraptured on finding me freed from the vexations[4] of a criminal charge, that I was again allowed to breathe the fresh atmosphere and permitted to return to my native country. I did not participate in these feelings, for to me the walls of a dungeon or a palace were alike hateful. The cup of life was poisoned forever, and although the sun shone upon me, as upon the happy and gay of heart, I saw around me nothing but a dense and frightful darkness, penetrated by no light but the glimmer of two eyes that glared[5] upon me. Sometimes they were the expressive eyes of Henry, languishing[6] in death, the dark orbs[7] nearly covered by the lids and the long black lashes that fringed them; sometimes it was the watery, clouded eyes of the monster, as I first saw them in my chamber at Ingolstadt.

My father tried to awaken in me the feelings of affection. He talked of Geneva, which I should soon visit, of Elizabeth and Ernest; but these words only drew deep groans from me. Sometimes, indeed, I felt a wish for happiness and thought with melancholy delight of my beloved cousin or longed, with a devouring *maladie du pays*[8], to see once more the blue lake and rapid Rhone[9], that had been so dear to me in early childhood; but my general state of feeling was a torpor[10] in which a prison was as welcome a residence as the divinest scene in nature; and these fits were seldom inter-

1 charge yourself with sth.: take sth. upon yourself **2** grand jury: (here) group of men of high standing who decide whether there is enough evidence to put an accused person on trial **3** reject the bill: *die Anklage niederschlagen*
4 vexation: worry, confusion **5** glare upon sb.: stare angrily at sb. **6** languish: become powerless/lifeless **7** orb: ball, (here) eye **8** maladie du pays (Fr.): homesickness **9** Rhone: river originating in France and flowing into Lake Geneva **10** torpor: inactivity, apathy

rupted but by paroxysms of anguish and despair. At these moments I often endeavoured to put an end to the existence I loathed, and it required unceasing attendance and vigilance[1] to restrain me from committing some dreadful act of violence.

Yet one duty remained to me, the recollection of which finally triumphed over my selfish despair. It was necessary that I should return without delay to Geneva, there to watch over the lives of those I so fondly loved and to lie in wait for the murderer, that if any chance led me to the place of his concealment, or if he dared again to blast[2] me by his presence, I might, with unfailing aim, put an end to the existence of the monstrous image which I had endued with the mockery of a soul still more monstrous. My father still desired to delay our departure, fearful that I could not sustain the fatigues of a journey, for I was a shattered wreck – the shadow of a human being. My strength was gone. I was a mere skeleton, and fever night and day preyed upon my wasted frame.

Still, as I urged our leaving Ireland with such inquietude[3] and impatience, my father thought it best to yield. We took our passage on board a vessel bound for Havre-de-Grâce[4], and sailed with a fair wind from the Irish shores. It was midnight. I lay on the deck looking at the stars and listening to the dashing of the waves. I hailed the darkness that shut Ireland from my sight, and my pulse beat with a feverish joy when I reflected that I should soon see Geneva. The past appeared to me in the light of a frightful dream; yet the vessel in which I was, the wind that blew me from the detested shore of Ireland, and the sea which surrounded me told me too forcibly that I was deceived by no vision and that Clerval, my friend and dearest companion, had fallen a victim to me and the monster of my creation. I repassed[5], in my memory, my whole life – my quiet happiness while residing with my family in Geneva, the death of my mother, and my departure for Ingolstadt. I remembered, shud-

1 vigilance: watchfulness, attention **2** blast sb.: attack sb. **3** inquietude: nervousness **4** Havre-de-Grâce: French port on the English channel (now: Le Havre) **5** repass sth.: *etw. Revue passieren lassen*

dering, the mad enthusiasm that hurried me on to the creation of my hideous enemy, and I called to mind the night in which he first lived. I was unable to pursue the train of thought; a thousand feelings pressed upon me, and I wept bitterly.

Ever since my recovery from the fever I had been in the custom of taking every night a small quantity of laudanum[1], for it was by means of this drug only that I was enabled to gain the rest necessary for the preservation of life. Oppressed by the recollection of my various misfortunes, I now swallowed double my usual quantity and soon slept profoundly. But sleep did not afford me respite from thought and misery; my dreams presented a thousand objects that scared me. Towards morning I was possessed by a kind of nightmare; I felt the fiend's grasp in my neck and could not free myself from it; groans and cries rang in my ears. My father, who was watching over me, perceiving my restlessness, awoke me; the dashing waves were around, the cloudy sky above, the fiend was not here: a sense of security, a feeling that a truce[2] was established between the present hour and the irresistible[3], disastrous future imparted[4] to me a kind of calm forgetfulness, of which the human mind is by its structure peculiarly susceptible[5].

1 laudanum ['lɔːdənəm]: in Shelley's time, a commonly used, opium-based drug to reduce pain and induce sleep **2** truce: temporary break from fighting during a war **3** irresistible: (here) unavoidable **4** impart sth. to sb.: give sth. to sb. **5** susceptible: open, receptive

Chapter 22

The voyage came to an end. We landed, and proceeded to Paris. I soon found that I had overtaxed[1] my strength and that I must repose before I could continue my journey. My father's care and attentions were indefatigable, but he did not know the origin of my sufferings and sought erroneous methods to remedy the incurable ill. He wished me to seek amusement in society. I abhorred the face of man. Oh, not abhorred! They were my brethren[2], my fellow beings, and I felt attracted even to the most repulsive among them, as to creatures of an angelic nature and celestial mechanism. But I felt that I had no right to share their intercourse. I had unchained an enemy among them whose joy it was to shed their blood and to revel in their groans. How they would, each and all, abhor me and hunt me from the world did they know my unhallowed acts and the crimes which had their source in me!

My father yielded at length to my desire to avoid society and strove by various arguments to banish my despair. Sometimes he thought that I felt deeply the degradation of being obliged to answer a charge of murder, and he endeavoured to prove to me the futility[3] of pride.

'Alas! my father,' said I, 'how little do you know me. Human beings, their feelings and passions, would indeed be degraded if such a wretch as I felt pride. Justine, poor unhappy Justine, was as innocent as I, and she suffered the same charge; she died for it; and I am the cause of this – I murdered her. William, Justine, and Henry – they all died by my hands.'

My father had often, during my imprisonment, heard me make the same assertion; when I thus accused myself, he sometimes

1 overtax your strength: make an effort that is too much for you **2** brethren (pl, old use, fml): brothers **3** futility: meaninglessness

seemed to desire an explanation, and at others he appeared to consider it as the offspring of delirium, and that, during my illness, some idea of this kind had presented itself to my imagination, the remembrance of which I preserved in my convalescence. I avoided explanation and maintained a continual silence concerning the wretch I had created. I had a persuasion that I should be supposed mad, and this in itself would forever have chained my tongue. But, besides, I could not bring myself to disclose a secret which would fill my hearer with consternation and make fear and unnatural horror the inmates of his breast. I checked, therefore, my impatient thirst for sympathy and was silent when I would have given the world to have confided the fatal secret. Yet, still, words like those I have recorded would burst uncontrollably from me. I could offer no explanation of them, but their truth in part relieved the burden of my mysterious woe.

Upon this occasion my father said, with an expression of unbounded wonder, 'My dearest Victor, what infatuation[1] is this? My dear son, I entreat you never to make such an assertion again.'

'I am not mad,' I cried energetically; 'the sun and the heavens, who have viewed my operations[2], can bear witness of my truth. I am the assassin of those most innocent victims; they died by my machinations. A thousand times would I have shed my own blood, drop by drop, to have saved their lives; but I could not, my father, indeed I could not sacrifice the whole human race.'

The conclusion of this speech convinced my father that my ideas were deranged[3], and he instantly changed the subject of our conversation and endeavoured to alter the course of my thoughts. He wished as much as possible to obliterate the memory of the scenes that had taken place in Ireland and never alluded to them or suffered me to speak of my misfortunes.

As time passed away I became more calm; misery had her dwelling in my heart, but I no longer talked in the same incoherent[4] man-

1 infatuation: foolishness, delusion **2** operation: (here) deed **3** deranged: disturbed **4** incoherent: lacking clarity and logic

ner of my own crimes; sufficient for me was the consciousness of them. By the utmost self-violence I curbed[1] the imperious[2] voice of wretchedness, which sometimes desired to declare itself to the whole world, and my manners were calmer and more composed[3] than they had ever been since my journey to the sea of ice.

A few days before we left Paris on our way to Switzerland I received the following letter from Elizabeth: –

MY DEAR FRIEND,

It gave me the greatest pleasure to receive a letter from my uncle dated at Paris; you are no longer at a formidable[4] distance, and I may hope to see you in less than a fortnight. My poor cousin, how much you must have suffered! I expect to see you looking even more ill than when you quitted Geneva. This winter has been passed most miserably, tortured as I have been by anxious suspense; yet I hope to see peace in your countenance and to find that your heart is not totally void of comfort and tranquillity.

Yet I fear that the same feelings now exist that made you so miserable a year ago, even perhaps augmented by time. I would not disturb you at this period, when so many misfortunes weigh upon you, but a conversation that I had with my uncle previous to his departure renders some explanation necessary before we meet.

Explanation! You may possibly say, What can Elizabeth have to explain? If you really say this, my questions are answered and all my doubts satisfied. But you are distant from me, and it is possible that you may dread and yet be pleased with this explanation; and in a probability of this being the case, I dare not any longer postpone writing what, during your absence, I have often wished to express to you but have never had the courage to begin.

You well know, Victor, that our union had been the favourite plan of your parents ever since our infancy. We were told this when young, and taught to look forward to it as an event that would cer-

1 curb sth. (v): hold sth. back, control sth. **2** imperious: domineering
3 composed: calm **4** formidable [fəˈmɪdəbl]: enormous

tainly take place. We were affectionate playfellows during childhood, and, I believe, dear and valued friends to one another as we grew older. But as brother and sister often entertain a lively affection towards each other without desiring a more intimate union, may not such also be our case? Tell me, dearest Victor. Answer me, I conjure you by our mutual happiness, with simple truth – Do you not love another?

You have travelled; you have spent several years of your life at Ingolstadt; and I confess to you, my friend, that when I saw you last autumn so unhappy, flying to solitude from the society of every creature, I could not help supposing that you might regret our connection and believe yourself bound in honour to fulfil the wishes of your parents, although they opposed themselves to your inclinations. But this is false reasoning. I confess to you, my friend, that I love you and that in my airy dreams of futurity[1] you have been my constant friend and companion. But it is your happiness I desire as well as my own when I declare to you that our marriage would render me eternally miserable unless it were the dictate[2] of your own free choice. Even now I weep to think that, borne down as you are by the cruellest misfortunes, you may stifle, by the word 'honour,' all hope of that love and happiness which would alone restore you to yourself. I, who have so disinterested[3] an affection for you, may increase your miseries tenfold by being an obstacle to your wishes. Ah! Victor, be assured that your cousin and playmate has too sincere a love for you not to be made miserable by this supposition. Be happy, my friend; and if you obey me in this one request, remain satisfied that nothing on earth will have the power to interrupt my tranquillity.

Do not let this letter disturb you; do not answer tomorrow, or the next day, or even until you come, if it will give you pain. My uncle will send me news of your health, and if I see but one smile on your

1 futurity: future events **2** dictate (n): order, command **3** disinterested: (here) selfless

lips when we meet, occasioned by this or any other exertion of mine, I shall need no other happiness.

ELIZABETH LAVENZA
Geneva, May 18th, 17–.

This letter revived in my memory what I had before forgotten, the threat of the fiend – 'I will be with you on your wedding-night!' Such was my sentence, and on that night would the daemon employ every art to destroy me and tear me from the glimpse[1] of happiness which promised partly to console my sufferings. On that night he had determined to consummate his crimes by my death. Well, be it so; a deadly struggle would then assuredly take place, in which if he were victorious[2] I should be at peace and his power over me be at an end. If he were vanquished[3], I should be a free man. Alas! what freedom? Such as the peasant enjoys when his family have been massacred before his eyes, his cottage burnt, his lands laid waste, and he is turned adrift[4], homeless, penniless, and alone, but free. Such would be my liberty except that in my Elizabeth I possessed a treasure, alas, balanced by those horrors of remorse and guilt which would pursue me until death.

Sweet and beloved Elizabeth! I read and reread her letter, and some softened feelings stole into my heart and dared to whisper paradisiacal dreams of love and joy; but the apple was already eaten, and the angel's arm bared[5] to drive me from all hope. Yet I would die to make her happy. If the monster executed his threat, death was inevitable; yet, again, I considered whether my marriage would hasten my fate. My destruction might indeed arrive a few months sooner, but if my torturer should suspect that I postponed it, influenced by his menaces, he would surely find other and perhaps more dreadful means of revenge. He had vowed to be with me on my

1 glimpse (n): (here) brief moment **2** victorious: winning **3** vanquish sb.: defeat sb. **4** turn sb. adrift: get rid of sb., cast off sb. **5** bared: *entblößt*; reference to the cherubim, angels who, after Adam and Eve had been driven out of Paradise, guarded the tree of life with drawn swords (see Genesis 3,24)

wedding-night, yet he did not consider that threat as binding him to peace in the mean time, for as if to show me that he was not yet satiated with blood, he had murdered Clerval immediately after the enunciation[1] of his threats. I resolved, therefore, that if my immediate union with my cousin would conduce either to hers or my father's happiness, my adversary's[2] designs[3] against my life should not retard it a single hour.

In this state of mind I wrote to Elizabeth. My letter was calm and affectionate. 'I fear, my beloved girl,' I said, 'little happiness remains for us on earth; yet all that I may one day enjoy is centred in you. Chase away your idle fears; to you alone do I consecrate my life and my endeavours for contentment. I have one secret, Elizabeth, a dreadful one; when revealed to you, it will chill your frame with horror, and then, far from being surprised at my misery, you will only wonder that I survive what I have endured. I will confide this tale of misery and terror to you the day after our marriage shall take place, for, my sweet cousin, there must be perfect confidence between us. But until then, I conjure you, do not mention or allude to it. This I most earnestly entreat, and I know you will comply.'

In about a week after the arrival of Elizabeth's letter we returned to Geneva. The sweet girl welcomed me with warm affection, yet tears were in her eyes as she beheld my emaciated frame and feverish cheeks. I saw a change in her also. She was thinner and had lost much of that heavenly vivacity that had before charmed me; but her gentleness and soft looks of compassion made her a more fit companion for one blasted and miserable as I was.

The tranquillity which I now enjoyed did not endure. Memory brought madness with it, and when I thought of what had passed, a real insanity possessed me; sometimes I was furious and burnt with rage, sometimes low and despondent. I neither spoke nor looked at anyone, but sat motionless, bewildered by the multitude of miseries that overcame me.

1 enunciation: announcement **2** adversary (n): enemy **3** design (n): plan

Elizabeth alone had the power to draw me from these fits; her gentle voice would soothe me when transported by passion and inspire me with human feelings when sunk in torpor. She wept with me and for me. When reason returned, she would remonstrate and endeavour to inspire me with resignation[1]. Ah! It is well for the unfortunate to be resigned, but for the guilty there is no peace. The agonies of remorse poison the luxury there is otherwise sometimes found in indulging the excess of grief.

Soon after my arrival my father spoke of my immediate marriage with Elizabeth. I remained silent.

'Have you, then, some other attachment?'

'None on earth. I love Elizabeth and look forward to our union with delight. Let the day therefore be fixed; and on it I will consecrate myself, in life or death, to the happiness of my cousin.'

'My dear Victor, do not speak thus. Heavy misfortunes have befallen us, but let us only cling closer to what remains and transfer our love for those whom we have lost to those who yet live. Our circle will be small but bound close by the ties of affection and mutual misfortune. And when time shall have softened your despair, new and dear objects of care will be born to replace those of whom we have been so cruelly deprived.'

Such were the lessons of my father. But to me the remembrance of the threat returned; nor can you wonder that, omnipotent as the fiend had yet been in his deeds of blood, I should almost regard him as invincible, and that when he had pronounced the words *'I shall be with you on your wedding-night,'* I should regard the threatened fate as unavoidable. But death was no evil to me if the loss of Elizabeth were balanced with it, and I therefore, with a contented and even cheerful countenance, agreed with my father that if my cousin would consent, the ceremony should take place in ten days, and thus put, as I imagined, the seal[2] to my fate.

1 resignation: attitude of enduring a miserable condition without attempting to change it **2** seal: *Siegel*

Great God! If for one instant I had thought what might be the hellish intention of my fiendish adversary, I would rather have banished myself forever from my native country and wandered a friendless outcast over the earth than have consented to this miserable marriage. But, as if possessed of magic powers, the monster had blinded me to his real intentions; and when I thought that I had prepared only my own death, I hastened that of a far dearer victim.

As the period fixed for our marriage drew nearer, whether from cowardice or a prophetic feeling, I felt my heart sink within me. But I concealed my feelings by an appearance of hilarity that brought smiles and joy to the countenance of my father, but hardly deceived the everwatchful and nicer[1] eye of Elizabeth. She looked forward to our union with placid contentment, not unmingled with a little fear, which past misfortunes had impressed, that what now appeared certain and tangible happiness might soon dissipate into an airy dream and leave no trace but deep and everlasting regret.

Preparations were made for the event, congratulatory visits were received, and all wore a smiling appearance. I shut up, as well as I could, in my own heart the anxiety that preyed there and entered with seeming earnestness into the plans of my father, although they might only serve as the decorations of my tragedy. Through my father's exertions a part of the inheritance of Elizabeth had been restored to her by the Austrian government. A small possession on the shores of Como[2] belonged to her. It was agreed that, immediately after our union, we should proceed to Villa Lavenza and spend our first days of happiness beside the beautiful lake near which it stood.

In the mean time I took every precaution to defend my person in case the fiend should openly attack me. I carried pistols and a dagger[3] constantly about me and was ever on the watch to prevent artifice[4], and by these means gained a greater degree of tranquillity. Indeed, as the period approached, the threat appeared more as a

1 nicer: (here) more accurate **2** Como: Lake Como, picturesque lake in Lombardy, northern Italy **3** dagger: sharp pointed knife **4** artifice: *Tücke*

delusion, not to be regarded as worthy to disturb my peace, while the happiness I hoped for in my marriage wore a greater appearance of certainty as the day fixed for its solemnisation drew nearer and I heard it continually spoken of as an occurrence which no accident could possibly prevent.

Elizabeth seemed happy; my tranquil demeanour contributed greatly to calm her mind. But on the day that was to fulfil my wishes and my destiny, she was melancholy, and a presentiment of evil pervaded her; and perhaps also she thought of the dreadful secret which I had promised to reveal to her on the following day. My father was in the mean time overjoyed and in the bustle[1] of preparation only recognised in the melancholy of his niece the diffidence[2] of a bride.

After the ceremony was performed a large party assembled at my father's, but it was agreed that Elizabeth and I should commence our journey by water, sleeping that night at Evian[3] and continuing our voyage on the following day. The day was fair, the wind favourable; all smiled on our nuptial[4] embarkation.

Those were the last moments of my life during which I enjoyed the feeling of happiness. We passed rapidly along; the sun was hot, but we were sheltered from its rays by a kind of canopy while we enjoyed the beauty of the scene, sometimes on one side of the lake, where we saw Mont Salêve, the pleasant banks of Montalègre[5], and at a distance, surmounting all, the beautiful Mont Blanc and the assemblage of snowy mountains that in vain endeavour to emulate[6] her; sometimes coasting[7] the opposite banks, we saw the mighty Jura opposing its dark side to the ambition that would quit its native country, and an almost insurmountable barrier to the invader who should wish to enslave it.

I took the hand of Elizabeth. 'You are sorrowful, my love. Ah! If you knew what I have suffered and what I may yet endure, you would

1 bustle: simultaneous noisy activities in a crowded place **2** diffidence: modesty, shyness **3** Evian: town on the shore of Lake Geneva **4** nuptial (adj): relating to marriage **5** Montalègre: town on the shore of Lake Geneva
6 emulate sth./sb.: imitate sth./sb. **7** coast (v): move along a coast/shore

endeavour to let me taste the quiet and freedom from despair that this one day at least permits me to enjoy.'

'Be happy, my dear Victor,' replied Elizabeth; 'there is, I hope, nothing to distress you; and be assured that if a lively joy is not painted in my face, my heart is contented. Something whispers to me not to depend too much on the prospect that is opened before us, but I will not listen to such a sinister[1] voice. Observe how fast we move along and how the clouds, which sometimes obscure and sometimes rise above the dome of Mont Blanc, render this scene of beauty still more interesting. Look also at the innumerable fish that are swimming in the clear waters, where we can distinguish every pebble[2] that lies at the bottom. What a divine day! How happy and serene all nature appears!'

Thus Elizabeth endeavoured to divert her thoughts and mine from all reflection upon melancholy subjects. But her temper was fluctuating; joy for a few instants shone in her eyes, but it continually gave place to distraction[3] and reverie.

The sun sank lower in the heavens; we passed the river Drance[4] and observed its path through the chasms[5] of the higher and the glens[6] of the lower hills. The Alps here come closer to the lake, and we approached the amphitheatre of mountains which forms its eastern boundary. The spire of Evian shone under the woods that surrounded it and the range of mountain above mountain by which it was overhung.

The wind, which had hitherto carried us along with amazing rapidity, sank at sunset to a light breeze; the soft air just ruffled the water and caused a pleasant motion among the trees as we approached the shore, from which it wafted the most delightful scent of flowers and hay. The sun sank beneath the horizon as we landed, and as I touched the shore I felt those cares and fears revive which soon were to clasp me and cling to me forever.

1 sinister: threatening, evil **2** pebble: small rounded stone **3** distraction: (here) uncertainty **4** Drance: river flowing into Lake Geneva **5** chasm: *Schlucht* **6** glen: narrow valley

Chapter 23

It was eight o'clock when we landed; we walked for a short time on the shore, enjoying the transitory light, and then retired to the inn and contemplated the lovely scene of waters, woods, and mountains, obscured in darkness, yet still displaying their black outlines.

The wind, which had fallen in the south, now rose with great violence in the west. The moon had reached her summit in the heavens and was beginning to descend; the clouds swept across it swifter than the flight of the vulture[1] and dimmed her rays, while the lake reflected the scene of the busy heavens, rendered still busier by the restless waves that were beginning to rise. Suddenly a heavy storm of rain descended.

I had been calm during the day, but so soon as night obscured the shapes of objects, a thousand fears arose in my mind. I was anxious and watchful, while my right hand grasped a pistol which was hidden in my bosom; every sound terrified me, but I resolved that I would sell my life dearly and not shrink from the conflict until my own life or that of my adversary was extinguished.

Elizabeth observed my agitation for some time in timid[2] and fearful silence, but there was something in my glance which communicated terror to her, and trembling, she asked, 'What is it that agitates you, my dear Victor? What is it you fear?'

'Oh! peace, peace, my love,' replied I; 'this night, and all will be safe; but this night is dreadful, very dreadful.'

I passed an hour in this state of mind, when suddenly I reflected how fearful the combat which I momentarily expected would be to my wife, and I earnestly entreated her to retire, resolving not to join her until I had obtained some knowledge as to the situation of my enemy.

1 vulture: *Geier* **2** timid: shy

She left me, and I continued some time walking up and down the passages of the house and inspecting every corner that might afford a retreat to my adversary. But I discovered no trace of him and was beginning to conjecture that some fortunate chance had intervened to prevent the execution of his menaces when suddenly I heard a shrill and dreadful scream. It came from the room into which Elizabeth had retired. As I heard it, the whole truth rushed into my mind, my arms dropped, the motion of every muscle and fibre was suspended[1]; I could feel the blood trickling in my veins and tingling in the extremities of my limbs. This state lasted but for an instant; the scream was repeated, and I rushed into the room.

Great God! why did I not then expire[2]! Why am I here to relate the destruction of the best hope and the purest creature on earth? She was there, lifeless and inanimate, thrown across the bed, her head hanging down and her pale and distorted features half covered by her hair. Everywhere I turn I see the same figure – her bloodless arms and relaxed form flung[3] by the murderer on its bridal bier[4]. Could I behold this and live? Alas! life is obstinate[5] and clings closest where it is most hated. For a moment only did I lose recollection; I fell senseless on the ground.

When I recovered I found myself surrounded by the people of the inn; their countenances expressed a breathless terror, but the horror of others appeared only as a mockery, a shadow of the feelings that oppressed me. I escaped from them to the room where lay the body of Elizabeth, my love, my wife, so lately living, so dear, so worthy. She had been moved from the posture in which I had first beheld her, and now, as she lay, her head upon her arm and a handkerchief thrown across her face and neck, I might have supposed her asleep. I rushed towards her and embraced her with ardour, but the deadly languor and coldness of the limbs told me that what I now held in my arms had ceased to be the Elizabeth whom I had

1 suspend: (here) cause to stop temporarily **2** expire: (here) die **3** fling sth. (flung – flung): throw sth. forcefully **4** bier: frame on which a dead person is placed and carried before the funeral **5** obstinate: stubborn, persistent

loved and cherished. The murderous mark of the fiend's grasp was on her neck, and the breath had ceased to issue from her lips.

While I still hung over her in the agony of despair, I happened to look up. The windows of the room had before been darkened, and I felt a kind of panic on seeing the pale yellow light of the moon illuminate the chamber. The shutters had been thrown back, and with a sensation of horror not to be described, I saw at the open window a figure the most hideous and abhorred. A grin was on the face of the monster; he seemed to jeer[1], as with his fiendish finger he pointed towards the corpse of my wife. I rushed towards the window, and drawing a pistol from my bosom, fired; but he eluded me, leaped from his station, and running with the swiftness of lightning, plunged into the lake.

The report[2] of the pistol brought a crowd into the room. I pointed to the spot where he had disappeared, and we followed the track with boats; nets were cast, but in vain. After passing several hours, we returned hopeless, most of my companions believing it to have been a form conjured up by my fancy. After having landed, they proceeded to search the country, parties going in different directions among the woods and vines.

I attempted to accompany them and proceeded a short distance from the house, but my head whirled round, my steps were like those of a drunken man, I fell at last in a state of utter exhaustion; a film covered my eyes, and my skin was parched with the heat of fever. In this state I was carried back and placed on a bed, hardly conscious of what had happened; my eyes wandered round the room as if to seek something that I had lost.

After an interval I arose, and as if by instinct, crawled into the room where the corpse of my beloved lay. There were women weeping around; I hung over it and joined my sad tears to theirs; all this time no distinct idea presented itself to my mind, but my thoughts rambled to various subjects, reflecting confusedly on my misfortunes and their cause. I was bewildered, in a cloud of wonder and

1 jeer (v): mock, ridicule **2** report (n): (here) explosive noise

horror. The death of William, the execution of Justine, the murder of Clerval, and lastly of my wife; even at that moment I knew not that my only remaining friends were safe from the malignity of the fiend; my father even now might be writhing under his grasp, and Ernest might be dead at his feet. This idea made me shudder and recalled me to action. I started up and resolved to return to Geneva with all possible speed.

There were no horses to be procured, and I must return by the lake; but the wind was unfavourable, and the rain fell in torrents. However, it was hardly morning, and I might reasonably hope to arrive by night. I hired men to row and took an oar myself, for I had always experienced relief from mental torment in bodily exercise. But the overflowing misery I now felt, and the excess of agitation that I endured rendered me incapable of any exertion. I threw down the oar, and leaning my head upon my hands, gave way to every gloomy idea that arose. If I looked up, I saw scenes which were familiar to me in my happier time and which I had contemplated but the day before in the company of her who was now but a shadow and a recollection. Tears streamed from my eyes. The rain had ceased for a moment, and I saw the fish play in the waters as they had done a few hours before; they had then been observed by Elizabeth. Nothing is so painful to the human mind as a great and sudden change. The sun might shine or the clouds might lower, but nothing could appear to me as it had done the day before. A fiend had snatched from me every hope of future happiness; no creature had ever been so miserable as I was; so frightful an event is single in the history of man.

But why should I dwell upon the incidents that followed this last overwhelming event? Mine has been a tale of horrors; I have reached their acme[1], and what I must now relate can but be tedious to you. Know that, one by one, my friends were snatched away; I was left desolate. My own strength is exhausted, and I must tell, in a few words, what remains of my hideous narration.

1 acme ['ækmi]: climax

I arrived at Geneva. My father and Ernest yet lived, but the former sunk under the tidings that I bore. I see him now, excellent and venerable old man! His eyes wandered in vacancy, for they had lost their charm and their delight – his Elizabeth, his more than daughter, whom he doted on with all that affection which a man feels, who in the decline of life, having few affections, clings more earnestly to those that remain. Cursed, cursed be the fiend that brought misery on his grey hairs and doomed him to waste in wretchedness! He could not live under the horrors that were accumulated around him; the springs[1] of existence suddenly gave way; he was unable to rise from his bed, and in a few days he died in my arms.

What then became of me? I know not; I lost sensation, and chains and darkness were the only objects that pressed upon me. Sometimes, indeed, I dreamt that I wandered in flowery meadows and pleasant vales with the friends of my youth, but I awoke and found myself in a dungeon. Melancholy followed, but by degrees I gained a clear conception of my miseries and situation and was then released from my prison. For they had called me mad, and during many months, as I understood, a solitary cell had been my habitation.

Liberty, however, had been a useless gift to me, had I not, as I awakened to reason, at the same time awakened to revenge. As the memory of past misfortunes pressed upon me, I began to reflect on their cause – the monster whom I had created, the miserable daemon whom I had sent abroad into the world for my destruction. I was possessed by a maddening rage when I thought of him, and desired and ardently prayed that I might have him within my grasp to wreak a great and signal revenge on his cursed head.

Nor did my hate long confine itself to useless wishes; I began to reflect on the best means of securing him; and for this purpose, about a month after my release, I repaired[2] to a criminal judge in the town and told him that I had an accusation to make, that I knew the

1 spring: (here) power, force **2** repair to: (here) go to

destroyer of my family, and that I required him to exert his whole authority for the apprehension of the murderer.

The magistrate listened to me with attention and kindness. 'Be assured, sir,' said he, 'no pains or exertions on my part shall be spared to discover the villain.'

'I thank you,' replied I; 'listen, therefore, to the deposition that I have to make. It is indeed a tale so strange that I should fear you would not credit it were there not something in truth which, however wonderful, forces conviction. The story is too connected to be mistaken for a dream, and I have no motive for falsehood.' My manner as I thus addressed him was impressive but calm; I had formed in my own heart a resolution to pursue my destroyer to death, and this purpose quieted my agony and for an interval reconciled[1] me to life. I now related my history briefly but with firmness and precision, marking the dates with accuracy and never deviating[2] into invective[3] or exclamation.

The magistrate appeared at first perfectly incredulous, but as I continued he became more attentive and interested; I saw him sometimes shudder with horror; at others a lively surprise, unmingled with disbelief, was painted on his countenance.

When I had concluded my narration I said, 'This is the being whom I accuse and for whose seizure[4] and punishment I call upon you to exert your whole power. It is your duty as a magistrate, and I believe and hope that your feelings as a man will not revolt from the execution of those functions on this occasion.'

This address[5] caused a considerable change in the physiognomy of my own auditor[6]. He had heard my story with that half kind of belief that is given to a tale of spirits and supernatural events; but when he was called upon to act officially in consequence, the whole tide of his incredulity returned. He, however, answered mildly, 'I would willingly afford you every aid in your pursuit, but the crea-

1 reconcile sb. to sth./sb.: re-establish harmony between sb. and sth./sb.
2 deviate: wander off **3** invective (n): insults and swearing **4** seizure: (here) arrest **5** address (n): (here) appeal **6** auditor: listener

ture of whom you speak appears to have powers which would put all my exertions to defiance[1]. Who can follow an animal which can traverse the sea of ice and inhabit caves and dens[2] where no man would venture to intrude? Besides, some months have elapsed since the commission of his crimes, and no one can conjecture to what place he has wandered or what region he may now inhabit.'

'I do not doubt that he hovers[3] near the spot which I inhabit, and if he has indeed taken refuge in the Alps, he may be hunted like the chamois and destroyed as a beast of prey[4]. But I perceive your thoughts; you do not credit my narrative and do not intend to pursue my enemy with the punishment which is his desert[5].'

As I spoke, rage sparkled in my eyes; the magistrate was intimidated[6]: – 'You are mistaken,' said he. 'I will exert myself, and if it is in my power to seize the monster, be assured that he shall suffer punishment proportionate to his crimes. But I fear, from what you have yourself described to be his properties[7], that this will prove impracticable; and thus, while every proper[8] measure is pursued, you should make up your mind to disappointment.'

'That cannot be; but all that I can say will be of little avail. My revenge is of no moment to you; yet, while I allow[9] it to be a vice, I confess that it is the devouring and only passion of my soul. My rage is unspeakable when I reflect that the murderer, whom I have turned loose upon society, still exists. You refuse my just demand; I have but one resource, and I devote myself, either in my life or death, to his destruction.'

I trembled with excess of agitation as I said this; there was a frenzy in my manner, and something, I doubt not, of that haughty[10] fierceness[11] which the martyrs of old[12] are said to have possessed. But

1 put sth. to defiance: defy sth., challenge sth.; (here) be stronger than sth. **2** den: resting place of a wild animal **3** hover (v): (here) linger, stay **4** beast of prey: animal that hunts and eats other animals **5** desert (n): (here) what sb. deserves **6** intimidate sb.: make sb. fearful and shy **7** property: (here) characteristic **8** proper: suitable **9** allow: (here) admit **10** haughty: (here) proud, fearless **11** fierceness: (here) boldness, determination **12** of old: in the old times

to a Genevan magistrate, whose mind was occupied by far other ideas than those of devotion[1] and heroism, this elevation[2] of mind had much the appearance of madness. He endeavoured to soothe me as a nurse does a child and reverted to my tale as the effects of delirium.

'Man,' I cried, 'how ignorant art thou in thy pride of wisdom! Cease; you know not what it is you say.'

I broke[3] from the house angry and disturbed and retired to meditate on some other mode of action.

1 devotion: passion **2** elevation: inspiration (by a noble cause) **3** break from sth.: rush out of sth.

Chapter 24

My present situation was one in which all voluntary thought was swallowed up and lost. I was hurried away by fury; revenge alone endowed me with strength and composure; it moulded my feelings and allowed me to be calculating and calm at periods when otherwise delirium or death would have been my portion.

My first resolution was to quit Geneva forever; my country, which, when I was happy and beloved, was dear to me, now, in my adversity, became hateful. I provided myself with a sum of money, together with a few jewels which had belonged to my mother, and departed.

And now my wanderings began which are to cease but with life[1]. I have traversed a vast portion of the earth and have endured all the hardships which travellers in deserts and barbarous countries are wont[2] to meet. How I have lived I hardly know; many times have I stretched my failing limbs upon the sandy plain and prayed for death. But revenge kept me alive; I dared not die and leave my adversary in being.

When I quitted Geneva my first labour was to gain some clue by which I might trace the steps of my fiendish enemy. But my plan was unsettled[3], and I wandered many hours round the confines of the town, uncertain what path I should pursue. As night approached I found myself at the entrance of the cemetery where William, Elizabeth, and my father reposed. I entered it and approached the tomb which marked their graves. Everything was silent except the leaves of the trees, which were gently agitated by the wind; the night was nearly dark, and the scene would have been solemn and affecting[4] even to an uninterested observer. The spirits of the departed

1 which are to cease but with life: which only death will end **2** be wont to do sth.: be used to do sth. **3** unsettled (adj): not fixed **4** affecting: touching

seemed to flit around and to cast a shadow, which was felt but not seen, around the head of the mourner.

The deep grief which this scene had at first excited quickly gave way to rage and despair. They were dead, and I lived; their murderer also lived, and to destroy him I must drag[1] out my weary existence. I knelt on the grass and kissed the earth and with quivering lips exclaimed, 'By the sacred earth on which I kneel, by the shades that wander near me, by the deep and eternal grief that I feel, I swear; and by thee, O Night, and the spirits that preside[2] over thee, to pursue the daemon who caused this misery, until he or I shall perish in mortal conflict. For this purpose I will preserve my life; to execute this dear revenge will I again behold the sun and tread the green herbage of earth, which otherwise should vanish from my eyes forever. And I call on you, spirits of the dead, and on you, wandering ministers of vengeance[3], to aid and conduct me in my work. Let the cursed and hellish monster drink deep of agony; let him feel the despair that now torments me.'

I had begun my adjuration[4] with solemnity and an awe which almost assured me that the shades of my murdered friends heard and approved my devotion, but the furies possessed me as I concluded, and rage choked my utterance.

I was answered through the stillness of night by a loud and fiendish laugh. It rang on my ears long and heavily; the mountains re-echoed it, and I felt as if all hell surrounded me with mockery and laughter. Surely in that moment I should have been possessed by frenzy and have destroyed my miserable existence but that my vow was heard and that I was reserved for vengeance[5]. The laughter died away, when a well-known and abhorred voice, apparently close to my ear, addressed me in an audible whisper, 'I am satisfied, miserable wretch! You have determined to live, and I am satisfied.'

1 drag sth. out: make sth. longer than necessary **2** preside over sth./sb.: have control over sth./sb. **3** ministers of vengeance: those who take revenge; reference to the furies *(Furien)* of Greek mythology **4** adjuration: prayer-like appeal **5** but that my … for vengeance: had my vow not been heard and had I not been kept alive to take revenge

I darted towards the spot from which the sound proceeded, but the devil eluded my grasp. Suddenly the broad disk of the moon arose and shone full upon his ghastly and distorted shape as he fled with more than mortal speed.

I pursued him, and for many months this has been my task. Guided by a slight clue, I followed the windings of the Rhone, but vainly. The blue Mediterranean appeared, and by a strange chance, I saw the fiend enter by night and hide himself in a vessel bound for the Black Sea[1]. I took my passage in the same ship, but he escaped, I know not how.

Amidst the wilds of Tartary[2] and Russia, although he still evaded me, I have ever followed in his track. Sometimes the peasants, scared by this horrid apparition, informed me of his path; sometimes he himself, who feared that if I lost all trace of him I should despair and die, left some mark to guide me. The snows descended on my head, and I saw the print of his huge step on the white plain. To you first entering on life, to whom care is new and agony unknown, how can you understand what I have felt and still feel? Cold, want, and fatigue were the least pains which I was destined to endure; I was cursed by some devil and carried about with me my eternal hell; yet still a spirit of good followed and directed my steps and when I most murmured[3] would suddenly extricate[4] me from seemingly insurmountable difficulties. Sometimes, when nature[5], overcome by hunger, sank under the exhaustion, a repast[6] was prepared for me in the desert that restored and inspirited me. The fare was, indeed, coarse, such as the peasants of the country ate, but I will not doubt that it was set there by the spirits that I had invoked to aid me. Often, when all was dry, the heavens cloudless, and I was parched by thirst, a slight cloud would bedim[7] the sky, shed the few drops that revived me, and vanish.

1 Black Sea: inland sea between southeast Europe and Asia **2** Tartary: now obsolete term for a vaguely defined area stretching from eastern Europe to the coast of the Asian Pacific, inhabited by the 'Tartars' **3** murmur: (here) complain **4** extricate sb. from sth.: free sb. from sth. **5** nature: (here) my strength **6** repast: meal **7** bedim sth.: darken sth.

I followed, when I could, the courses of the rivers; but the daemon generally avoided these, as it was here that the population of the country chiefly collected. In other places human beings were seldom seen, and I generally subsisted on the wild animals that crossed my path. I had money with me and gained the friendship of the villagers by distributing it; or I brought with me some food that I had killed, which, after taking a small part, I always presented to those who had provided me with fire and utensils for cooking.

My life, as it passed thus, was indeed hateful to me, and it was during sleep alone that I could taste joy. O blessed sleep! Often, when most miserable, I sank to repose, and my dreams lulled me even to rapture. The spirits that guarded me had provided these moments, or rather hours, of happiness that I might retain strength to fulfil my pilgrimage. Deprived of this respite, I should have sunk under my hardships. During the day I was sustained and inspirited by the hope of night, for in sleep I saw my friends, my wife, and my beloved country; again I saw the benevolent countenance of my father, heard the silver tones of my Elizabeth's voice, and beheld Clerval enjoying health and youth. Often, when wearied by a toilsome[1] march, I persuaded myself that I was dreaming until night should come and that I should then enjoy reality in the arms of my dearest friends. What agonising fondness did I feel for them! How did I cling to their dear forms, as sometimes they haunted even my waking hours, and persuade myself that they still lived! At such moments vengeance, that burned within me, died in my heart, and I pursued my path towards the destruction of the daemon more as a task enjoined by heaven, as the mechanical impulse of some power of which I was unconscious, than as the ardent desire of my soul.

What his feelings were whom I pursued I cannot know. Sometimes, indeed, he left marks in writing on the barks of the trees or cut in stone that guided me and instigated my fury. 'My reign is not yet over' – these words were legible[2] in one of these inscriptions – 'you live, and my power is complete. Follow me; I seek the everlast-

1 toilsome: difficult and exhausting **2** legible: readable

ing ices of the north, where you will feel the misery of cold and frost, to which I am impassive[1]. You will find near this place, if you follow not too tardily[2], a dead hare[3]; eat and be refreshed. Come on, my enemy; we have yet to wrestle for our lives, but many hard and miserable hours must you endure until that period shall arrive.'

Scoffing[4] devil! Again do I vow vengeance; again do I devote thee, miserable fiend, to torture and death. Never will I give up my search until he or I perish; and then with what ecstasy shall I join my Elizabeth and my departed friends, who even now prepare for me the reward of my tedious toil and horrible pilgrimage!

As I still pursued my journey to the northward, the snows thickened and the cold increased in a degree almost too severe to support. The peasants were shut up in their hovels, and only a few of the most hardy ventured forth to seize the animals whom starvation had forced from their hiding-places to seek for prey. The rivers were covered with ice, and no fish could be procured; and thus I was cut off from my chief article of maintenance[5].

The triumph of my enemy increased with the difficulty of my labours. One inscription that he left was in these words: 'Prepare! Your toils only begin; wrap yourself in furs and provide food, for we shall soon enter upon a journey where your sufferings will satisfy my everlasting hatred.'

My courage and perseverance were invigorated[6] by these scoffing words; I resolved not to fail in my purpose, and calling on heaven to support me, I continued with unabated[7] fervour to traverse immense deserts, until the ocean appeared at a distance and formed the utmost boundary of the horizon. Oh! how unlike it was to the blue seasons of the south! Covered with ice, it was only to be distinguished from land by its superior wildness and ruggedness. The Greeks wept for joy when they beheld the Mediterranean

1 impassive: (here) insensitive **2** tardily: belated **3** hare: *(Feld-)Hase* **4** scoff (v): express contempt and mockery **5** article of maintenance: (here) source of nourishment **6** invigorate sb./sth.: give energy to sb./sth. **7** unabated: unreduced

from the hills of Asia, and hailed with rapture the boundary[1] of their toils. I did not weep, but I knelt down and with a full heart thanked my guiding spirit for conducting me in safety to the place where I hoped, notwithstanding my adversary's gibe[2], to meet and grapple with him.

Some weeks before this period I had procured a sledge[3] and dogs and thus traversed the snows with inconceivable speed. I know not whether the fiend possessed the same advantages, but I found that, as before I had daily lost ground in the pursuit, I now gained[4] on him, so much so that when I first saw the ocean he was but one day's journey in advance, and I hoped to intercept him before he should reach the beach. With new courage, therefore, I pressed on, and in two days arrived at a wretched hamlet[5] on the seashore. I inquired of the inhabitants concerning the fiend and gained accurate information. A gigantic monster, they said, had arrived the night before, armed with a gun and many pistols, putting to flight the inhabitants of a solitary cottage through fear of his terrific appearance. He had carried off their store of winter food, and placing it in a sledge, to draw which he had seized on a numerous drove[6] of trained dogs, he had harnessed[7] them, and the same night, to the joy of the horror-struck villagers, had pursued his journey across the sea in a direction that led to no land; and they conjectured that he must speedily be destroyed by the breaking of the ice or frozen by the eternal frosts.

On hearing this information I suffered a temporary access[8] of despair. He had escaped me, and I must commence a destructive and almost endless journey across the mountainous ices of the ocean, amidst cold that few of the inhabitants could long endure and which I, the native of a genial and sunny climate, could not hope to survive. Yet at the idea that the fiend should live and be

1 boundary: (here) end **2** gibe: mockery **3** sledge: *Schlitten* **4** gain on sb.: get clother to sb. **5** hamlet: small village **6** drove (n): *Rudel* **7** harness (v): put on strong leather bands around an animal so that it can pull a vehicle **8** access (n): (here) fit

triumphant, my rage and vengeance returned, and like a mighty tide, overwhelmed every other feeling. After a slight repose, during which the spirits of the dead hovered round and instigated me to toil and revenge, I prepared for my journey.

I exchanged my land-sledge for one fashioned[1] for the inequalities of the frozen ocean, and purchasing a plentiful stock of provisions[2], I departed from land.

I cannot guess how many days have passed since then, but I have endured misery which nothing but the eternal sentiment of a just retribution[3] burning within my heart could have enabled me to support. Immense and rugged mountains of ice often barred up my passage, and I often heard the thunder of the ground sea, which threatened my destruction. But again the frost came and made the paths of the sea secure.

By the quantity of provision which I had consumed, I should guess that I had passed three weeks in this journey; and the continual protraction[4] of hope, returning back upon the heart, often wrung[5] bitter drops of despondency and grief from my eyes. Despair had indeed almost secured her prey, and I should soon have sunk beneath this misery. Once, after the poor animals that conveyed me had with incredible toil gained the summit of a sloping ice mountain, and one, sinking under his fatigue, died, I viewed the expanse before me with anguish, when suddenly my eye caught a dark speck upon the dusky plain. I strained my sight[6] to discover what it could be and uttered a wild cry of ecstasy when I distinguished a sledge and the distorted proportions of a well-known form within. Oh! with what a burning gush did hope revisit my heart! Warm tears filled my eyes, which I hastily wiped away, that they might not intercept the view I had of the daemon; but still my sight was dimmed by

1 fashion sth. for sth.: make sth. suitable for sth. **2** provision: food supply **3** retribution: revenge **4** protraction: *Hinauszögern* **5** wring sth. from sth. (wrung – wrung): (here) extract sth. from sth. **6** strain your sight: make an effort to see

the burning drops, until, giving way to the emotions that oppressed me, I wept aloud.

But this was not the time for delay; I disencumbered[1] the dogs of their dead companion, gave them a plentiful portion of food, and after an hour's rest, which was absolutely necessary, and yet which was bitterly irksome to me, I continued my route. The sledge was still visible, nor did I again lose sight of it except at the moments when for a short time some ice-rock concealed it with its intervening[2] crags[3]. I indeed perceptibly gained on it, and when, after nearly two days' journey, I beheld my enemy at no more than a mile distant, my heart bounded within me.

But now, when I appeared almost within grasp of my foe, my hopes were suddenly extinguished, and I lost all trace of him more utterly than I had ever done before. A ground sea was heard; the thunder of its progress, as the waters rolled and swelled beneath me, became every moment more ominous and terrific. I pressed on, but in vain. The wind arose; the sea roared; and, as with the mighty shock of an earthquake, it split and cracked with a tremendous and overwhelming sound. The work was soon finished; in a few minutes a tumultuous sea rolled between me and my enemy, and I was left drifting on a scattered piece of ice that was continually lessening and thus preparing for me a hideous death. In this manner many appalling hours passed; several of my dogs died, and I myself was about to sink under the accumulation of distress when I saw your vessel riding at anchor and holding forth to me hopes of succour and life. I had no conception that vessels ever came so far north and was astounded at the sight. I quickly destroyed part of my sledge to construct oars, and by these means was enabled, with infinite fatigue, to move my ice raft in the direction of your ship. I had determined, if you were going southwards, still to trust myself to the mercy of the seas rather than abandon my purpose. I hoped to induce you to grant me a boat with which I could pursue my enemy. But your

1 disencumber sth./sb.: unburden sth./sb. **2** intervene: (here) block the sight
3 crag: *(hier) Zacke*

direction was northwards. You took me on board when my vigour was exhausted, and I should soon have sunk under my multiplied hardships into a death which I still dread, for my task is unfulfilled.

Oh! when will my guiding spirit, in conducting me to the daemon, allow me the rest I so much desire; or must I die, and he yet live? If I do, swear to me, Walton, that he shall not escape, that you will seek him and satisfy my vengeance in his death. And do I dare to ask of you to undertake my pilgrimage, to endure the hardships that I have undergone? No; I am not so selfish. Yet, when I am dead, if he should appear, if the ministers of vengeance should conduct him to you, swear that he shall not live – swear that he shall not triumph over my accumulated woes and survive to add to the list of his dark crimes. He is eloquent and persuasive, and once his words had even power over my heart; but trust him not. His soul is as hellish as his form, full of treachery and fiendlike malice. Hear him not; call on the manes[1] of William, Justine, Clerval, Elizabeth, my father, and of the wretched Victor, and thrust your sword into his heart. I will hover near and direct the steel aright[2].

Walton, *in continuation.*

August 26th, 17–.

You have read this strange and terrific story, Margaret; and do you not feel your blood congeal[3] with horror, like that which even now curdles mine? Sometimes, seized with sudden agony, he could not continue his tale; at others, his voice broken, yet piercing, uttered with difficulty the words so replete with anguish. His fine and lovely eyes were now lighted up with indignation, now subdued to downcast[4] sorrow and quenched in infinite wretchedness. Sometimes he commanded his countenance and tones and related the most horrible incidents with a tranquil voice, suppressing every mark of agitation; then, like a volcano bursting forth, his face would

1 manes (pl): spirits of the dead **2** aright: correctly **3** congeal [kənˈdʒiːl]: harden **4** downcast: miserable

suddenly change to an expression of the wildest rage as he shrieked out imprecations[1] on his persecutor.

His tale is connected and told with an appearance of the simplest truth, yet I own to you that the letters of Felix and Safie, which he showed me, and the apparition of the monster seen from our ship, brought to me a greater conviction of the truth of his narrative than his asseverations[2], however earnest and connected. Such a monster has, then, really existence! I cannot doubt it, yet I am lost in surprise and admiration. Sometimes I endeavoured to gain from Frankenstein the particulars of his creature's formation, but on this point he was impenetrable.

'Are you mad, my friend?' said he. 'Or whither does your senseless curiosity lead you? Would you also create for yourself and the world a demoniacal enemy? Peace, peace! Learn my miseries and do not seek to increase your own.'

Frankenstein discovered that I made notes concerning his history; he asked to see them and then himself corrected and augmented them in many places, but principally in giving the life and spirit to the conversations he held with his enemy. 'Since you have preserved my narration,' said he, 'I would[3] not that a mutilated[4] one should go down to posterity.'

Thus has a week passed away, while I have listened to the strangest tale that ever imagination formed. My thoughts and every feeling of my soul have been drunk up by the interest for my guest which this tale and his own elevated and gentle manners have created. I wish to soothe him, yet can I counsel[5] one so infinitely miserable, so destitute[6] of every hope of consolation, to live? Oh, no! The only joy that he can now know will be when he composes his shattered spirit to peace and death. Yet he enjoys one comfort, the offspring of solitude and delirium; he believes that when in dreams he holds

1 imprecation: curse **2** asseveration: affirmation **3** would (old use): want **4** mutilated: crippled **5** counsel sb. to do sth.: advise sb. to do th. **6** destitute of sth.: without sth.

converse[1] with his friends and derives from that communion consolation for his miseries or excitements to his vengeance, that they are not the creations of his fancy, but the beings themselves who visit him from the regions of a remote world. This faith gives a solemnity to his reveries that render them to me almost as imposing[2] and interesting as truth.

Our conversations are not always confined to his own history and misfortunes. On every point of general literature he displays unbounded knowledge and a quick and piercing apprehension. His eloquence is forcible[3] and touching; nor can I hear him, when he relates a pathetic[4] incident or endeavours to move the passions of pity or love, without tears. What a glorious creature must he have been in the days of his prosperity, when he is thus noble and godlike in ruin! He seems to feel his own worth and the greatness of his fall.

'When younger,' said he, 'I believed myself destined for some great enterprise. My feelings are profound, but I possessed a coolness of judgment that fitted me for illustrious achievements. This sentiment of the worth of my nature supported me when others would have been oppressed, for I deemed it criminal to throw away in useless grief those talents that might be useful to my fellow creatures. When I reflected on the work I had completed, no less a one than the creation of a sensitive and rational animal, I could not rank myself with the herd of common projectors[5]. But this thought, which supported me in the commencement of my career, now serves only to plunge me lower in the dust. All my speculations and hopes are as nothing, and like the archangel who aspired to omnipotence[6], I am chained in an eternal hell. My imagination was vivid, yet my powers of analysis and application were intense; by the union of these qualities I conceived the idea and executed the creation of a man. Even now I cannot recollect without passion my reveries while the work

1 hold converse: talk **2** imposing: impressive, fascinating **3** forcible: convincing **4** pathetic: pitiful **5** projector: sb. who makes unrealistic plans
6 archangel who aspired to omnipotence: reference to satan in Milton's *Paradise Lost*

was incomplete. I trod[1] heaven in my thoughts, now exulting in my powers, now burning with the idea of their effects. From my infancy I was imbued with high hopes and a lofty ambition; but how am I sunk! Oh! my friend, if you had known me as I once was, you would not recognise me in this state of degradation. Despondency rarely visited my heart; a high destiny seemed to bear me on, until I fell, never, never again to rise.'

Must I then lose this admirable being? I have longed for a friend; I have sought one who would sympathise with and love me. Behold, on these desert seas I have found such a one, but I fear I have gained him only to know his value and lose him. I would reconcile him to life, but he repulses[2] the idea.

'I thank you, Walton,' he said, 'for your kind intentions towards so miserable a wretch; but when you speak of new ties and fresh affections, think you that any can replace those who are gone? Can any man be to me as Clerval was, or any woman another Elizabeth? Even where the affections are not strongly moved by any superior excellence, the companions of our childhood always possess a certain power over our minds which hardly any later friend can obtain. They know our infantine[3] dispositions, which, however they may be afterwards modified, are never eradicated; and they can judge of our actions with more certain conclusions as to the integrity of our motives. A sister or a brother can never, unless indeed such symptoms have been shown early, suspect the other of fraud[4] or false dealing, when another friend, however strongly he may be attached, may, in spite of himself, be contemplated with suspicion. But I enjoyed friends, dear not only through habit and association, but from their own merits; and wherever I am, the soothing voice of my Elizabeth and the conversation of Clerval will be ever whispered in my ear. They are dead, and but one feeling in such a solitude can persuade me to preserve my life. If I were engaged in any high

1 tread [tred] (trod – trod): walk **2** repulse sth.: reject sth. **3** infantine: childish
4 fraud: deceit, trickery

undertaking or design, fraught[1] with extensive utility to my fellow creatures, then could I live to fulfil it. But such is not my destiny; I must pursue and destroy the being to whom I gave existence; then my lot on earth will be fulfilled and I may die.'

September 2nd.

MY BELOVED SISTER,

I write to you, encompassed by peril and ignorant whether I am ever doomed to see again dear England and the dearer friends that inhabit it. I am surrounded by mountains of ice which admit[2] of no escape and threaten every moment to crush my vessel. The brave fellows whom I have persuaded to be my companions look towards me for aid, but I have none to bestow. There is something terribly appalling in our situation, yet my courage and hopes do not desert me. Yet it is terrible to reflect that the lives of all these men are endangered through me. If we are lost, my mad schemes are the cause.

And what, Margaret, will be the state of your mind? You will not hear of my destruction, and you will anxiously await my return. Years will pass, and you will have visitings of despair and yet be tortured by hope. Oh! my beloved sister, the sickening failing of your heart-felt expectations is, in prospect[3], more terrible to me than my own death. But you have a husband and lovely children; you may be happy. Heaven bless you and make you so!

My unfortunate guest regards me with the tenderest compassion. He endeavours to fill me with hope and talks as if life were a possession which he valued. He reminds me how often the same accidents have happened to other navigators who have attempted this sea, and in spite of myself, he fills me with cheerful auguries[4]. Even the sailors feel the power of his eloquence; when he speaks, they no longer despair; he rouses their energies, and while they hear his voice they believe these vast mountains of ice are molehills

1 fraught with sth.: full of sth. **2** admit of sth.: make sth. possible **3** prospect (n): (here) vision of future events **4** augury: prediction, prophecy

which will vanish before the resolutions of man. These feelings are transitory; each day of expectation delayed fills them with fear, and I almost dread a mutiny[1] caused by this despair.

September 5th.

A scene has just passed of such uncommon interest that, although it is highly probable that these papers may never reach you, yet I cannot forbear recording it.

We are still surrounded by mountains of ice, still in imminent danger of being crushed in their conflict. The cold is excessive, and many of my unfortunate comrades have already found a grave amidst this scene of desolation. Frankenstein has daily declined in health; a feverish fire still glimmers in his eyes, but he is exhausted, and when suddenly roused to any exertion, he speedily sinks again into apparent lifelessness.

I mentioned in my last letter the fears I entertained of a mutiny. This morning, as I sat watching the wan[2] countenance of my friend – his eyes half closed and his limbs hanging listlessly – I was roused by half a dozen of the sailors, who demanded admission into the cabin. They entered, and their leader addressed me. He told me that he and his companions had been chosen by the other sailors to come in deputation to me to make me a requisition which, in justice, I could not refuse. We were immured in ice and should probably never escape, but they feared that if, as was possible, the ice should dissipate and a free passage be opened, I should be rash enough to continue my voyage and lead them into fresh dangers, after they might happily have surmounted this. They insisted, therefore, that I should engage with a solemn promise that if the vessel should be freed I would instantly direct my course southwards.

This speech troubled me. I had not despaired, nor had I yet conceived the idea of returning if set free. Yet could I, in justice, or even in possibility, refuse this demand? I hesitated before I answered, when Frankenstein, who had at first been silent, and indeed appeared

1 mutiny: rebellion **2** wan [wɒn]: pale

hardly to have force enough to attend, now roused himself; his eyes sparkled, and his cheeks flushed with momentary vigour. Turning towards the men, he said –

'What do you mean? What do you demand of your captain? Are you, then, so easily turned from your design? Did you not call this a glorious expedition? And wherefore was it glorious? Not because the way was smooth and placid as a southern sea, but because it was full of dangers and terror, because at every new incident your fortitude was to be called forth and your courage exhibited, because danger and death surrounded it, and these you were to brave and overcome. For this was it a glorious, for this was it an honourable undertaking. You were hereafter to be hailed as the benefactors of your species, your names adored as belonging to brave men who encountered death for honour and the benefit of mankind. And now, behold, with the first imagination of danger, or, if you will, the first mighty and terrific trial of your courage, you shrink away and are content to be handed[1] down as men who had not strength enough to endure cold and peril; and so, poor souls, they were chilly and returned to their warm firesides. Why, that requires not this preparation; ye need not have come thus far and dragged your captain to the shame of a defeat merely to prove yourselves cowards. Oh! be men, or be more than men. Be steady[2] to your purposes and firm as a rock. This ice is not made of such stuff as your hearts may be; it is mutable and cannot withstand[3] you if you say that it shall not. Do not return to your families with the stigma of disgrace marked on your brows. Return as heroes who have fought and conquered and who know not what it is to turn their backs on the foe.'

He spoke this with a voice so modulated[4] to the different feelings expressed in his speech, with an eye so full of lofty design and heroism, that can you wonder that these men were moved? They looked at one another and were unable to reply. I spoke; I told them to retire

1 be handed down as sth./sb.: be remembered in history as sth./sb. **2** steady to sth.: faithful to sth. **3** withstand sth./sb.: resist sth./sb. **4** modulated to sth.: adapted to sth.

and consider of what had been said, that I would not lead them farther north if they strenuously[1] desired the contrary, but that I hoped that, with reflection, their courage would return.

They retired and I turned towards my friend, but he was sunk in languor and almost deprived of life.

How all this will terminate, I know not, but I had rather die than return shamefully, my purpose unfulfilled. Yet I fear such will be my fate; the men, unsupported by ideas of glory and honour, can never willingly continue to endure their present hardships.

September 7th.

The die is cast[2]; I have consented to return if we are not destroyed. Thus are my hopes blasted by cowardice and indecision; I come back ignorant and disappointed. It requires more philosophy than I possess to bear this injustice with patience.

September 12th.

It is past; I am returning to England. I have lost my hopes of utility and glory; I have lost my friend. But I will endeavour to detail these bitter circumstances to you, my dear sister; and while I am wafted towards England and towards you, I will not despond.

September 9th, the ice began to move, and roarings like thunder were heard at a distance as the islands split and cracked in every direction. We were in the most imminent[3] peril, but as we could only remain passive, my chief attention was occupied by my unfortunate guest whose illness increased in such a degree that he was entirely confined to his bed. The ice cracked behind us and was driven with force towards the north; a breeze sprang from the west, and on the 11th the passage towards the south became perfectly free. When the sailors saw this and that their return to their native country was apparently assured, a shout of tumultuous joy broke from them, loud and long-continued. Frankenstein, who was doz-

1 strenuously: energetically **2** The die is cast: *Der Würfel ist gefallen.*
3 imminent: immediate

ing, awoke and asked the cause of the tumult. 'They shout,' I said, 'because they will soon return to England.'

'Do you, then, really return?'

'Alas! yes; I cannot withstand their demands. I cannot lead them unwillingly to danger, and I must return.'

'Do so, if you will; but I will not. You may give up your purpose, but mine is assigned to me by heaven, and I dare not. I am weak, but surely the spirits who assist my vengeance will endow me with sufficient strength.' Saying this, he endeavoured to spring from the bed, but the exertion was too great for him; he fell back and fainted.

It was long before he was restored, and I often thought that life was entirely extinct. At length he opened his eyes; he breathed with difficulty and was unable to speak. The surgeon[1] gave him a composing draught and ordered us to leave him undisturbed. In the mean time he told me that my friend had certainly not many hours to live.

His sentence was pronounced, and I could only grieve[2] and be patient. I sat by his bed, watching him; his eyes were closed, and I thought he slept; but presently he called to me in a feeble voice, and bidding me come near, said,

'Alas! the strength I relied on is gone; I feel that I shall soon die, and he, my enemy and persecutor, may still be in being. Think not, Walton, that in the last moments of my existence I feel that burning hatred and ardent desire of revenge I once expressed; but I feel myself justified in desiring the death of my adversary. During these last days I have been occupied in examining my past conduct; nor do I find it blamable. In a fit of enthusiastic madness I created a rational creature and was bound towards him to assure, as far as was in my power, his happiness and well-being. This was my duty, but there was another still paramount[3] to that. My duties towards the beings of my own species had greater claims to my attention because they included a greater proportion of happiness or misery. Urged by this view, I refused, and I did right in refusing, to create

1 surgeon: doctor **2** grieve: feel deep sadness, mourn **3** paramount to sth.: (here) more important than sth.

a companion for the first creature. He showed unparalleled malignity and selfishness in evil; he destroyed my friends; he devoted to destruction beings who possessed exquisite sensations, happiness, and wisdom; nor do I know where this thirst for vengeance may end. Miserable himself that he may render no other wretched, he ought to die. The task of his destruction was mine, but I have failed. When actuated[1] by selfish and vicious motives, I asked you to undertake my unfinished work, and I renew this request now, when I am only induced by reason and virtue.

'Yet I cannot ask you to renounce[2] your country and friends to fulfil this task; and now that you are returning to England, you will have little chance of meeting with him. But the consideration of these points, and the well balancing of what you may esteem your duties, I leave to you; my judgment and ideas are already disturbed by the near approach of death. I dare not ask you to do what I think right, for I may still be misled by passion.

'That he should live to be an instrument of mischief disturbs me; in other respects, this hour, when I momentarily expect my release, is the only happy one which I have enjoyed for several years. The forms of the beloved dead flit before me, and I hasten to their arms. Farewell, Walton! Seek happiness in tranquillity and avoid ambition, even if it be only the apparently innocent one of distinguishing[3] yourself in science and discoveries. Yet why do I say this? I have myself been blasted in these hopes, yet another may succeed.'

His voice became fainter as he spoke, and at length, exhausted by his effort, he sank into silence. About half an hour afterwards he attempted again to speak but was unable; he pressed my hand feebly, and his eyes closed forever, while the irradiation of a gentle smile passed away from his lips.

Margaret, what comment can I make on the untimely extinction of this glorious spirit? What can I say that will enable you to understand the depth of my sorrow? All that I should express would be

1 actuate: motivate **2** renounce sth.: give sth. up **3** distinguish yourself: stand out, make a name for youself

inadequate and feeble. My tears flow; my mind is overshadowed by a cloud of disappointment. But I journey towards England, and I may there find consolation.

I am interrupted. What do these sounds portend[1]? It is midnight; the breeze blows fairly, and the watch on deck scarcely stir. Again there is a sound as of a human voice, but hoarser; it comes from the cabin where the remains of Frankenstein still lie. I must arise and examine. Good night, my sister.

Great God! what a scene has just taken place! I am yet dizzy with the remembrance of it. I hardly know whether I shall have the power to detail it; yet the tale which I have recorded would be incomplete without this final and wonderful catastrophe.

I entered the cabin where lay the remains of my ill-fated[2] and admirable friend. Over him hung a form which I cannot find words to describe – gigantic in stature, yet uncouth and distorted in its proportions. As he hung over the coffin, his face was concealed by long locks of ragged hair; but one vast hand was extended, in colour and apparent texture[3] like that of a mummy. When he heard the sound of my approach, he ceased to utter exclamations of grief and horror and sprung towards the window. Never did I behold a vision so horrible as his face, of such loathsome yet appalling hideousness. I shut my eyes involuntarily and endeavoured to recollect what were my duties with regard to this destroyer. I called on him to stay.

He paused, looking on me with wonder, and again turning towards the lifeless form of his creator, he seemed to forget my presence, and every feature and gesture seemed instigated by the wildest rage of some uncontrollable passion.

'That is also my victim!' he exclaimed. 'In his murder my crimes are consummated; the miserable series of my being is wound[4] to its close! Oh, Frankenstein! Generous and self-devoted[5] being! What does it avail that I now ask thee to pardon me? I, who irretrievably

1 portend [pɔːˈtend]: indicate **2** ill-fated: unlucky **3** texture: surface structure
4 wind to a close (wound – wound): come to an end **5** self-devoted: selfless

destroyed thee by destroying all thou lovedst. Alas! he is cold, he cannot answer me.'

His voice seemed suffocated, and my first impulses, which had suggested to me the duty of obeying the dying request of my friend in destroying his enemy, were now suspended by a mixture of curiosity and compassion. I approached this tremendous being; I dared not again raise my eyes to his face, there was something so scaring and unearthly in his ugliness. I attempted to speak, but the words died away on my lips. The monster continued to utter wild and incoherent self-reproaches. At length I gathered resolution to address him in a pause of the tempest of his passion: 'Your repentance,' I said, 'is now superfluous[1]. If you had listened to the voice of conscience and heeded the stings of remorse before you had urged your diabolical vengeance to this extremity, Frankenstein would yet have lived.'

'And do you dream?' said the daemon. 'Do you think that I was then dead to agony and remorse? – He,' he continued, pointing to the corpse, 'he suffered not in the consummation of the deed – oh! not the ten-thousandth portion of the anguish that was mine during the lingering[2] detail of its execution. A frightful selfishness hurried me on, while my heart was poisoned with remorse. Think you that the groans of Clerval were music to my ears? My heart was fashioned to be susceptible of love and sympathy, and when wrenched[3] by misery to vice and hatred, it did not endure the violence of the change without torture such as you cannot even imagine.

'After the murder of Clerval I returned to Switzerland, heartbroken and overcome. I pitied Frankenstein; my pity amounted to horror; I abhorred myself. But when I discovered that he, the author at once of my existence and of its unspeakable torments, dared to hope for happiness, that while he accumulated wretchedness and despair upon me he sought his own enjoyment in feelings and passions from the indulgence of which I was forever barred, then impo-

1 superfluous [suːˈpɜːfluəs]: not necessary, redundant **2** lingering: *(hier) schleichend* **3** wrench sth.: pull and strain sth. violently

tent[1] envy and bitter indignation filled me with an insatiable[2] thirst for vengeance. I recollected my threat and resolved that it should be accomplished. I knew that I was preparing for myself a deadly torture, but I was the slave, not the master, of an impulse which I detested yet could not disobey. Yet when she died! – nay, then I was not miserable. I had cast off all feeling, subdued all anguish, to riot in the excess of my despair. Evil thenceforth became my good. Urged thus far, I had no choice but to adapt my nature to an element which I had willingly chosen. The completion of my demoniacal design became an insatiable passion. And now it is ended; there is my last victim!'

I was at first touched by the expressions of his misery; yet, when I called to mind what Frankenstein had said of his powers of eloquence and persuasion, and when I again cast my eyes on the lifeless form of my friend, indignation was rekindled[3] within me. 'Wretch!' I said. 'it is well that you come here to whine[4] over the desolation that you have made. You throw a torch into a pile of buildings, and when they are consumed, you sit among the ruins and lament the fall. Hypocritical[5] fiend! If he whom you mourn still lived, still would he be the object, again would he become the prey, of your accursed vengeance. It is not pity that you feel; you lament only because the victim of your malignity is withdrawn from your power.'

'Oh, it is not thus – not thus,' interrupted the being; 'yet such must be the impression conveyed to you by what appears to be the purport of my actions. Yet I seek not a fellow-feeling in my misery. No sympathy may I ever find. When I first sought it, it was the love of virtue, the feelings of happiness and affection with which my whole being overflowed, that I wished to be participated. But now that virtue has become to me a shadow, and that happiness and affection are turned into bitter and loathing despair, in what should I seek for sympathy? I am content to suffer alone while my sufferings shall endure; when I die, I am well satisfied that abhorrence and oppro-

1 impotent: powerless **2** insatiable: not to be satisfied **3** rekindle: renew
4 whine over sth.: complain about sth. **5** hypocritical: *scheinheilig, heuchlerisch*

brium[1] should load my memory. Once my fancy was soothed with dreams of virtue, of fame, and of enjoyment. Once I falsely hoped to meet with beings who, pardoning my outward form, would love me for the excellent qualities which I was capable of unfolding. I was nourished with high thoughts of honour and devotion. But now crime has degraded me beneath the meanest animal. No guilt, no mischief, no malignity, no misery, can be found comparable to mine. When I run over the frightful catalogue of my sins, I cannot believe that I am the same creature whose thoughts were once filled with sublime and transcendent[2] visions of the beauty and the majesty of goodness. But it is even so; the fallen angel becomes a malignant devil. Yet even that enemy of God and man had friends and associates in his desolation; I am alone.

'You, who call Frankenstein your friend, seem to have a knowledge of my crimes and his misfortunes. But in the detail which he gave you of them he could not sum up the hours and months of misery which I endured wasting in impotent passions. For while I destroyed his hopes, I did not satisfy my own desires. They were forever ardent and craving; still I desired love and fellowship, and I was still spurned. Was there no injustice in this? Am I to be thought the only criminal, when all humankind sinned against me? Why do you not hate Felix, who drove his friend from his door with contumely[3]? Why do you not execrate the rustic who sought to destroy the saviour of his child? Nay, these are virtuous and immaculate[4] beings! I, the miserable and the abandoned, am an abortion, to be spurned at, and kicked, and trampled on. Even now my blood boils at the recollection of this injustice.

'But it is true that I am a wretch. I have murdered the lovely and the helpless; I have strangled the innocent as they slept and grasped to death his throat who never injured me or any other living thing. I have devoted[5] my creator, the select specimen of all that is wor-

1 opprobium: disgrace **2** transcendent: supernatural **3** contumely ['kɒntjʊmɪlɪ] (n): mockery, contempt **4** immaculate: faultless **5** devote sb. to sth.: consign sb. to sth., hand over sb. to sth.

thy of love and admiration among men, to misery; I have pursued him even to that irremediable[1] ruin. There he lies, white and cold in death. You hate me, but your abhorrence cannot equal that with which I regard myself. I look on the hands which executed the deed; I think on the heart in which the imagination of it was conceived and long for the moment when these hands will meet my eyes, when that imagination will haunt my thoughts no more.

'Fear not that I shall be the instrument of future mischief. My work is nearly complete. Neither yours nor any man's death is needed to consummate the series[2] of my being and accomplish that which must be done, but it requires my own. Do not think that I shall be slow to perform this sacrifice[3]. I shall quit your vessel on the ice raft which brought me thither[4] and shall seek the most northern extremity of the globe; I shall collect my funeral pile[5] and consume to ashes this miserable frame, that its remains may afford no light to any curious and unhallowed wretch who would create such another as I have been. I shall die. I shall no longer feel the agonies which now consume me or be the prey of feelings unsatisfied, yet unquenched. He is dead who called me into being; and when I shall be no more, the very remembrance of us both will speedily vanish. I shall no longer see the sun or stars or feel the winds play on my cheeks. Light, feeling, and sense will pass away; and in this condition must I find my happiness. Some years ago, when the images which this world affords first opened upon me, when I felt the cheering warmth of summer and heard the rustling of the leaves and the warbling of the birds, and these were all to me, I should have wept to die; now it is my only consolation. Polluted by crimes and torn by the bitterest remorse, where can I find rest but in death?

'Farewell! I leave you, and in you the last of humankind whom these eyes will ever behold. Farewell, Frankenstein! If thou wert yet alive and yet cherished[6] a desire of revenge against me, it would

1 irremediable: hopeless **2** series: *(hier) Lauf* **3** sacrifice (n): act of giving sth. up **4** thither: there **5** funeral pile: *Scheiterhaufen* **6** cherish sth.: (here) have sth.

be better satiated in my life than in my destruction. But it was not so; thou didst seek my extinction, that I might not cause greater wretchedness; and if yet, in some mode unknown to me, thou hadst not ceased to think and feel, thou wouldst not desire against me a vengeance greater than that which I feel. Blasted as thou wert, my agony was still superior to thine, for the bitter sting of remorse will not cease to rankle[1] in my wounds until death shall close them forever.

'But soon,' he cried with sad and solemn enthusiasm, 'I shall die, and what I now feel be no longer felt. Soon these burning miseries will be extinct. I shall ascend my funeral pile triumphantly and exult in the agony of the torturing flames. The light of that conflagration[2] will fade away; my ashes will be swept into the sea by the winds. My spirit will sleep in peace, or if it thinks, it will not surely think thus. Farewell.'

He sprung from the cabin window as he said this, upon the ice raft which lay close to the vessel. He was soon borne away by the waves and lost in darkness and distance.

1 rankle: (here) hurt **2** conflagration: great fire

Additional Texts

The Modern Prometheus *Maurice Hindle*

[W]e need look no further than the novel's subtitle – *The Modern Prometheus* — to discover *Frankenstein*'s main theme: the aspiration of modern masculinist scientists to be technically creative divinities[1]. Who was Prometheus? There are two versions of the Prometheus story, which Mary Shelley manages to combine into one. The first and most famous is that in which the Prometheus of Greek mythology, a rebellious Titan, steals fire from Olympus in order to succour and save humankind. [...] The later, Roman, elaboration of the Promethean legend rendered by Ovid (whose *Metamorphoses* she had been reading in 1815), has Prometheus as *plasticator*, a figure who *creates and manipulates* men into life, rather than 'saves' them:

> Whether with particles of heavenly fire,
> The God of Nature did his soul inspire;
> Or earth, but new divided from the sky,
> And, pliant[2], still retain'd th'ethereal[3] energy:
> Which wise Prometheus temper'd[4] into paste,
> And, mix't with living streams, the godlike image caste[5] ...
> From such rude principles our form began;
> And earth was metamorphosed into man.

Rather than take up Ovid's 'ethereal energy' speculation, Mary Shelley chose to focus on the 'particles of heavenly fire' aspect, the means whereby Prometheus quickened his clay images into life. As we know, the 'real' means by which she imagined life could be bestowed on an assembled corpse in her book was through the 'galvanizing' use of electricity. Humphry Davy, pioneer of electro-

1 divinity: god **2** pliant: able to be bent or formed **3** ethereal: heavenly, immaterial **4** temper sth.: mix sth. **5** caste sth.: form sth.

chemistry and discoverer of potassium[1] and sodium[2], was a famous experimental chemist whom Percy Shelley admired (as he did the poet-botanist Erasmus Darwin) and who had been a visitor to the Godwin household in Mary's childhood. It was books by Davy, his *Elements of Chemical Philosophy* (1812) and an earlier publication, *A Discourse, Introductory to a Course of Lectures on Chemistry* (1802), that Mary was reading in October and November 1816. The tone and content of some of Davy's 'progressive' views will repay attention, as they embody much the same message that Frankenstein was so entranced by in the momentous 'panegyric' on chemistry delivered by Professor Waldman at Ingolstadt University. Davy claims that 'science has done much for man, but it is capable of doing still more'. More specifically, Waldman feels that 'Chemistry is that branch of natural philosophy in which the greatest improvements have been and may be made' (p. 63). When he claims that the modern masters of science have acquired almost 'unlimited powers', Frankenstein's whole being is numbed as if by sudden religious conversion:

> ... soon my mind was filled with one thought, one conception, one purpose. So much has been done, exclaimed the soul of Frankenstein, – more, far more, will I achieve; treading in the steps already marked, I will pioneer a new way, explore unknown powers, and unfold to the world the deepest mysteries of creation. (p. 61)

Familiar rhetoric to watchers of Frankenstein films today, but quite new in Mary Shelley's era. The voice of the 'real' scientist, Humphry Davy, is not far behind (or rather, in front) in its enthusiasm:

> Science has ... bestowed upon [man] powers which may be called almost creative; which have enabled him to change and modify the beings surrounding him, and by his experiments

1 potassium: *Kalium* **2** sodium: *Natrium*

> to interrogate[1] nature with power, not simply as a scholar, passive and seeking only to understand her operations, but rather as a master, active with his own instruments ... who would not be ambitious of becoming acquainted with the most profound secrets of nature; of ascertaining[2] her hidden operations; and of exhibiting to man that system of knowledge which relates so intimately to their own physical and moral constitution?

From the evidence of *Frankenstein*, of course we know that Mary Shelley was not ambitious in that way, for one, and in fact sought to warn the world away from those dangers inherent in the type of attitude Davy was espousing[3].

It was, then, the Promethean 'maker', 'artist', 'shaper' of men in a scientist-hero guise that interested Mary Shelley and which should preoccupy us; for is it not the modern experience of feeling manipulated by forces larger than ourselves (which are nevertheless humanly managed) – Big Science, technology, the 'machinery' of State, globalization, the mass media, and so on – that links the lay[4] person's predicament[5] with that of Frankenstein's Creature, he who has been put together from dead human parts and then infused with 'a spark of being' without having any say in the form or purpose of his own genesis[6]?

From. Maurice Hindle: 'Introduction'. In: Mary Shelley: Frankenstein. *Edited with an Introduction and Notes by Maurice Hindle. London: Penguin, 2003. Pp. XXVII–XXX. – Copyright © Maurice Hindle 1985, 1992, 2003.*

1 interrogate sth.: (here) examine sth. by posing questions **2** ascertain sth.: find sth. out with certainty **3** espouse sth.: speak up for sth. publicly **4** lay (adj): (here) nonexpert **5** predicament: condition **6** genesis: coming into being

Who put the spark in Frankenstein's monster?

Jamie Doward

→ praises the book
→ similarity to today's society → still relevant

On the 200th anniversary of Mary Shelley's gothic horror, a new edition discusses its roots in experiments with electricity on the dead

It is one of the most famous novels of all time, often cited as the first work of science fiction, with a genesis almost as well known as its terrifying central character.

Mary Shelley's *Frankenstein: or the Modern Prometheus* was published 200 years ago in 1818, when she was just 21. It was the result of a challenge laid down in 1816 by Lord Byron, when Shelley and her lover – later her husband – Byron's fellow poet Percy Bysshe Shelley were holidaying at Lake Geneva in Switzerland.

The party had hoped for good weather, but the eruption of a volcano in the East Indies in 1815, the greatest event of its kind in recorded history, had ushered[1] in three years of bone-chilling cold that killed crops and cast a shadow across Europe. As they huddled for warmth around a fire one night, Byron suggested each of them should write a horror story.

For days Shelley suffered writer's block until she came up with the idea of a scientist who reanimated a creature stitched together from body parts, only to be horrified by his success. Some believe Shelley was inspired by a trip to Germany, where she is thought to have learned the legend of Frankenstein Castle and one of its 17th-century inhabitants, an alchemist called Johann Conrad Dippel, who was rumoured to have exhumed[2] bodies for experimentation.

But it now appears Shelley's true source of inspiration for Victor Frankenstein's monster was considerably closer to home. In a foreword to a new edition of the classic, to be published by Oxford University Press next month, Nick Groom, of Exeter University, some-

1 usher in sth.: mark the beginning of sth. **2** exhume sb.: dig up a dead person's body from its grave

times referred to as the 'Prof of Goth', suggests it was her husband's fascination with galvanism – chemically generated electricity – that sparked her imagination.

Percy Shelley, one of Britain's most cherished Romantic poets and author of the celebrated sonnet Ozymandias, was fascinated by science, in particular the creation of electricity. 'He was very excited by galvanic apparatus,' Groom explained. 'His sister, Helen, would recall that he would, as she put it, "practise electricity upon us". He used to make all the family sit around the dining room table holding hands, and he'd turn up with some brown paper, a bottle and a wire and they'd all get electrocuted[1].'

On one occasion Percy even threatened to electrocute the son of his scout[2] at Oxford University.

Mary and Percy enjoyed a symbiotic[3] working relationship. She corrected his proofs[4] and he helped edit *Frankenstein*. But Groom is clear that the book was, contrary to what some have argued, Mary's creation. 'The work is by her and should be attributed to her.'

Sent down[5] in 1811 from Oxford for co-authoring a pamphlet on atheism, Percy attended anatomy classes for a term at St Bartholomew's hospital in London. 'One of the things she would have got from talking to her husband about laboratories was that they were really filthy places,' Groom said. 'The cadavers would be in a state of advanced putrefaction[6] when they arrived. These were not antiseptic places full of chaps in white coats. They were unpleasant. The word filthy turns up a lot in Frankenstein. There was something really disreputable[7] about medical science, which Mary Shelley is fascinated in.'

She would have been aware of notorious[8] public experiments involving galvanism. 'There was a particularly chilling one in London in 1803 when galvanism was used on the body of an executed

1 electrocute sb.: (here) send electricity through sb.'s body **2** scout (n): (here) housekeeper **3** symbiotic: cooperative **4** proof: (here) copy of a text used for making corrections before publication **5** send down sb.: (here) expel sb. **6** putrefaction: decay **7** disreputable: disgraceful, shady **8** notorious: *berüchtigt*

criminal,' Groom said. 'The very first thing that happened was that the corpse opened its eyes. A very Frankenstein moment.'

At the time Mary was writing, the rights of animals had become a concern for many of the intelligentsia. 'The being that Victor creates knows he's not human but still believes that he should have rights,' Groom said. 'Part of the conundrum[1] of the novel is, do you afford comparable rights to non-human sentient[2] creatures?'

Two centuries on, the novel continues to shape contemporary thinking, Groom suggested, posing questions about matters such as artificial intelligence and genetic modification.

But Mary's astonishing foresight has yet to be fully recognised.

'Her reputation has been overtaken by the films, which have oversimplified these questions in ways that don't really reflect the sophistication[3] of her novel,' Groom said. 'Boris Karloff's monster has none of the subtlety that the being has in the novel. He's not a zombie, he's intelligent and sentient.

'People need to see this as a novel for today. It's very much entangled[4] with the pressing questions of humanity, which still concern us.'

Jamie Doward: 'Who put the spark in Frankenstein's monster?', The Guardian, *4 March 2018.*

1 conundrum: intricate and difficult problem **2** sentient ['sentiənt]: capable of having feelings **3** sophistication: (here) knowledge and understanding of a complicated subject **4** entangled with sth.: closely connected to sth.

Our Posthuman Future *Francis Fukuyama*

Consider the following three scenarios, all of which are distinct[1] possibilities that may unfold over the next generation or two.

The first has to do with new drugs. As a result of advances in neuropharmacology, psychologists discover that human personality is much more plastic[2] than formerly believed. It is already the case that psychotropic[3] drugs such as Prozac and Ritalin can affect traits like self-esteem and the ability to concentrate, but they tend to produce a host of unwanted side effects and hence are shunned[4] except in cases of clear therapeutic need. But in the future, knowledge of genomics[5] permits pharmaceutical companies to tailor drugs very specifically to the genetic profiles of individual patients and greatly minimize unintended side effects. Stolid[6] people can become vivacious; introspective ones extroverted; you can adopt one personality on Wednesday and another for the weekend. There is no longer any excuse for anyone to be depressed or unhappy; even 'normally' happy people can make themselves happier without worries of addiction, hangovers, or long-term brain damage.

In the second scenario, advances in stem cell research allow scientists to regenerate virtually any tissue[7] in the body, such that life expectancies are pushed well above 100 years. If you need a new heart or liver, you just grow one inside the chest cavity[8] of a pig or cow; brain damage from Alzheimer's and stroke can be reversed. The only problem is that there are many subtle and some not-so-subtle aspects of human aging that the biotech industry hasn't quite figured out how to fix: people grow mentally rigid[9] and increasingly fixed in their views as they age, and try as they might, they can't make themselves sexually attractive to each other and continue to

1 distinct: (here) realistic **2** plastic: (here) able to be formed and changed **3** psychotropic: mood-altering **4** shun sth.: avoid sth. **5** genomics: area of biotechnology that focuses on DNA mapping **6** stolid: unemotional **7** tissue: *Gewebe* **8** chest cavity: *Brustraum* **9** rigid: inflexible

long for partners of reproductive age. Worst of all, they just refuse to get out of the way, not just of their children, but their grandchildren and great-grandchildren. On the other hand, so few people have children or any connection with traditional reproduction that it scarcely seems to matter.

In a third scenario, the wealthy routinely screen embryos before implantation so as to optimize the kind of children they have. You can increasingly tell the social background of a young person by his or her looks and intelligence; if someone doesn't live[1] up to social expectations, he tends to blame bad genetic choices by his parents rather than himself. Human genes have been transferred to animals and even to plants, for research purposes and to produce new medical products; and animal genes have been added to certain embryos to increase their physical endurance[2] or resistance to disease. Scientists have not dared to produce a full-scale chimera[3], half human and half ape, though they could; but young people begin to suspect that classmates who do much less well than they do are in fact genetically not fully human. Because, in fact, they aren't. [...]

Toward the very end of his life, Thomas Jefferson[4] wrote, 'The general spread of the light of science has already laid open to every view the palpable[5] truth, that the mass of mankind has not been born with saddles on their backs, nor a favored few booted and spurred[6], ready to ride them legitimately, by the grace of God.' The political equality enshrined in the Declaration of Independence rests on the empirical fact of natural human equality. We vary greatly as individuals and by culture, but we share a common humanity that allows every human being to potentially communicate with and enter into a moral relationship with every other human being on the planet. The ultimate question raised by biotechnology is, What will happen

1 live up to sth.: meet the standards of sth. **2** endurance: *Ausdauer* **3** chimera: organism composed of (genetic) material of multiple species **4** Thomas Jefferson (1743–1826): Founding Father and third president of the United States **5** palpable: unmistakable, simple **6** booted and spurred: equipped with boots and spurs (*Sporen*) to urge on a horse

to political rights once we are able to, in effect, breed some people with saddles on their backs, and others with boots and spurs?

From: Francis Fukuyama: Our Posthuman Future. Consequences of the Biotechnology Revolution. *New York: Farrar, Straus and Giroux, 2002. Pp. 8–10. – Copyright © 2002 by Francis Fukuyama.*

The Frankenstein Prophecy *Yuval Noah Harari*

In 1818 Mary Shelley published *Frankenstein*, the story of a scientist who tries to create a superior being and instead creates a monster. In the last two centuries, this story has been told over and over again in countless variations. It has become a central pillar[1] of our new scientific mythology. At first sight, the Frankenstein story appears to warn us that if we try to play God and engineer life we will be punished severely. Yet the story has a deeper meaning.

The Frankenstein myth confronts *Homo sapiens* with the fact that the last days are fast approaching. Unless some nuclear or ecological catastrophe destroys us first, the pace of technological development will soon lead to the replacement of *Homo sapiens* by completely different beings who possess not only different physiques, but also very different cognitive and emotional worlds. This is something most Sapiens find extremely disconcerting. We like to believe that in the future people just like us will travel from planet to planet in fast spaceships. We don't like to contemplate the possibility that in the future, beings with emotions and identities like ours will no longer exist, and our place will be taken by alien life forms whose abilities dwarf[2] our own.

We seek comfort in the fantasy that Dr Frankenstein can create only terrible monsters, whom we would have to destroy in order to save the world. We like to tell the story that way because it implies that we are the best of all beings, that there never was and never will be something better than us. Any attempt to improve us will inevitably fail, because even if our bodies might be improved, you cannot touch the human spirit.

We would have a hard time swallowing the fact that scientists could engineer spirits as well as bodies, and that future Dr Frankensteins could therefore create something truly superior to us,

1 pillar: *Säule* **2** dwarf sth.: make sth. appear smaller/inferior in comparison

something that will look at us as condescendingly[1] as we look at the Neanderthals.

We cannot be certain whether today's Frankensteins will indeed fulfil this prophecy. [...] History teaches us that what seems to be just around the corner may never materialise[2] due to unforeseen barriers, and that other unimagined scenarios will in fact come to pass. When the nuclear age erupted in the 1940s, many forecasts were made about the future nuclear world of the year 2000. When sputnik and Apollo 11 fired the imagination of the world, everyone began predicting that by the end of the century, people would be living in space colonies on Mars and Pluto. Few of these forecasts came true. On the other hand, nobody foresaw the Internet.

[...] What we should take seriously is the idea that the next stage of history will include not only technological and organisational transformations, but also fundamental transformations in human consciousness and identity. And these could be transformations so fundamental that they will call the very term 'human' into question. How long do we have? No one really knows. As already mentioned, some say that by 2050 a few humans will already be a-mortal. Less radical forecasts speak of the next century, or the next millennium. Yet from the perspective of 70,000 years of Sapiens history, what are a few centuries?

If the curtain is indeed about to drop on Sapiens history, we members of one of its final generations should devote some time to answering one last question: what do we want to become? This question, sometimes known as the Human Enhancement[3] question, dwarfs the debates that currently preoccupy politicians, philosophers, scholars and ordinary people. After all, today's debate between today's religions, ideologies, nations and classes will in all likelihood disappear along with *Homo sapiens*. If our successors indeed function on a different level of consciousness (or perhaps

1 condescending: showing a superior attitude towards sb./sth. **2** materialise: come true, come into being **3** enhancement: improvement

possess something beyond consciousness that we cannot even conceive[1]), it seems doubtful that Christianity or Islam will be of interest to them, that their social organisation could be Communist or capitalist, or that their genders could be male or female.

And yet the great debates of history are important because at least the first generation of these gods would be shaped by the cultural ideas of their human designers. Would they be created in the image of capitalism, of Islam, or of feminism? The answer to this question might send them careening[2] in entirely different directions.

Most people prefer not to think about it. Even the field of bioethics prefers to address another question: 'What is it forbidden to do?' Is it acceptable to carry our genetic experiments on living human beings? On aborted[3] fetuses? On stem cells? Is it ethical to clone sheep? And chimpanzees? And what about humans? All of these are important questions, but it is naive to imagine that we might simply hit the brakes and stop the scientific projects that are upgrading *Homo sapiens* into a different kind of being. For these projects are inextricably meshed together with the Gilgamesh Project[4]. Ask scientists why they study the genome, or try to connect a brain to a computer, or try to create a mind inside a computer. Nine out of ten times you'll get the same standard answer: we are doing it to cure diseases and save human lives. Even though the implications of creating a mind inside a computer are far more dramatic than curing psychiatric illnesses, this is the standard justification given, because nobody can argue with it. This is why the Gilgamesh Project is the flagship of science. It serves to justify everything science does. Dr Frankenstein piggybacks[5] on the shoulders of Gilgamesh. Since it is impossible to stop Gilgamesh, it is also impossible to stop Dr Frankenstein.

1 conceive: imagine **2** careen (v): move forward in an uncontrolled way **3** abort: *abtreiben* **4** Gilgamesh Project: the scientific quest for immortality; refers to King Gilgamesh of Uruk who, according to Babylonian myth, travelled to the end of the universe in order to find a way to defeat death **5** piggyback: move by being carried on sb.'s shoulders

The only thing we can try to do is to influence the direction scientists are taking. But since we might soon be able to engineer[1] our desires too, the real question facing us is not 'What do we want to become?', but 'What do we want to want?' Those who are not spooked by this question probably haven't given it enough thought.

From: Yuval Noah Harari: Sapiens. A Brief History of Humankind. *London: Vintage, 2015. Pp. 461–464. – Copyright © Yuval Noah Harari 2011.*

1 engineer sth.: (here) manipulate sth. by technical means

The Author

Richard Rothwell: 'Mary Wollstonecraft Shelley' (Oil on canvas, 1840)

Mary Shelley was born as Mary Godwin on August 30, 1797 in London. She was the daughter of two writers: the political philosopher William Godwin and the women's rights activist Mary Wollstonecraft. Although the latter died only eleven days after her daughter's birth, Mary Shelley loved her mother dearly and held her in high esteem throughout her life. At a time when women writers were still frowned upon, Ms Wollstonecraft's personality and legacy can be counted as one of the main catalysts for her daughter's literary ambitions.

Young Mary Godwin grew up in difficult and poor conditions. After the death of her mother, her father found it hard to cope with the task of bringing up his two daughters alone. In 1801, he remarried, but family life was much strained by constant arguments between Mary, her stepmother and her two stepsiblings.

When Mary was 16, she met Percy Bysshe Shelley, an aristocrat who was to emerge as one of the leading poets of English Romanticism and was a frequent guest at the Godwins' place. He revered William Godwin's philosophical work, but soon he took even greater interest in the bright and pretty Mary. However, a grave problem stood in the way of Mary and Percy's happiness: Shelley was married and had a young son. The lovers fled to Paris, then to Germany via Switzerland and – much in the spirit of Romanticsm – enjoyed their unbounded happiness to the fullest. When their savings were exhausted, they made their way back home to London in the autumn of 1814, where Mary found out that she was pregnant.

After an acrimonious divorce that only came to an end with the suicide of Percy's first wife, Percy was finally free to remarry in 1816. Mary went through four pregnancies, but only one child, Percy Florence, who was born in 1819, survived into adulthood. After the death of her baby daughter Clara in 1815, Mary noted in her diary: 'Sunday, March 19. – Dream that my little baby came to life again; that it had only been cold, and that we rubbed it before the fire, and it lived. Awake, and find no baby.'

Thanks to Percy, Mary had a number of influential and famous friends. Her husband's best friend was Lord Byron, whom some literary scholars deem the greatest English poet after Shakespeare. In 1816, Mary, Percy and two friends spent about two months with Lord Byron in his villa on Lake Geneva, reading horror stories to each other during the stormy nights. Encouraged by her friends, Mary let her imagination run wild and wrote her own horror story which developed into *Frankenstein*. The novel was first published – anonymously – in 1818. After her husband's death in 1822, Mary made some changes to the original text and republished it in 1823 and 1831. It was not until the second edition that she was given full credit as the author.

In the years after the creation of *Frankenstein*, Mary Shelley continued to write novels, biographies, stories and travel books, and edited the works of her deceased husband. Like *Frankenstein*, many of her later novels, such as *Valperga, or the Life and Adventures of Castruccio, Prince of Lucca* (1823), *The Last Man* (1826) and *The Fortunes of Perkin Warbeck* (1830), are set in mainland Europe and have a historical background. They laid the foundation for the genre of the gothic novel and ushered in science fiction literature. Her stories are characterized by a blend of skepticism about and fascination with scientific progress.

Mary Shelley died on February 1, 1851, aged 53, in London.